1-2-3® Business Formula Handbook

Ron Person

Que™ Corporation
Indianapolis, Indiana

Library of Congress Catalog No.: 85-63876
ISBN 0-88022-198-4

90 89 88 87 86   8 7 6 5 4 3 2 1

Interpretation of the printing code: the rightmost double-digit number is the year of the book's printing; the rightmost single-digit number, the number of the book's printing. For example, a printing code of 87-4 shows that the fourth printing of the book occurred in 1987.

About the Author

Ron Person

Ron Person of Santa Rosa, California, a former industry analyst for Texas Instruments, is a trainer and consultant in the field of software applications for finance and marketing. His clients include businesses and professionals throughout San Francisco and the North Bay area. He earned his master's degree in business administration in marketing from Hardin-Simmons University in Abilene, Texas; a master of science degree in physics from the Ohio State University in Columbus, Ohio; and a bachelor of science degree in physics from the United States Air Force Academy in Colorado Springs, Colorado. Mr. Person is the author of *Macintosh Game Animation, Animation Magic with Your Apple* IIe *and* IIc, and *Animation Magic with Your IBM PC and PC*jr, all published by Osborne/McGraw-Hill.

Product Director
David P. Ewing

Editorial Director
David F. Noble, Ph.D.

Managing Editor
Gregory Croy

Editors
Kathie-Jo Arnoff
Jeannine Freudenberger, M.A.
Pamela Fullerton

Technical Editor
G. Kent Holloway

Technical Consultant
Thomas W. Carlton

Table of Contents

5   Statistics and Database Analysis 159

x

Trademark Acknowledgments

Composed by Que Corporation in
Garamond

Cover designed by
Listenberger Design Associates

Conventions Used in This Book

A number of conventions are used in the *1-2-3 Business Formula Handbook* to help you better understand the book.

1. References to keys are as they appear on the keyboard of the IBM Personal Computer. Direct quotations of words that appear on the screen are spelled as they appear on the screen and are printed in a `special typeface`.

2. The first letter of each command from 1-2-3's menu system appears in boldface: /**R**ange **F**ormat **C**urrency. Abbreviated commands appear as in the following example: /rfc. **Range Format Currency** indicates that you type /rfc to select this command if you were entering it manually. The first letter of menu choices also appears in boldface: **C**opy.

3. Words printed in uppercase include range names (SALES), functions (@PMT), modes (READY), and cell references (A1..G5).

4. The function keys, F1 through F10, are used for special situations in 1-2-3. In the text, the function key number usually is followed by the name in parentheses: F10 (Graph).

5. Ctrl-Break indicates that you press the Ctrl key and hold it down while you press the Break key. Other hyphenated key combinations, such as Alt-F10, are performed in the same manner.

6. Key sequences, such as End+Home, are performed by pressing and releasing each key in turn.

Conventions that pertain to macros deserve special mention here:

1. Macro names (Alt-character combinations) appear with the backslash (\) and single character in lowercase: \a. In this macro command example, the \ indicates that you press the Alt key and hold it down while you press the A key.

2. All /x macro commands, such as /xm or /xn, appear in lowercase, but macro commands from Release 2's command language within braces are uppercase: {WAIT}.

3. 1-2-3 menu keystrokes in a macro line are in lowercase: /rnc.

4. Range names within macros are in uppercase: /rncTEST.

5. In macros, representation of cursor keys, such as {DOWN}; function keys, such as {CALC}; and editing keys, such as {DEL}, appear in uppercase letters and are surrounded by braces.

6. Enter is represented by the tilde (~). (Note that throughout the text, Enter is used instead of Return.)

Introduction

The *1-2-3 Business Formula Handbook* adds power to Lotus® 1-2-3®. This handbook for advanced Lotus 1-2-3 users contains frequently used financial and marketing-analysis formulas and techniques for solving problems with the 1-2-3 spreadsheet. Spreadsheet models in the book demonstrate formulas that solve problems as varied as lease analysis, rate of return from complex cash flows, stock-market charting, and survey analysis.

Through sample problems, each formula's limitations and assumptions are explained. You can use the formulas just as they are or incorporate them into your own spreadsheets. Macros are built invisibly as you create the spreadsheet. Even if you are not familiar with macros, you can use all the formulas in this book.

A tool for business and investment, the *1-2-3 Business Formula Handbook* is a book you should keep on your bookshelf next to your dictionary and 1-2-3 reference manual. Whether you are a business person, investor, analyst, or researcher, you can find valuable information in this book. Formulas and templates (prepared spreadsheets) in the book solve problems ranging from simple compound interest to many types of annuities, such as mortgages and sinking funds. The formulas you often need are explained and assembled in a form you can use in 1-2-3. For example, a chapter on trends analysis gives you the power to calculate unknown data and forecast near-term futures. A chapter on statistics and survey analysis shows you how to improve on 1-2-3's statistical functions, how to find quality control levels with a probability template, how to chart a histogram from text information in your database, and even how to generate a matrix showing multiple cross sections of your database.

Although this book is written for Release 2, many templates in the book can be used with both Release 2 and Release 1A. Using the formulas in each section and the conversion information in three appendixes, you can convert templates and macros that contain Release 2 functions so that they work with Release 1A.

What Is in This Book?

The *1-2-3 Business Formula Handbook* covers three major business and investment areas: financial analysis, trend analysis and forecasting, and database analysis. Each example throughout the book includes an explanation of how the formula or technique is used, a sample problem, the formula and its assumptions, a print of the template screen, and the template cell listing. To help you create the template, range names and major formulas are listed separately. The print of the template screen shows you how the template appears when complete.

Chapters 1 and 2 present hints and tips for using the templates and formulas in your own 1-2-3 spreadsheets. These chapters tell you how to enter and edit complex formulas, how to use the iteration (circular reference) method of finding solutions, how to increase performance, and how to share data among spreadsheets.

Monitoring your business is easier when you use the financial ratios described in Chapter 3. They provide an excellent way to track your business progress. The chapter is devoted to financial formulas used to solve simple problems like compound interest or more complex problems like the rate of return on a lease. Fourteen different financial management formulas and methods help you use 1-2-3 to calculate investments, leases, business and personal loans, sinking funds, and mortgages.

The mortgage schedule template begins printing at any date you select, thereby saving your patience and your paper. You can calculate terms for add-on interest loans (installment loans) or for any term in an amortized loan. One template even calculates the unknown interest from the monetary terms. The formulas in this chapter also can handle balloon payments for present value annuities as well as for mortgages.

In addition to templates for present value annuities, Chapter 3 provides templates you can use to solve for any term in a future value annuity. Those templates are handy for finding the interest rate required to meet a sinking fund or for calculating the rate of return you need to meet your retirement goals. The templates use the new 1-2-3 Release 2 functions—@TERM, @RATE, and @CRATE. The text provides formulas that show you how to adjust the templates for Release 1A.

Eliminating inherent problems with the 1-2-3 internal rate of return function, @IRR, the Financial Management Rate of Return template calculates an accurate rate of return no matter how complex the cash flow. Using the model, you can even select the saving rate and the reinvestment rate used for cash outlays and positive cash flows.

If you need to find a trend hidden in a collection of data, consult Chapter 4. The chapter demonstrates curve-fitting techniques that can reduce a cloud of data into an equation and a suitable curve. The formulas and templates fit six different types of curves to your collection of data and give you the equations that describe those curves. Explanations included with each formula and template help you decide which type of curve to use. Chapter 4 also demonstrates how to find cyclical patterns, an aid in identifying business and investment cycles. The smoothing techniques show you how to get rid of the "static" in data so that long-term trends are visible.

Chapter 5 can help you find the gold hidden in your database. Most people get so overloaded with information that they cannot see the relationships and patterns hidden in the information. Using a technique known as cross-tabulation, you can cross-reference one field in your database against any other field. For example, you can see the answers to as many as 30 questions at a time. You can view the answers to questions such as "What products do my top salespeople sell the most?" or "Do the customers shopping on different days of the week come from different areas of town?"

You also can learn from Chapter 5 how you can improve the accuracy of the 1-2-3 @STD and @VAR functions. The chapter shows you how you can use simple statistics and probability to predict failure rates and improve quality control.

Appendix A contains a reference list of private and government bureaus that gather and analyze many types of industrial, demographic, and financial information. Also included are sources for the financial ratios used by competitive industries. This information can help you analyze market and industry trends, profile your customers, and gain a perspective on your competitors. These low-cost sources can save you an immense amount of work and expense. Appendix B lists references that give more in-depth information and additional formulas on the subjects covered in the *1-2-3 Business Formula Handbook*.

Appendix C includes a cross-reference guide for Release 2 and Release 1A macros. Appendix D lists important 1-2-3 Release 1A macros. Release 1A users should substitute these macros for the Release 2 macros used in the templates. Appendix E gives the 1-2-3 Release 1A formulas for creating a linear regression template.

Who Should Use This Book?

If you are an advanced user of Lotus 1-2-3, the *1-2-3 Business Formula Handbook* can save you time. The text gives you the major financial and mathematical tools needed to build investment, business, and marketing analysis models in 1-2-3.

You save time and avoid errors by using the *1-2-3 Business Formula Handbook* as a reference guide for important financial, trend, and statistical formulas. You can use the formulas and templates exactly as listed in the book, or you can integrate them into your own spreadsheets. Companies with many 1-2-3 users can maintain standards and reduce inaccuracies in spreadsheets by designating the *1-2-3 Business Formula Handbook* as the standard reference source for 1-2-3 formulas. Less experienced 1-2-3 users as well as some advanced users can learn by examining the macros and studying the discussions of iterative methods in Chapters 1 and 2.

A Note to Release 1A and Release 2 Users

Users of both Release 1A and Release 2 can create their own spreadsheets with the formulas and techniques presented in this book. Many of the templates run in both Release 1A and Release 2. Other templates are designed for Release 2, but can be converted to Release 1A. To help Release 1A users to convert Release 2 templates, the book offers three appendixes. Appendix C compares old and new macro commands. Appendix D contains complete Release 1A macros for templates with more complex macros. And Appendix E gives the 1-2-3 Release 1A formulas for creating a linear regression template.

What Do You Need To Use This Book?

The templates in this book were designed on an IBM® Personal Computer and run in the minimum memory required by Lotus 1-2-3 Release 1A or Release 2. Templates that analyze a database may require more memory if the database is large.

How Can You Learn More about 1-2-3?

Two other Que books make excellent companions to the *1-2-3 Business Formula Handbook*. While the *1-2-3 Business Formula Handbook* provides financial and management analysis formulas and techniques, *1-2-3 for Business* by Leith Anderson, and Douglas Ford Cobb offers 14 interesting and useful business applications for 1-2-3. A more general text, *Using 1-2-3* by Geoffrey T. LeBlond and Douglas Ford Cobb, concentrates on the fundamentals of 1-2-3.

For users who want to learn more about 1-2-3's macros, Que offers two more books. *1-2-3 Macro Library* by David P. Ewing is an easy-to-use reference that contains more than 100 examples of 1-2-3 macros. *1-2-3 Financial Macros* by Thomas W. Carlton expands on the applications introduced in *1-2-3 Macro Library* and shows how to develop complex spreadsheet and database models controlled by macros.

If you would like to receive a continual flow of information about 1-2-3, you should consider subscribing to Que's publication, *Absolute Reference: The Journal for 1-2-3 and Symphony Users*. For more on this exciting opportunity, see the announcement inside the back cover of this book.

1

1-2-3 Formula Basics

1-2-3 can solve problems that would be difficult and time-consuming to do by hand or with reference tables. The more difficult those problems are to calculate, the more valuable 1-2-3 becomes to you. Helping you solve difficult problems is also what makes the *1-2-3 Business Formula Handbook* valuable. The formulas and techniques presented in this book add more power to 1-2-3. With these formulas, templates, and techniques, the program gives you timely answers you otherwise may not have.

To use the full power of 1-2-3, you must enter and debug formulas. Although these formulas at first may appear complex, the hints and tips in this chapter help you to enter and debug formulas and to use new programming techniques.

Constructing Formulas

The formulas in 1-2-3 cells are coded instructions that tell 1-2-3 how to operate on numbers or text. Formulas can calculate a numeric value, make changes to a string of text, or determine a TRUE (1) or FALSE (0) condition. Formula instructions are written with operators (signs) and functions that control the number and text operations.

Operators and functions reference information by the addresses of the cells where the information is stored. These addresses can be relative or absolute. Relative addresses (for example, A7) locate information by position relative to the cell containing the formula. If a formula containing A7 is copied one column to the right, A7 becomes B7. On the other hand, absolute addresses reference an exact row or column and do not change when copied to a new location. If a formula containing the absolute address A7 is copied one column to the right, the cell referenced is still A7. Dollar signs in an address indicate that the row, column, or both are absolute addresses.

Formulas are constructed according to specific rules. A formula must contain fewer than 241 characters. If a cell address is the first entry in a formula, the formula must begin with a plus sign (+). 1-2-3 recognizes a cell's contents as a formula only when the entry begins with a number or one of the following symbols:

. + – (@ # $

Formulas normally are not displayed on the screen; only the results of the calculations are shown. You can see a formula in a cell by moving the cursor to that cell; the formula appears in the edit line at the top of the screen. You also can display formulas by formatting cells with the /Range Format Text command.

Precedence of Operations

Formulas that contain many functions and operators can produce different answers depending on which order the functions and operators calculate. Understanding the precedence of operations is important in creating correct formulas. Lotus 1-2-3 formulas always perform calculations in the order given in table 1.1.

Calculations with high precedence numbers are executed before calculations with low numbers. In a formula, 1-2-3 executes from left to right all calculations with the same precedence level before executing calculations in the next precedence level.

Enclosing sections of a formula in parentheses changes the order of precedence by making the enclosed section calculate as a single entity. Parentheses force 1-2-3 to calculate the innermost parentheses section first, then the next higher section, and so on. For example, in the formula

$$INT/(1-(1+INT)^{-N})$$

the (1+INT) term is added, and the result is raised to the –N power. That result is subtracted from 1, and, finally, INT is divided by the result of the subtraction.

Even if all functions and operators are correct, formulas that use parentheses incorrectly will produce incorrect answers. Checking parentheses for errors is explained later in this chapter.

Table 1.1
Precedence of Operations

Precedence Number	Operator	Operation
7	^	Exponentiation (to the power of)
6	+, −	Positive, negative
5	*, /	Multiplication and division
4	+, −	Addition and subtraction
3	>=	Greater than or equal to
3	<=	Less than or equal to
3	< >	Not equal to
3	=, >, <	Equal to, greater than, less than
2	#NOT#	Logical NOT
1	&	Combining strings of text
1	@functions	Numeric and text functions
1	#AND#	Logical AND
1	#OR#	Logical OR

Range Names in Formulas

Range names—the text names (such as PROFIT) assigned to a single cell or an area of cells on a spreadsheet—are important in designing large spreadsheets and entering complex formulas. You can use assigned range names in formulas instead of using conventional 1-2-3 cell addresses in order to make your formulas and functions simpler and to make your spreadsheets self-documenting.

Using range names, you can insert or delete rows of data within the ranges you have defined, without disturbing your formulas and functions. You must be careful, however, when you delete data on the first or last row in a named range. Doing so changes the boundaries of the range and destroys the accuracy of your formulas and functions. If this occurs, you must delete the range name and re-create it. In the formulas that contained that range name, you then must replace the ERR message with the corrected range name.

By assigning descriptive names to the ranges on your spreadsheets, you can make your spreadsheets self-documenting. When you use range names that describe the information in the ranges, you usually don't need to list the addresses and functions of each formula. For example, the formula

(CURRENTASSETS–INVENTORY)/CURRENTLIABIL

is much easier to understand and to document than

(A47–C36)/B16

You can record the cell addresses assigned to each range name in either of two ways. Using the first method, you type each range name in capital letters as a label next to the cell being named. You then use /Range Name Label to change each label into a range name that describes the adjacent cell. The /rnl command gives you the options of making the label the name of the cell above, below, to the right, or to the left of the cell containing the label. Aside from recording the cell addresses, this method also helps you create the range names. Another advantage of this method is that you can identify range names by looking at the display.

With this first method, you also can create many range names at once by putting all the labels in a row or column. The Compound Interest template in Chapter 3, for example, has the labels FV, PV, INT, and N in a single row (see fig. 3.1). Using /Range Name Label Down across these four labels creates all four range names at once. However, /rnl can label only a single cell adjacent to each label. The command cannot give a range name to an area of cells.

The second method of documenting range names is to create a table of range names and their cell addresses. Lotus 1-2-3 Release 2 creates this table for you when you issue the /Range Name Table command. Be careful where you position the cursor. The cursor marks the upper left corner of a two-column table of range names and cell addresses. When you execute /rnt, the table covers the existing display in the cursor's column and the column to the right. The table covers as many rows as there are range names.

You should create the range names before you enter any formulas using the names. If you have not created a range name, however, you still can enter the name within a formula by entering the formula as a label, with an apostrophe (') at the beginning of the formula. After the range name is created, remove the apostrophe from the formula.

Entering Long Formulas

Long complex formulas are easier to enter, to understand, and to test when they are created in sections. Creating formulas in sections, using a few simple techniques, can save you time and reduce errors.

One technique for entering long formulas is to break the formulas into manageable sections with parentheses. Whether or not the parentheses are needed for calculation precedence, they can be used to group sections of a formula. You can think of the sections as sentences in a paragraph, with each section containing one logical entity. You will find that you can enter sections in parentheses more easily than you can enter a long continuous formula.

You can use another time- and error-saving technique for creating long formulas or for creating a number of formulas that share common sections. You can type sections of a formula in separate cells and assign range names to the cells. Then you can use those range names in place of the formula sections. This technique, which is used in the Quadratic Regression template, saves considerable typing time and reduces errors (see fig. 4.12).

Finding errors is easier when you enter formulas in pieces. When you enter formulas that contain a large number of parentheses or similar range names, you are more likely to make mistakes. These formulas usually are easiest to enter in sections that are valid by themselves. For example, you can enter just the divisor in a complex division problem. If a section is accepted by 1-2-3, you know that the section has no typographical errors. If 1-2-3 refuses to accept your latest addition, you know that an error is in the last section you entered.

Editing and Correcting Formulas

If you enter a long formula and 1-2-3 won't accept it, don't despair. You don't have to press Esc and start over. Although 1-2-3 is not helpful in pointing out errors, you can edit and correct your formulas without redoing all your work. Pressing the F2 (Edit) key puts the program in Edit mode, where you can use the cursor keys to move the cursor inside the formula and make corrections without erasing all your work. Some tips for making the editing process easier follow.

Correcting Formulas as Labels

If an error in a formula isn't immediately apparent, you can change the formula to a label, use the techniques in the following sections to discover the error, and then change the label back to a formula. Although 1-2-3 will not accept an incorrect formula, the program will accept the entry as a label. By changing your formula to a label, you can save the formula and avoid retyping it. If you're not already in Edit mode, press the F2 (Edit) key. Then press the Home key to move the cursor to the first character in the formula. Type an apostrophe (') in that location and press Enter. Your formula is entered in the cell as a label. After you have corrected the error, you can change the entry from a label back to a formula by removing the apostrophe and pressing Enter.

Another technique for correcting formulas is to copy the formula to another location and use the copy to test for errors. By changing a formula to a label, you can copy the formula to another location without changing relative addresses. First, remove the apostrophe from the copy of the formula in order to re-create the formula. Second, use the techniques described in the following sections to check for errors. Finally, remove integral pieces from the formula and see whether 1-2-3 accepts the formula. When 1-2-3 accepts the formula, you know that the last section removed contains the error. When you find the error, you can return to the original formula and make the correction. If 1-2-3 still does not accept the formula, check for additional errors.

Finding Common Errors in Formulas

Sometimes a formula is accepted by 1-2-3 and appears to be correct, yet produces incorrect answers. The most likely causes for these errors are incorrect data, a parenthesis in the wrong place, or incorrectly assigned range names. Finding these types of errors is often a process of elimination. The following sections give you some guidelines for finding these errors.

Finding Parentheses Errors

When 1-2-3 refuses to accept a formula that looks correct, the most likely error is unmatched parentheses—an unequal number of left and right parentheses. To find whether your parentheses are matched, start from the left and, working to the right, count all left (opening) parentheses. Remember that number. Then start at the right and work left, counting all right (closing) parentheses. If the numbers don't match, the parentheses don't either.

Find the unmatched parenthesis by working from the inside set of parentheses to the outside. In long complex formulas, the easiest way is to print the formula (using Cell-Formula printing mode) and make check marks over each matched pair of parentheses. One of the most frequent locations for an unmatched parenthesis is the last group of right parentheses in a formula nested inside a 1-2-3 @ function.

Finding Range Name Errors

Although range names are a great help when you are typing formulas, 1-2-3 refuses formulas that have errors in range names. When you press Enter, 1-2-3 beeps and sets the cursor on the offending range name. To correct a range name error, change the formula to a label by inserting an apostrophe before the formula and pressing Enter. Then check the range names by one of two methods.

One way to check a range name is to press F5 (GoTo), type the range name, and press Enter. The cursor moves to the named cell or the upper left cell of the range. Another method is to highlight the named cell or the complete area by issuing the /Range Name Create command and selecting the range name in question. Hold down the Ctrl key and press Break to exit without changing the name or area. If the range or name is incorrect, delete the range name with /Range Name Delete. Then you can re-create the range name. If the range name doesn't exist, create it.

Range names that have had the first or last anchor cell erased still may appear as range names, but they are invalid. This happens most frequently when rows are deleted in a database. If you suspect that this has happened, delete the name, and re-create it.

If database analysis templates are not analyzing all the data rows, you should check the database range name. Rows inserted at either end of the database range may not be included in the range name.

In 1-2-3 Release 2, you can display a table of all range names and their addresses. Move the cursor to a clear area of the spreadsheet and issue the /Range Name Table command. The displayed table shows all the range names and their addresses. Improperly assigned range names show as errors. The table does not update automatically when you change range names; you must re-create the table with the /rnt command.

Building the Templates in This Book

The *1-2-3 Business Formula Handbook* includes lists of all the cell entries that create the templates. To create each template, consult the list of cells, which you can find at the end of the discussion about the template. Before you create a template from a cell listing, examine the screen display to see how the finished template appears. When you are familiar with how labels and data are arranged, create the template using the steps outlined in the following paragraphs.

1. Begin by adjusting the column widths as recommended in the instructions for creating the template. Nonstandard column widths also are shown at the beginning of each cell listing. For example, [W12] represents a column width of 12.

2. Enter all the labels. The labels, by furnishing reference points, act as a skeleton for the rest of your entries. Labels in the cell listings are preceded by an apostrophe ('), quotation mark ("), or a circumflex (^). These marks indicate, respectively, left-justified, right-justified, or centered labels.

3. Enter the numbers (called values in 1-2-3). In templates that use circular references, some formulas must be entered with values in place, or the formulas produce errors.

   Templates that use circular references contain formulas that refer to the cell containing the formula. This reference can be immediate or through a chain of other cells. If any cell in the chain produces an ERR message because a value the formula needs doesn't exist, then all the formulas in the chain will produce ERRs. Once this cycle of ERRs starts, entering a value will not correct the problem. Methods of entering circular reference formulas are described later in this chapter.

4. Create range names after labels and values are entered. If you don't create the range names used in the formulas, the formulas are not accepted by 1-2-3. Range names are listed within the explanation section of each template.

You can create range names in either of two ways. The first method is to move the cursor to the cell address given in the listing and then issue the command /**R**ange Name Create. Type the name of the range in uppercase letters and press Enter. If the range is a single cell, press Enter again. If the range is an area, type a period (.) to anchor the upper left cell; then move the cursor to the lower right cell of the area and press Enter.

Some templates, for example, that compound interest (see fig. 3.1), are designed so that you can create range names quickly using a second method. When you select /**R**ange Name **L**abel **D**own and highlight the labels above the named cells, 1-2-3 uses the highlighted labels as names for the cells below each label.

5. The next step is entering formulas. You can enter formulas exactly as they appear in the cell listings. The major formulas in a template also are given in the discussion of each template.

6. You always must save the template before testing it. You also should save a template approximately every 15 minutes as you are building it. Note that on rare occasions, incorrect macros may erase (destroy) a spreadsheet during testing.

7. The final step in creating a template is testing. Each section in this handbook has one or more sample problems you can use to test the template. If the formulas or macros do not work correctly, double-check the values you entered. If the data is correct, use /**P**rint **P**rinter **O**ptions **O**ther **C**ell-Formulas to print a list of cells you can check against the list of cells in this book.

Improving Your Spreadsheets with Template Techniques

The templates demonstrate a number of techniques you may find helpful for improving your own spreadsheets. One technique is to use the @IF statement to decide which formulas to solve. Formulas with insufficient data display NA. A second technique, iteration, solves problems by repeatedly estimating the answer. The iteration technique solves problems for which you do not have a formula. A third technique uses the {RECALC} or {RECALCCOL} macro commands to increase the speed of calculations in large spreadsheets.

Deciding Which Formulas To Solve

You can build simple decision making into your templates with the @IF function. One decision the template can make is to determine which formulas have enough data to be solved. One way that the template can make this decision is to have the operator enter the data with zeros for the unknown data. In the Compound Interest template, for example, when a zero is entered for PV in the KNOWN row, the present value formula attempts to solve for an unknown PV (see fig. 3.1). This function is

@IF(PV=0,FV*(1+INT)^−N,@NA)

If the PV cell in the KNOWN row contains a number, the formula doesn't try to solve for an answer that's already known; instead, the formula displays NA. In Release 2 of 1-2-3, you can enter text in place of the @NA function, for example, "Not Appropriate".

Sometimes zero is a valid number in the data cell. This case causes the function just described to solve for an answer at the wrong time. In those situations, 1-2-3 should test more than one data-entry cell before deciding which formula to solve. The template for the present value of an annuity with known interest works this way (see fig. 3.7).

Many annuities do not have a balloon payment. In those cases, the data in the range BLN is frequently zero. That zero throws off the preceding formula. To test when BLN should be solved, you need an @IF function that checks for the other data involved. You need a condition that specifies that "BLN is zero and all other terms in the formula are not zero." A statement like this can be described in 1-2-3 by using logical #AND#, #OR#, and #NOT# functions. The function that solves for BLN in figure 3.7 becomes

@IF(BLN=0#AND#PV<>0#AND#PMT<>0#AND#N<>0,(PV−PMT*ICALC)/
(1+INT)^−N,@NA)

Solving Problems with Iteration

Some problems do not have a discrete formula that produces an exact, easy-to-calculate answer. Solving these problems requires calculus or differential equations, which 1-2-3 is not equipped to handle. However, the following trick lets you use 1-2-3 to solve many of these problems.

The trick uses a technique called iteration, which means making repeated estimates of an answer so that each estimate is closer to the solution than the previous one. The template uses circular reference, indicated by the CIRC indicator, to use the program's preceding guess as the base for the next guess.

An obvious question is "How can 1-2-3 know that the estimates are getting closer?" A template like the future value of an annuity due (see fig. 3.10) works by using different estimated interest rates, INT, to solve the function @FV(PMT,INT,N). When the estimated interest rate produces an @FV answer that is the same as the known value of FV, the estimated interest rate must be the true interest rate for the annuity. To make this happen, the template must start with your initial guess of the interest rate, calculate @FV, and then adjust the next interest estimate according to whether @FV is above or below FV.

The templates using iteration and circular reference use similar range names and methods. The range names that most of these templates use are given in table 1.2.

Table 1.2
Iteration and Circular Reference Range Names

Range Name	Contents
ESTINT	Your initial estimate of the unknown value
INT	@IF(COUNT<2,ESTINT,NEXT INT) The final answer
CALCCLR	0 or 1
COUNTER	@IF(CALCCLR=1,COUNTER+1,0)
FIRST INCR	+ESTINT/2
NEXT INCR	@IF(CALCCLR=0,ESTINT, @IF(FV>CALC FV,LAST INCR,LAST INCR/2))
NEXT INT	@IF(FV>CALC FV,INT+LAST INCR,INT−LAST INCR)
CALC FV	@IF(CALCCLR=0,0.001,@FV(PMT,INT,N))
LAST INCR	@IF(COUNTER<2,FIRST INCR,NEXT INCR)

The @IF functions are used in NEXT INCR and CALC FV to make sure that these cells always have a value, even when you are constructing the template and when the macro clears the previous answer. If at any time the cells do not contain a value, the circular reference produces an ERR.

The template fine tunes the estimated interest starting with the estimated interest, EST INT, that you enter. The template uses this interest rate to calculate the value CALC FV from @FV. If CALC FV is smaller than FV, a small increment is added to the interest rate, and the calculation is repeated. This small increment, LAST INCR, starts with an initial value, FIRST INCR, of half the initial interest.

If CALC FV is larger than FV, the estimated interest rate is too large. To compensate, two things must happen: the estimated interest rate, NEXT INT, must return to its original value; and the next increment, NEXT INCR, must be reduced to one-half of the previous increment, LAST INCR.

In this way, the estimated interest rate increases with large steps as long as the calculated future value, CALC FV, does not exceed the true FV. If CALC FV is larger than FV, the estimated interest rate goes back to a value that produced a smaller CALC FV, reduces the size of the interest increment, and tries again.

The formula in NEXT INCR cuts the interest increment in half when FV is greater than CALC FV. The formula in NEXT INT adds the LAST INCR to the estimated interest if FV is greater than CALC FV and subtracts LAST INCR if FV is less than CALC FV.

As CALC FV gets closer to FV, the increments become smaller. Additional iterations (recalculations) bring the estimated interest closer and closer to the real interest. The accuracy level of the iteration is displayed on some templates next to the label Accuracy.

In some equations, you may need to determine whether the calculated value, in this case @FV, is smaller than the known value. The deciding factor is whether an increase in the estimated interest causes the calculated value to increase or decrease.

In templates with iteration formulas, the macro uses {RECALCCOL} to recalculate the template until the difference between the true FV and CALC FV, using the estimated interest, is less than 1/10 of a cent. If this limit isn't reached, the template recalculates 100 times. (The Release 1A iteration macro listed in Appendix D recalculates the template 50 times without checking the accuracy of the answer.)

The iteration macro begins by making CALCCLR equal zero. This setting prepares the template to solve a new problem by setting COUNTER equal to zero, NEXT INCR equal to your initial interest estimate, and CALC FV equal to an arbitrary 0.001. CALC FV initially is set to an arbitrary number so that an error (ERR) is not produced in NEXT INCR and NEXT INT.

The next step of the macro sets CALCCLR equal to one. Each iteration now adds one to COUNTER. The next two recalculations return the cell values to starting values. When COUNTER is greater than two, LAST INCR reflects the last value used in NEXT INCR. The value in LAST INCR remembers the last adjustment added to the estimated interest.

If the template uses {RECALCCOL} or {RECALC}, the iteration cells (shown in table 1.2) must be in the same order as shown in the templates. The information in the iteration cells is calculated in the same order as the cell sequence, because {RECALCCOL} and {RECALC} use column and row calculation, respectively. The CIRC indicator is not displayed when you use {RECALCCOL} or {RECALC}. If your template uses natural order calculations, you can place the iteration cells in any order.

Increasing Calculation Speed

Some iteration problems are solved slowly because the entire spreadsheet must be recalculated. The templates given in this handbook speed up the process by using {RECALCCOL} and {RECALC}. These two macros are available only with 1-2-3 Release 2. A method for increasing iteration speed for 1-2-3 Release 1A is explained in Chapter 2.

The annuity template uses the {RECALCCOL} macro to recalculate only a selected area of the spreadsheet. This practice increases the speed because only certain formulas are recalculated. When you use {RECALCCOL} or {RECALC}, you must be sure that all formulas used by the calculations are within the range specified. The macro

{RECALCCOL C19..C42,@ABS(FV–CALC FV)<.001,100}

recalculates the area between C19 and C42 until the difference between FV and CALC FV is less than 1/10 of a cent or until 100 recalculations have been performed. The conditional statement @ABS(FV–CALC FV) also improves performance because the statement stops the iteration process as soon as the answer is close enough to the accuracy specified.

Always do a final {CALC} in a macro after using the {RECALCCOL} or {RECALC} macros. The final {CALC} integrates the results from the partial calculations with the rest of the spreadsheet.

Conclusion

This chapter has provided formula entry and "debugging" tips as well as information on how to record spreadsheet comments, solve difficult problems, and improve performance. The tips on entering formulas and finding formula errors are easy to use and should soon become part of your everyday Lotus 1-2-3 procedures.

Explaining your spreadsheet and its assumptions is almost as important as programming the spreadsheet correctly from the start. If you follow the documenting tips in this chapter, future changes will be easier to make. Using these documenting tips also will reduce the chance of someone using the spreadsheet incorrectly or interpreting the results wrong.

The iteration method gives you the ability to solve problems that don't have a formula or that must be estimated. Iteration is a powerful technique.

When your spreadsheet has many equations or a large database, 1-2-3 may slow down. The techniques in the "Improving Your Spreadsheets with Template Techniques" section will help you speed up your spreadsheets.

2

Using the Templates
and Formulas

You can use the templates and formulas in the *1-2-3 Business Formula Handbook* in three ways. You can use the templates just as they are, to work as "calculator type" problem solvers. You can use the templates as they are, but link them through 1-2-3 to data in other spreadsheets and databases. Finally, you can rewrite the templates and formulas and integrate them into your own spreadsheets. This chapter explains how you can do all three of these efficiently.

Using Templates
as Customized Calculators

You can use the templates in this handbook to do financial or trend-analysis work the same way you use a special-function calculator. You can protect the templates and add instructions to them so that operators do not need to be familiar with Lotus 1-2-3.

To set up a template so that operators can enter information in data cells and view the answer, but perform no other functions, follow these steps.

1. Create, test, and save the template as explained in this handbook.

2. Unprotect all data-entry cells by using /**Range** Unprotect. At the upper left corner of each screen area, where the answers display, also unprotect a cell. This last

unprotected cell lets the operator move the cursor to the answer portion of the template. In most cases, this cell is A1.

3. Move the cursor to a portion of the template that you have reserved for macros and enter the following macro. Assign the range names \0 and AGAIN to the two cells to the right of the cells containing these labels. Assign the range name SAFECELL to a single cell off screen. \0 is an autoexecuting macro that runs immediately when the template loads.

CONTROLLED INPUT MACRO (AUTOEXECUTING)

```
\0        ~
AGAIN     /ri{HOME}.{END}{HOME}~
          /xc\templatemacro~          or {CALC}
          {GOTO}cell address to display answers~
          /xlSolve another problem? (Y/N): ~SAFECELL~
          {IF SAFECELL="Y"}/xgAGAIN~
          /wey
```

This macro executes automatically when the template is recalled with **/File Retrieve**. After the file is loaded, the /ri command limits cursor movement and data entry to unprotected cells. When Esc or Enter is pressed without data entry, the /xc command executes the macro that solves the template. The template macro must end with /xr to return control to the autoexecuting macro, \0.

If you have no macro for the template, use the {CALC} command. The program then moves the cursor to the answer area and asks whether the operator wants to solve another problem. If the operator presses Y and then Enter, the template operates again. If the operator presses any other key followed by Enter, the template is erased.

4. After entering the macro, protect the entire spreadsheet by selecting **/Worksheet Global Protection Enable**.

5. Save the template with the **/File Save** command and then test the template.

Linking Your Data and Databases to a Template

Templates can access information on other spreadsheets easily. This capability is particularly valuable if you want to analyze a large database in another spreadsheet.

The following instructions and short macro provide an easy way to bring into the template data from other spreadsheets. The template results then can be transported to another spreadsheet just as easily.

1. In the spreadsheet containing the data or database, create a range name for each data cell or database area that will be transferred. Use specific, easily remembered names and write the names down for later reference.

2. Save the data spreadsheet with its range names. If some of the range names include data calculated by a numeric or text formula, save the entire spreadsheet with the /File Xtract Values command. If you fail to perform this step, the formulas will produce wrong answers when transferred to the template.

3. Load the template into 1-2-3.

4. Transfer the data from the spreadsheet to your template.

   a. Erase the data areas in the template so that new and old data are not mingled.

   b. Increase the number of rows in the template's database areas if necessary. Use /Worksheet Insert Row to insert rows in the middle of database ranges.

   c. Place the cursor where you want the upper left corner of the incoming data area. If the incoming data needs to be changed from horizontal to vertical format or vice versa, move the cursor to a free area of the template so that you can use the /Range Transpose command to reorganize the data. (This command is available only in Release 2.)

   d. Select /File Combine Copy Named/Specified-Range and enter the name of the range being brought in and the name of the data spreadsheet that holds the data.

Loading information to a template is easy with the following macro. You enter the macro as labels on the template being loaded. Then give the cell to the right of \l the range name \l.

INFORMATION LOADER

\l   /fccn{?}~{?}~
            {?}~
            /xg\l~

This macro prompts you for the range name and then for the file name of the incoming data. After the incoming data loads at the cursor location, the macro pauses for you to move the cursor to the next receiving cell. When the cursor is positioned for the next incoming data, press Enter. To start the macro, press Alt-l. To stop, press Ctrl-Break.

Range names are not transferred with the incoming data. You must create new, named ranges to replace range names from the data spreadsheet. Before creating new range names, make sure the names you plan to use do not already exist.

Formula data must be converted to values on the original spreadsheet before the data can be transferred. If the incoming data causes an ERR message or if a formula is transferred instead of a value, the data will be wrong. To convert a formula in a single cell to data, you can locate the cursor on the cell and then press F2 (Edit) followed by F9 (Calc). The easiest way to convert all formulas to values is to save the spreadsheet with the /File Xtract Values command.

Using Templates and Formulas in Your Spreadsheets

You can enter the formulas in this handbook into your own spreadsheets easily by merging the templates with your spreadsheets. After the two files are combined, you can redesign the template portion so that it best fits your needs.

Moving a Template to a Spreadsheet

You can enter the templates as listed and then redesign them to fit your specific needs. You also can use /File Combine Copy Entire to load an entire template into your spreadsheet. The formulas automatically adjust their relative and absolute addresses to their new locations in your spreadsheet. After the template is loaded, you must reenter range names.

The /Move command moves formulas and areas while maintaining correct range names and addresses. If you use the /Copy command, however, you must take precautions, because range names and relative addresses in formulas change. You can copy formulas without changing them by first putting an apostrophe in front of them so that they become labels. The iteration calculations used in some templates must keep the same relative positions to work correctly when using {RECALC} or {RECALCCOL}.

A few macros in this book contain relative cell addresses. The addresses used in macros do not change because macros are labels, and labels do not change when copied or moved. You must change these addresses to reflect new locations.

Entering Formulas in a Spreadsheet

If you enter formulas directly from this handbook, you must create the range names before you enter the formulas. Formulas that are copied from another spreadsheet do not bring their range names with them. You must re-create the range names.

Formulas from the *1-2-3 Business Formula Handbook* can be used in your own spreadsheets as long as you adhere to the assumptions and restrictions shown with them. Some of these formulas and solution methods are accurate only within the data and solution boundaries given.

If you use the iteration method in your own spreadsheets, include all the range names and formulas, as shown in Chapter 1. If you use {RECALC} or {RECALCCOL}, the iteration formulas must be in the same column and row order as they are in the list of cells. If you use natural-order calculation with {CALC}, the order can vary.

Increasing Calculation Speed

Many templates in the *1-2-3 Business Formula Handbook* contain multiple calculations, as the Cross-Tabulation template does, or use 100 recalculations, as the templates using the iteration method do. If you add calculations to the templates or use the iteration methods inside large spreadsheets, the calculation time can become very long.

You can increase performance in these situations by calculating only the necessary areas involved and recalculating the fewest necessary number of times. For example,

> {RECALC C23..D43,(PMT<200),100}

recalculates by row the area between C23 and D43 until PMT is less than 200 or until the program has performed 100 calculations, whichever occurs first.

{RECALC} and {RECALCCOL} calculate by row and column order, respectively. Therefore, iterative methods, described in Chapter 1, must perform calculations in the correct row or column order. When you use {RECALC} or {RECALCCOL}, be sure that you always follow the macro with {CALC}, which incorporates the newly calculated values into the entire spreadsheet.

If you use 1-2-3 Release 1A, you can speed up performance by extracting the iteration area and calculating that portion as a separate spreadsheet (see Chapter 1). When the section has finished calculating, you can merge it back into the original spreadsheet.

Before extracting the iteration area with this method, make sure that you have saved your worksheet. Then create a range name encompassing the iteration area and all the values, formulas, and macros used in the iteration process. Use /File Xtract Formulas to extract this area to a daughter spreadsheet file. The commands prompt for the range name of the extracted area and a new file name. Erase the current spreadsheet (the mother spreadsheet) and load the daughter spreadsheet just created. Execute it as you do normally.

When the daughter spreadsheet finishes calculating, save it to disk with /File Save. Restart the mother spreadsheet and position the cursor by pressing F5 (GoTo) and typing the range name of the extracted area. The cursor moves to the upper left corner of the extracted area. Then use /File Combine Copy Entire to copy the entire daughter spreadsheet back into the mother spreadsheet. Be sure to press F9 (Calc) once to incorporate the iteration result into the mother spreadsheet.

Avoiding Spreadsheet Pitfalls

Spreadsheets, like the Golem of Hebrew folklore, can be a powerful helpmate, or they can be a destructive force. When you accept the results of a spreadsheet as accurate without rigorous examination, you are asking for disaster. A former product manager for a now defunct personal computer manufacturer confided that when times got lean, his section had been asked to cut their budget by $120,000. He related that the cut wasn't as difficult as it first appeared. On reexamining the section's 1-2-3 marketing expense model, he found a $40,000 error that now helped the company. Although that particular error was in his favor, any error that gives you an unrealistic appraisal can hurt the company.

Three types of spreadsheet problems can cause disaster. The first problem is when the formulas, assumptions, and models a spreadsheet is based on are incorrect. A second problem is when a spreadsheet that once may have been correct has assumptions and models that don't match the new time or situation. A third problem is when a spreadsheet that was created for a specific type of data is used with a different type of data.

Beware of other spreadsheet pitfalls and learn to avoid them. The *1-2-3 Business Formula Handbook* gives you many correct formulas. Use the formulas in the handbook and watch out for problems such as data changes and out-of-date spreadsheets.

Documenting a Spreadsheet

Documenting a spreadsheet or template is a job that few enjoy, but everyone should do. Nearly all spreadsheets and templates are used by others, are modified in the future, and evolve from a simple template into a complex model. Trying to modify a template or spreadsheet that you created weeks or months ago sometimes is a difficult and confusing task, especially if many of the assumptions you made and methods you used were not documented. What was an obvious assumption at the time of creation becomes a mystery with the passage of time.

The problem of poor or missing documentation becomes apparent when you attempt to modify a spreadsheet or template created by someone else. In addition to having a different logical flow, another person's spreadsheet may contain undocumented assumptions. Should you violate one of those assumptions, the entire spreadsheet may produce errors. The problem of proliferating errors and inaccurate spreadsheets becomes particularly severe in large companies. Without a manager to control "officially sanctioned" spreadsheets, many bad spreadsheets can pervade a company. Inaccurate models, wrong assumptions, and improper modifications rapidly undo the advantages of 1-2-3.

When you report the results of any spreadsheet, you always should include the assumptions on which the spreadsheet is based. This lets those using the results understand how the model may differ from real-world expectations. Including the assumptions is a way of alerting others that they may be operating under different assumptions or that the report is out-of-date because the assumptions are no longer valid.

Displaying Instructions and Assumptions

You can display instructions and assumptions in a number of ways so that they are easy to find. One of the simplest techniques is to assign to a full-sized-screen area of the spreadsheet the name HELP and to display instructions in that HELP area. Operators then can display that area at any time by pressing F5 (GoTo), typing *help*, and pressing Enter. Using another method, you can name a portion of the spreadsheet ASSUMPTIONS and include there all the important assumptions and limitations for the template. Using a third method, you can highlight hidden critical instructions or assumptions by unprotecting the cell with /**R**ange Unprotect.

1-2-3 Release 2 can hide columns you select with the /**W**orksheet Column **H**ide command. Place assumptions or explanations in a column adjacent to the range name or formula being described and hide the column. The worksheet can then operate with the comments hidden until you want to see them.

The range name table, created with the /**R**ange Name **T**able command, is another important part of the documentation for your spreadsheet. The range name table displays a two-column list of all range names and their cell locations. Keep in mind that the table does not update itself automatically. You must re-create the table when you add or delete range names.

Conclusion

The formulas and templates in the *1-2-3 Business Formula Handbook* are building blocks that you can use to build larger and more valuable spreadsheets. The techniques and macros in this chapter have shown you how to use the book's templates by themselves, how to use them with data from other spreadsheets, and how to use them within larger spreadsheets that you build. The chapter's suggestions on documentation and performance will help keep your spreadsheets accurate and improve their speed.

3
Financial Management Formulas

No businessperson can afford to undervalue the role of financial analysis. Effective financial, managerial, marketing, and production decisions are made only in the light of accurate financial planning and analysis. Factors such as the cost of capital, asset management, and changing inflation have as great an impact on small proprietorships as on large multinational firms. By using 1-2-3 models that incorporate standard financial formulas, the small-business owner and the corporate manager alike can predict the effects that changing financial patterns might have on their businesses.

This chapter presents 1-2-3 templates for financial management formulas that compare and convert interest rates, analyze loans, calculate different types of annuities, and analyze complex cash flows. Each section of the chapter includes both the formulas and their assumptions. You can use the complete templates as they are or incorporate the formulas into your own spreadsheets.

With the Compound Interest and interest-rate conversion templates, you can determine how your fixed investments will grow at different interest rates or what length of time an investment requires to reach a specific amount. With the interest-rate conversion template, you can compare bank rates or money market rates to find the best rate of return even if the investments compound with different periods.

The loan templates provide loan schedules and information on amortized loans, such as mortgages. In addition, these templates calculate add-on interest-rate installment loans, also known as consumer loans. The Rule of 78s template calculates the amount needed for early payoff of an add-on interest-rate loan.

Complex investments yield complex cash flows, which the 1-2-3 @IRR is not equipped to handle. That function also has a strategic flaw of which all investors should be aware. Both of these problems are overcome with the Financial Management Rate of Return template. That template solves for the rate of return from complex cash flows.

Many investments—such as mortgages, sinking funds, and leases—involve annuities. An annuity is a string of fixed deposits or fixed payments that may yield a large single amount at the end. Annuities may differ according to whether payments are made at the beginning of each period or at the end. The four annuity templates presented here calculate any unknown term. They even calculate the interest rate when given the annuity's dollar and term amounts.

Ratio analysis can help you monitor your business activity, growth, profitability, and competitive position. If your accountant or bookkeeper has been handing you a stack of financial reports, but has not been helping you "fine tune" your business, you need to look at ratio analysis. The ratio analysis formulas presented in this chapter are easy to follow. They can use information from your balance sheet and income statement and can help you monitor your business performance.

Creating the Financial Management Templates

When you create the financial management templates, use the following steps. Step 3 is particularly important; you must enter a zero (0) in the CALCCLR range in templates that use the iteration method.

1. Change column widths to the widths shown in the listing, such as [W5], then enter and justify the labels and section lines for the entire spreadsheet. The labels and lines will act as a skeleton from which you can locate other parts of the template. Use the figure of each template to get an idea of how labels are arranged. Lines between sections are easiest to enter using the repeat command, for example, \=.

2. Enter and format numbers from the template cell listing. Numbers in the listings are usually data for the sample problem. Entering the numbers will help you see the addresses to be used by range names.

3. In templates that use iteration, make sure that you have entered a zero (0) in the cell given the range name CALCCLR. These templates, like the unknown interest of annuities templates, must have a zero in CALCCLR before formulas are entered. Without this zero, a circular error will occur.

4. Create the range names used in the formulas. The range names must be created before entering formulas that use those names. The range names used in each template are listed in the "Creating the Template" section that relates to each template. The skeleton of labels and numbers you have entered will guide you in creating range names. Create range names with the /Range Name Create command. In Release 2, you can review range names and their addresses by issuing the /Range Name Table command. In Release 1A, issue the /rnc command and select a range name with the cursor and Enter keys; this procedure displays the address assigned to the selected name.

5. After creating the range names, enter the formulas. Major formulas are given in the "Financial Formulas" section that relates to each template as well as in the listing. Each of the four annuity templates listed can solve for two different types of annuities, depending on which set of formulas is inserted. Chapters 1 and 2 describe how to enter and correct formulas efficiently. After entering a long or complex formula, you should save the template to disk.

6. When everything is entered, *don't* run your template. For most templates, you will want to unprotect the data entry cells (the cells shown in the listing with a U) with the /Range Unprotect command and then protect the entire spreadsheet with /Worksheet Global Protection. You always should save your template before testing. Although the calculations in this chapter are straightforward, some templates that use macros may erase data and formulas or create errors when tested. Having an original in these cases can save you unnecessary work.

7. If you have entered the data values shown in the cell listing, the template will execute the sample problem. If the answers are different from the answers shown in the

figure of the template, check the data, then check the
range names, and finally print and check the formulas.
Chapters 1 and 2 offer tips on how to check formulas.

Compound Interest

The relationship between time and money is fundamental to finance.
You'd rather have a dollar today than the same dollar two years from
now.

The simplest expression of money's relationship to time is compound
interest—putting a fixed deposit in a fixed-interest investment with
the understanding that the investment will grow over time. Using a
compound interest formula, you can calculate how much your deposit
will grow. You also can use the formula to compare the value of an
investment today to its value in the future. The 1-2-3 Compound Interest template calculates any of the four variables involved in compound interest when you supply three known variables. In the
following sample problem, the Compound Interest template calculates the length of time needed for an investment to build up to a specific amount.

Making Your Money Grow

Suppose that you have won $5,000 in a radio station giveaway. You
want to put your winnings in a money market fund and let the sum
accumulate interest until the total reaches $9,000. If the money mar-
ket fund earns 8 percent compounded monthly, how long will you
have to wait before you have $9,000?

Compound interest investments accumulate interest on a fixed deposit of money, which is the *present value*, over a set *period* of time.
The amount to which the deposit grows is known as the *future value*.
The *interest* earned is calculated not only on the initial deposit but also
on the interest earned during each period. In the sample problem,
your initial deposit, the present value, is $5,000. You want your in-
vestment to grow to $9,000, the future value. The money market in-
terest rate is 8 percent annually, which is .67 percent per month. The
Compound Interest template (see fig. 3.1) shows that at this rate of
compounding, you will have to wait 88 months to accumulate $9,000.

Fig. 3.1. Compound Interest template.

```
       A        B        C         D        E      F      G      H
 1
 2 COMPOUND INTEREST
 3 =====================================================================
 4 Enter the three known values.
 5 Enter interest as the decimal interest per period. (15%/12 mo.=.0125)
 6 Enter a zero in the KNOWN row for the unknown value.
 7 ---------------------------------------------------------------------
 8             PV       FV        INT       N
 9 KNOWN:   5000.00  9000.00     0.67%      0
10
11 SOLUTION:    NA       NA        NA       88
12
13
```

Financial Formulas

The compound interest problem involves four different values: present value, future value, interest, and period. If any three values are known, the fourth may be calculated. Depending on which value is unknown, the compound interest formula will take one of the following forms.

$$FV=PV(1+INT)^N$$

$$PV=FV(1+INT)^{-N}$$

$$INT=((FV/PV)^{1/N}-1)$$

$$N=\ln(FV/PV)/\ln(1+INT)$$

When you use these formulas in the 1-2-3 Compound Interest template, also use range names with the same names as the variables. This convention helps you enter formulas easily and accurately. The variables and range names in the formulas and template are straightforward. PV stands for the present value, or the principal initially invested. FV is the future value of the investment. INT is the interest rate per period, which is entered as a decimal; and N is the number of periods the investment is compounded.

If you are using Release 2 of 1-2-3, you can use two functions in place of the INT and N formulas listed previously. (Release 1A users should use the previous formulas.)

$$INT=@RATE(FV,PV,N)$$

$$N=@CTERM(INT,FV,PV)$$

Creating the Template

Before you enter the formulas, you must create the range names used in the formulas. Creating these range names will make formulas easier to enter and to understand. The range names and their addresses are given in the following list.

Address	Range Name
B9	PV
C9	FV
D9	INT
E9	N

The 1-2-3 template encloses each compound interest formula in an @IF function, which determines the appropriate formula for calculating the answer. The following formulas solve for each variable:

Term	Address	Formulas
PV	B11	@IF(PV=0,FV*(1+INT)^-N,@NA)
FV	C11	@IF(FV=0,PV*(1+INT)^N,@NA)
INT	D11	@IF(INT=0,@RATE(FV,PV,N),@NA)
N	E11	@IF(N=0,@CTERM(INT,FV,PV),@NA)

If you are using 1-2-3 Release 1A, you must make the following substitutions because you do not have the @RATE and @CTERM functions.

Term	Address	Formulas
INT	D11	@IF(INT=0,(FV/PV)^(1/N)-1,@NA)
N	E11	@IF(N=0,@LN(FV/PV)/@LN(1+INT),@NA)

When the entry in the cell labeled PV is zero, for example, the PV formula in cell B11 is solved because PV is the *unknown value*. Cells containing numbers for the other variables hold *known values*, so the template displays NA in corresponding cells in the SOLUTION row.

When you create the template, leave the column widths set at 9. Be sure to create the range names before you enter the formulas. You also must unprotect the cells labeled U in list of cells 3.1. Use /**Range** Un-protect to unprotect cells or cell ranges. Then type the cell listings exactly as shown in list of cells 3.1. When you have finished entering the cell listings, protect the template with /**Worksheet** Global Protection Enable and save it to disk.

Once the template is saved, check it with the sample problem to see whether the template works correctly (see fig. 3.1). Enter three of the four known values under their appropriate labels in the row labeled

KNOWN. Enter a zero in the KNOWN row under the label of the unknown value. Enter interest as a decimal figure. The interest rate is the interest per period, so divide annual rates by the number of periods in a year. For example, for quarterly compounding, divide the annual rate by four. After you enter the knowns and the zero, the answer is displayed below the zero in the SOLUTION row. NA is displayed below the known values.

Tricks, Traps, and Assumptions

You can compare single-deposit investments by reducing all the investments to their future values. If the risk for the investments is the same, the investment with the highest future value will yield the best return.

The compound interest formula works for a single investment only when that investment is made at the beginning of the term and the interest rate remains constant. In investments where the interest rate fluctuates, you must recalculate when the rate changes. Use the future value at the point of change as the new present value and recalculate the compound interest from that point forward.

If you add constant amounts to your investment each period, use one of the annuity templates described later in this chapter.

Dollar values for FV and PV may vary slightly when you enter three of four known values in different combinations. This difference occurs because N is displayed as an integer number when solved for, but the division actually may have a remainder. You do not enter this remainder when you enter N as a known; this causes the difference in FV and PV dollar values.

List of Cells 3.1

```
A2:  PR [W9] 'COMPOUND INTEREST
A3:  PR [W9] \=
B3:  PR \=
C3:  PR \=
D3:  PR [W9] \=
E3:  PR \=
F3:  PR \=
G3:  PR \=
H3:  PR \=
A4:  PR [W9] ^Enter the three known values.
A5:  PR [W9] ^Enter interest as the decimal interest per period. (15%/12 mo.=.0125)
A6:  PR [W9] ^Enter a zero in the KNOWN row for the unknown value.
A7:  PR [W9] \-
B7:  PR \-
C7:  PR \-
D7:  PR [W9] \-
E7:  PR \-
F7:  PR \-
G7:  PR \-
H7:  PR \-
B8:  PR "PV
C8:  PR "FV
D8:  PR [W9] "INT
E8:  PR "N
A9:  PR [W9] 'KNOWN:
B9:  (F2) U 5000
C9:  (F2) U 9000
D9:  (P2) U [W9] 0.08/12
E9:  (F0) U 0
A11: PR [W9] ^SOLUTION:
B11: (F2) PR @IF(PV=0,FV*(1+INT)^-N,@NA)
C11: (F2) PR @IF(FV=0,PV*(1+INT)^N,@NA)
D11: (P2) PR [W9] @IF(INT=0,@RATE(FV,PV,N),@NA)
E11: (F0) PR @IF(N=0,@CTERM(INT,FV,PV),@NA)
```

Annual Percentage Rate (APR)

Comparing different types of investments is a difficult task, particularly when many different compounding periods are involved. When each investment has its own compounding period, the task can seem like comparing apples to oranges. For example, accounts in banks and savings and loan companies compound monthly or quarterly; bonds return dividends semiannually or annually; and some investments compound continuously. To compare these investments, the different stated rates and compounding periods have to be reduced to a common rate and period. The common rate used most often is the *effective rate*, also known as the *annual percentage rate* (APR).

Shopping for the Best Investment

Suppose that you have to choose between two different investment opportunities that appear to have the same risks. One investment has a stated interest rate (*nominal interest rate*) of 12 percent compounded semiannually. The other investment's nominal rate is 11.5 percent compounded monthly. Although the percentage rates of the two investments are only half a percent apart, the compounding periods can make a significant difference in their effective, or annual, percentage rates (APR). Which of these investments has the greater yield?

The 1-2-3 Interest Rate Conversion template (see fig. 3.2) calculates two different effective, or annual, interest rates (APR). Cells A1..G15 solve for investments compounded periodically during a year, while cells A18..G29 solve for investments compounded continuously. You can see in the upper portion of the template in figure 3.2 that 12 percent compounded semiannually yields an effective rate of 12.36 percent. This rate is higher than 11.5 percent compounded monthly. If these second figures were entered, the template would show that 11.5 percent yields an effective rate of 12.13 percent.

With the lower part of the template, you can compare investments that compound continuously. Continuous compounding adds interest to the principal amount continually throughout the year rather than adding interest at certain points such as monthly or quarterly. For example, the lower part of figure 3.2 shows that a nominal rate of 5.25 percent compounded continuously is the equivalent of 5.39 percent APR.

Financial Formulas

If the nominal rate compounds periodically during the year, the formulas that convert between nominal and effective (APR) rate are

$$NOMPER=N*((APRPER+1)^{1/N}-1)$$

$$APRPER=(1+NOMPER/N)^{N}-1$$

NOMPER is the nominal, or stated, interest rate per period, and APRPER is the effective, or annual, percentage rate per period. N is the number of compounding periods in a year.

```
        A         B         C         D         E         F         G         H
 1
 2  INTEREST RATE CONVERSION
 3  ============================================================================
 4  PERIODIC COMPOUNDING
 5  ----------------------------------------------------------------------------
 6  Enter the known interest rate as a decimal in the KNOWN row.
 7  Enter the unknown interest rate as a zero in the KNOWN row.
 8  The number of periods must be entered.
 9  ----------------------------------------------------------------------------
10                      NOMINAL            EFFECTIVE          PERIODS/
11                        RATE               RATE               YEAR
12
13  KNOWN:                0.12                 0                  2
14
15  SOLUTION:             NA               0.1236
16
17
18  ============================================================================
19  CONTINUOUS COMPOUNDING
20  ----------------------------------------------------------------------------
21  Enter the known interest rate as a decimal in the KNOWN row.
22  Enter the unknown interest rate as a zero in the KNOWN row.
23  ----------------------------------------------------------------------------
24                      NOMINAL            EFFECTIVE
25                        RATE               RATE
26
27  KNOWN:               0.0525               0
28
29  SOLUTION:             NA               0.0539
30
31
32
33
34
35
36
```

Fig. 3.2. Interest Rate Conversion template.

When the nominal rate compounds continuously, use the following conversion formulas:

NOMCONT=In(APRCONT+1)

APRCONT=exp(NOMCONT)–1

In these formulas, NOMCONT is the nominal, or stated, interest rate, and APRCONT is the effective, or annual, percentage rate for continuous compounding.

Creating the Template

You can convert interest rates easily by using the formulas along with a few @IF functions and range names. The formulas use range names to identify cells holding information. Using range names makes formulas easier to enter and debug. The range names used in the template and their addresses are

Address	Range Name
C13	NOMPER
C27	NOMCONT
E13	APRPER
E27	APRCONT
G13	N

The formulas that use these range names are contained inside @IF functions. The main formulas are

Term	Address	Formulas
NOMPER	C15	@IF(NOMPER=0,N*((APRPER+1)^(1/N)−1),@NA)
APRPER	E15	@IF(APRPER=0,(1+NOMPER/N)^N−1,@NA)
NOMCONT	C29	@IF(NOMCONT=0,@LN(APRCONT+1),@NA)
APRCONT	E29	@IF(APRCONT=0,@EXP(NOMCONT)−1,@NA)

The @IF functions determine which formula does the calculating. Only a formula that has a zero in the KNOWN row is calculated. For example, if E13 (APRPER) contains zero, the formula in cell E15 solves for APRPER. If E13 contains a number, the label NA is displayed in the SOLUTION row, because a solution isn't appropriate.

When you create the Interest Rate Conversion template, leave the column widths set at 9. Be sure you create the range names before you enter formulas that use those range names. Use the /Range Unprotect command to unprotect the cells preceded by U in the listing (see list of cells 3.2). Then enter the formulas as shown. After creating the spreadsheet, protect it with the /Worksheet Global Protection Enable command and save the template to disk.

Use the sample problem to check the formulas. To use the template, enter the known interest rate as a decimal in the KNOWN row under the appropriate label. Be sure to enter the number of periods per year. Enter a zero in the KNOWN row under the label of the unknown rate. Your answer will appear in the SOLUTION row.

Continuously compounding interest rates are converted in the same manner. Enter the known rate as a decimal in the KNOWN row in the lower half of the template. Continuous compounding does not have a number of periods per year. Enter zero under the label of the unknown term in the KNOWN row, and your answer will appear in the SOLUTION row.

Tricks, Traps, and Assumptions

When comparing investments, you must consider more than the effective rate. Differences between rates of returns must be weighed against the risk involved with each investment.

Usually, the estimated rate of return for an investment is higher when an investment is riskier. Investors require a higher rate of return to offset the chance of losing their money. For example, a passbook savings account insured by the FDIC may return only 5.25 percent because the investment is insured against loss. At the same time, an investment such as a second mortgage may return 14 percent because the chance of losing the original funds is greater. Every person must decide how much is worth risking for greater gain.

List of Cells 3.2

```
A2:  PR 'INTEREST RATE CONVERSION
A3:  PR \=
B3:  PR \=
C3:  PR \=
D3:  PR \=
E3:  PR \=
F3:  PR \=
G3:  PR \=
H3:  PR \=
A4:  PR 'PERIODIC COMPOUNDING
A5:  PR \-
B5:  PR \-
C5:  PR \-
D5:  PR \-
E5:  PR \-
F5:  PR \-
G5:  PR \-
H5:  PR \-
A6:  PR 'Enter the known interest rate as a decimal in the KNOWN row.
A7:  PR 'Enter the unknown interest rate as a zero in the KNOWN row.
A8:  U 'The number of periods must be entered.
A9:  PR \-
B9:  PR \-
C9:  PR \-
D9:  PR \-
E9:  PR \-
F9:  PR \-
G9:  PR \-
H9:  PR \-
C10: PR "NOMINAL
E10: PR "EFFECTIVE
G10: PR "PERIODS/
C11: PR "RATE
E11: PR "RATE
G11: PR "YEAR
A13: PR 'KNOWN:
C13: U 0.12
E13: U 0
G13: U 2
A15: PR 'SOLUTION:
```

```
C15: (F4) PR @IF(NOMPER=0,N*((APRPER+1)^(1/N)-1),@NA)
E15: (F4) PR @IF(APRPER=0,(1+NOMPER/N)^N-1,@NA)
A18: PR \=
B18: PR \=
C18: PR \=
D18: PR \=
E18: PR \=
F18: PR \=
G18: PR \=
H18: PR \=
A19: PR 'CONTINUOUS COMPOUNDING
A20: PR \-
B20: PR \-
C20: PR \-
D20: PR \-
E20: PR \-
F20: PR \-
G20: PR \-
H20: PR \-
A21: PR 'Enter the known interest rate as a decimal in the KNOWN row.
A22: PR 'Enter the unknown interest rate as a zero in the KNOWN row.
A23: PR \-
B23: PR \-
C23: PR \-
D23: PR \-
E23: PR \-
F23: PR \-
G23: PR \-
H23: PR \-
C24: PR "NOMINAL
E24: PR "EFFECTIVE
C25: PR "RATE
E25: PR "RATE
A27: PR 'KNOWN:
C27: U 0.0525
E27: U 0
A29: PR 'SOLUTION:
C29: (F4) PR @IF(NOMCONT=0,@LN(APRCONT+1),@NA)
E29: (F4) PR @IF(APRCONT=0,@EXP(NOMCONT)-1,@NA)
```

Add-On Interest Installment Loans

Smaller loans, for purchases such as boats and furniture, sometimes are made as installment loans with add-on interest. Add-on interest installment loans cost the borrower nearly twice as much as amortized loans with the same stated interest rate. This difference occurs because the installment loan borrower pays interest on the entire value of the initial loan over the life of the loan, but the amortized loan borrower pays interest only on the loan's remaining unpaid balance.

The Add-On Interest Installment Loan template can help you shop for better loan rates. The template calculates the payments and finance charges for an installment loan and gives you the annual percentage rate (APR) for the loan. You can use the APR to determine which loan gives you the lowest actual rate.

Finding the Best Loan Rates

Suppose that you have found the furniture you want for your den, but you are not sure how to finance the purchase. You can get a loan from your credit union for 18 percent APR, or you can get an installment loan from the store with an add-on interest rate of 12 percent for 1 year. You plan to purchase $3,000 worth of furniture this Saturday, 10 days before the end of the month. What are the face value and monthly payment for the installment loan? Should you choose the store's installment plan or the credit union loan?

At a 12 percent add-on interest rate, the face value of the store's loan is $3,369.86 with monthly payments of $280.82. The fact that the loan started 10 days before the first of the next month has been figured into the payments. You can see from figure 3.3 that the 12 percent add-on rate is the same as a 20.92 percent APR. Therefore, you should purchase the furniture through your credit union at 18 percent APR.

Financial Formulas

The face value of an add-on interest installment loan is the sum of the loan amount and the interest charges. For example, a 12-month loan of $8,000 at a 10 percent add-on rate has a face value of $8,800. The monthly payment is $733.00 ($8,800 divided by 12 months). The face value for an $8,000 loan at 10 percent for 2 years is $9,600 ($8,000 + $800 + $800).

The finance charges on most installment loans also include the number of days until the first of the next month. The following formula is used:

FC=LOAN*INTAO*(N/12+DAYS/365)

In this formula, FC is the finance charge, LOAN is the loan amount, INTAO is the add-on interest, and DAYS is the number of days remaining until the start of the next month. DAYS must be between 0 and 30. N is the number of monthly payments.

You calculate the monthly payment for an installment loan by dividing the loan's face amount by the number of monthly payments:

PMT=(LOAN+FC)/N

The annual percentage rate (APR) cannot be calculated directly. The iterative method described in Chapter 1 must be used. This method makes repeated estimates of the APR until the program finds a rate that

```
        A           B            C            D            E         F      G
 1
 2  ADD-ON INTEREST INSTALLMENT LOAN
 3  ============================================================================
 4  DATA ENTRY: LOAN VALUES
 5  ----------------------------------------------------------------------------
 6  Enter the known values for the add-on interest loan.
 7              Loan amount          3000.00
 8              Add-on rate             0.12 (Annual decimal rate)
 9              Periods                   12 (Total number)
10              Days to EOM               10 (0 to 30)
11
12  Press Alt-c to calculate a new APR.
13
14  ============================================================================
15  CALCULATED LOAN VALUES
16  ----------------------------------------------------------------------------
17              Finance charge        369.86
18              Payment               280.82
19              Repaid amount        3369.86 (Total in life of loan)
20              APR                   0.2092 (Annual Percentage Rate)
21
22  ============================================================================
23  CALCULATIONS
24  ----------------------------------------------------------------------------
25  CALCCLR is 1 when complete. To clear manually, enter 0, press F9 twice.
26              CALCCLR                    0
27
28  Each iteration (counter) increments the calculated interest rate.
29  Calculations are in decimal numbers, not percentages.
30      COUNTER                       37
31    FIRST INCR                   0.005
32
33  Next increment and interest used to calculate PMT
34      NEXT INCR   0.0000006104
35      NEXT INT    0.0174353027
36
37  Calculated value of PMT from 1st calculated interest
38      CALC PMT    280.82086198                      0.0010558299
39
40  Increment last added to calculated interest rate
41      LAST INCR   0.0000006104
42
43  ============================================================================
44                  CLEAR AND CALC MACRO
45  \c              {HOME}{BLANK A20}                      Position screen, erase warning
46                  {LET CALCCLR,0}{CALC}                  Set up to clear old values
47                  {RECALCCOL B30..B41}{RECALCCOL B30..B41}  Recalculate to clear
48                  {LET CALCCLR,1}                        Accept new values
49                  {RECALCCOL B30..B41}                   Prepare new values in cells
50                  {RECALCCOL B30..B41,@ABS(PMT-CALC PMT)<.001,100}  Iterative recalc until solved
51                  {CALC}                                 Calc rest of spreadsheet
52                  {GOTO}APR~                             Cursor on answer
53                  {IF FIRST INCR/NEXT INCR<=10}{WRONG}
54
55                  INCORRECT ANSWER: Interest or loan is too small to solve.
56  WRONG           {LET A20,"Incorrect!"}
57                  {GOTO}A20~
58                  {BEEP}
59
60
61
62
63
64
65
66
67
```

*Fig. 3.3. Add-On Interest
Installment Loan template.*

produces the same monthly payment as the monthly payment for the installment loan. The formula used to calculate the payment with APR is

$$PMT_{APR}=LOAN*(APR/(1-(1+APR)^{-N}))*(1+APR)^{(DAYS*12/365)}$$

Creating the Template

Before you enter the formulas for the Add-On Interest Installment Loan template, you need to create the following range names:

Address	Range Name
B30	COUNTER
B31	FIRST INCR
B34	NEXT INCR
B35	NEXT INT
B38	CALC PMT
B41	LAST INCR
B45	\C
B56	WRONG
C7	LOAN
C8	INTAO
C9	N
C10	DAYS
C17	FC
C18	PMT
C19	REPAY
C20	APR
C26	CALCCLR

The main formulas in this template and their locations are given in the following list:

Term	Address	Formula
FC	C17	+LOAN*INTAO*(N/12+DAYS/365)
PMT	C18	(LOAN+FC)/N
Repaid amount	C19	+PMT*N
APR	C20	@IF(CALCCLR=1,12*NEXT INT,@NA)
CALC PMT	B38	@IF(CALCCLR=0,0.001,LOAN*(NEXT INT/ (1-(1+NEXT INT)^-N))*(1+NEXT INT)^ (DAYS*12/365))

Using the iteration method, 1-2-3 makes repeated estimates of the APR, adjusting each estimate until the estimated APR is as accurate as desired. Cell B31 holds the initial APR estimate, which is one-half of the monthly add-on interest rate. The formula in cell B38 uses this initial estimate to calculate a value that is already known, the monthly payment (PMT). If the calculated payment is greater than or less than the true payment, the estimated APR is adjusted. These adjustments bring the estimated APR closer and closer to an APR that produces the same payment as the payment using the add-on interest method. The more the estimation process repeats, the more accurate the estimated APR becomes. The iteration process is discussed in more detail in Chapter 1.

The \c macro repeatedly calculates the PMT equation in cell B38. The PMT calculated uses the formula in cell B38 as PMT_{APR}. The \c macro, beginning at cell B45, first clears old estimations by setting the cell CALCCLR to zero and recalculating twice with {RECALCCOL B30..B41}.

The {RECALCCOL} command in cell B50 recalculates the spreadsheet area between B30 and B41 until one of two conditions is satisfied: either the true and estimated value of PMT are within one-tenth of a cent, or the area has been recalculated 100 times.

1-2-3 Release 1A users can use this template with the iteration macro listed in Appendix D. That macro should replace the macro in list of cells 3.3 completely for Release 1A users.

Before entering the cell listings, change the column widths so that columns A and B are 14, C is 15, D is 17, and E is 12. Be sure that the cells marked with a U and cell A20 are unprotected. Cell A20 displays the warning Incorrect when a solution is out of bounds.

In addition, before you enter the data and formulas given in list of cells 3.3, make sure that you enter the CALCCLR value in C26 as zero. This entry causes the circular reference formulas initially to display constant values and so prevents an ERR condition. After entering the template, protect it with /Worksheet Global Protection Enable, and save the template to disk.

After the template is saved, you can test the program with the sample data shown in figure 3.3. Make sure the template is set to manual recalculation with one iteration. In cells C7 through C10, enter the initial loan amount, add-on interest rate, number of monthly payments, and number of days until the first of the next month. The finance charge, face value, and monthly payment are displayed immediately. You must hold down the Alt key and press C to update the APR.

Tricks, Traps, and Assumptions

Add-on installment loans cost the borrower nearly twice the rate of an amortized loan with the same stated interest rate. Before initiating an add-on installment loan, calculate the annual percentage rate (APR) and compare the amount to other forms of credit. Installment lenders are required by law to display the APR in boldface figures on all installment loan contracts. Lenders may use either an exact APR, as calculated by the template, or an approximation.

In most financial calculations, including add-on installment loans, months are assumed to be 30 days in length.

For more information on installment loans, see the next section concerning rebates on installment loans (Rule of 78s).

List of Cells 3.3

```
A2:  PR [W14] 'ADD-ON INTEREST INSTALLMENT LOAN
A3:  PR [W14] \=
B3:  PR [W14] \=
C3:  PR [W15] \=
D3:  PR [W17] \=
E3:  PR [W12] \=
A4:  PR [W14] 'DATA ENTRY: LOAN VALUES
A5:  PR [W14] \-
B5:  PR [W14] \-
C5:  PR [W15] \-
D5:  PR [W17] \-
E5:  PR [W12] \-
A6:  PR [W14] 'Enter the known values for the add-on interest loan.
B7:  PR [W14] 'Loan amount
C7:  (F2) U [W15] 3000
B8:  PR [W14] 'Add-on rate
C8:  U [W15] 0.12
D8:  PR [W17] '(Annual decimal rate)
B9:  PR [W14] 'Periods
C9:  (F0) U [W15] 12
D9:  PR [W17] '(Total number)
B10: PR [W14] 'Days to EOM
C10: (F0) U [W15] 10
D10: PR [W17] '(0 to 30)
A12: U [W14] 'Press Alt-c to calculate a new APR.
A14: PR [W14] \=
B14: PR [W14] \=
C14: PR [W15] \=
D14: PR [W17] \=
E14: PR [W12] \=
A15: PR [W14] 'CALCULATED LOAN VALUES
A16: PR [W14] \-
B16: PR [W14] \-
C16: PR [W15] \-
D16: PR [W17] \-
E16: PR [W12] \-
B17: PR [W14] 'Finance charge
C17: (F2) PR [W15] +LOAN*INTAO*(N/12+DAYS/365)
B18: PR [W14] 'Payment
```

```
C18: (F2) PR [W15] (LOAN+FC)/N
B19: PR [W14] 'Repaid amount
C19: (F2) PR [W15] +PMT*N
D19: PR [W17] '(Total in life of loan)
B20: PR [W14] 'APR
C20: (F4) PR [W15] @IF(CALCCLR=1,12*NEXT INT,@NA)
D20: PR [W17] '(Annual Percentage Rate)
A22: PR [W14] \=
B22: PR [W14] \=
C22: PR [W15] \=
D22: PR [W17] \=
E22: PR [W12] \=
A23: PR [W14] 'CALCULATIONS
A24: PR [W14] \-
B24: PR [W14] \-
C24: PR [W15] \-
D24: PR [W17] \-
E24: PR [W12] \-
A25: PR [W14] 'CALCCLR is 1 when complete. To clear manually, enter 0, press F9 twice.
B26: PR [W14] 'CALCCLR
C26: U [W15] 0
A28: PR [W14] 'Each iteration (counter) increments the calculated interest rate.
A29: PR [W14] 'Calculations are in decimal numbers, not percentages.
A30: PR [W14] "COUNTER
B30: PR [W14] @IF(CALCCLR=1,COUNTER+1,0)
A31: PR [W14] "FIRST INCR
B31: PR [W14] +INTA0/24
A33: PR [W14] 'Next increment and interest used to calculate PMT
A34: PR [W14] "NEXT INCR
B34: PR [W14] @IF(PMT>CALC PMT,LAST INCR,LAST INCR/2)
A35: PR [W14] "NEXT INT
B35: PR [W14] @IF(CALCCLR=0,INTA0/12,@IF(PMT>CALC PMT,NEXT INT+LAST INCR,NEXT INT-LAST INCR))
A37: PR [W14] 'Calculated value of PMT from 1st calculated interest
A38: PR [W14] "CALC PMT
B38: (G) PR [W14] @IF(CALCCLR=0,0.001,LOAN*(NEXT INT/(1-(1+NEXT INT)^-N))*(1+NEXT INT)^(DAYS*12/365))
D38: PR [W17] @ABS(PMT-CALC PMT)
A40: PR [W14] 'Increment last added to calculated interest rate
A41: PR [W14] "LAST INCR
B41: PR [W14] @IF(COUNTER<2,FIRST INCR,NEXT INCR)
A43: PR [W14] \=
B43: PR [W14] \=
C43: PR [W15] \=
D43: PR [W17] \=
E43: PR [W12] \=
B44: PR [W14] 'CLEAR AND CALC MACRO
A45: PR [W14] '\c
B45: PR [W14] '{HOME}{BLANK A20}
F45: PR 'Position screen, erase warning
B46: PR [W14] '{LET CALCCLR,0}{CALC}
F46: PR 'Set up to clear old values
B47: PR [W14] '{RECALCCOL B30..B41}{RECALCCOL B30..B41}
F47: PR 'Recalculate to clear
B48: PR [W14] '{LET CALCCLR,1}
F48: PR 'Accept new values
B49: PR [W14] '{RECALCCOL B30..B41}
F49: PR 'Prepare new values in cells
B50: PR [W14] '{RECALCCOL B30..B41,@ABS(PMT-CALC PMT)<.001,100}
F50: PR 'Iterative recalc until solved
B51: PR [W14] '{CALC}
F51: PR 'Calc rest of spreadsheet
B52: PR [W14] '{GOTO}APR~
F52: PR 'Cursor on answer
B53: PR [W14] '{IF FIRST INCR/NEXT INCR<=10}{WRONG}
B55: PR [W14] 'INCORRECT ANSWER: Interest or loan is too small to solve.
A56: PR [W14] 'WRONG
B56: PR [W14] '{LET A20,"Incorrect!"}
B57: PR [W14] '{GOTO}A20~
B58: PR [W14] '{BEEP}
```

Rule of 78s: Interest Rebates

When you pay off an add-on interest loan or an installment loan early, you don't owe the entire balance of the loan's face value. In fact, you usually owe much less. The face value of an add-on interest loan is the loan amount plus the finance charge. When you pay off a loan early, you haven't kept the money for the full term of the loan, so you don't owe the full finance charge. But how much do you owe?

Paying Off Add-On Interest Loans Early

Suppose that you will get a Christmas bonus of $4,500, and the first thing you plan to do with the bonus is pay off the installment loan on the boat you bought last summer. The $6,000 boat loan was for 24 months at 10 percent per year add-on interest. Payments started on July 1. How much will you have left from your Christmas bonus when you pay off the loan on January 15?

The finance charge for the loan is $1,200 (2 years times 10 percent times $6,000), which makes the loan's face value $7,200. The monthly payments of $300 are calculated by dividing the $7,200 face value by 24 months. You will make the January 1 payment before paying off the loan, so the 7th payment will be the last payment you make. Figure 3.4 shows that you will receive a rebate of $612. This rebate is subtracted from the balance of the loan's face value. You must pay $4,488.00 to pay off the loan. You will have $12 left from your bonus to spend as you choose.

Financial Formulas

If the loan isn't kept for the full term, some of the interest in the face value hasn't been earned. This unearned interest is calculated by the following formula:

REBATE=FC*(N–LASTN)*(N–LASTN+1)/(N(N+1))

The actual balance owed on the loan is calculated by this formula:

BALANCE=PMT*(N–LASTN)–REBATE

In these formulas, FC is the finance charge for the full term of the loan. N is the number of periods in the loan, and LASTN is the number of

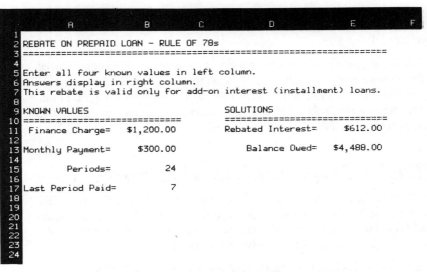

```
              A              B         C            D             E          F
 1
 2 REBATE ON PREPAID LOAN - RULE OF 78s
 3 =================================================================
 4
 5 Enter all four known values in left column.
 6 Answers display in right column.
 7 This rebate is valid only for add-on interest (installment) loans.
 8
 9 KNOWN VALUES                          SOLUTIONS
10 =============================         =============================
11  Finance Charge=    $1,200.00         Rebated Interest=      $612.00
12
13 Monthly Payment=      $300.00            Balance Owed=     $4,488.00
14
15         Periods=           24
16
17 Last Period Paid=           7
18
19
20
21
22
23
24
```

Fig. 3.4. Rebate on Prepaid Loan –
Rule of 78s template.

the last payment that was made. PMT is the amount of the monthly payment.

Creating the Template

This template is short and straightforward. The variables all are given range names to make the formulas easier to understand. The range names and their locations are

Address	Range Name
B11	FC
B13	PMT
B15	N
B17	LASTN
E11	REBATE

The formulas used in the 1-2-3 template appear the same as they do in the financial formulas presented in the last section. The formulas and their locations are

Term	Address	Range Name
REBATE	E11	+FC*(N–LASTN)*(N–LASTN+1)/(N*(N+1))
BALANCE	E13	+PMT*(N–LASTN)–REBATE

Before you enter list of cells 3.4, change the column widths so that column A is 17, columns B and E are 12, column C is 8, and column D is 18. Create the range names and then type the cell listings. Use /Range Unprotect to unprotect those cells in the list of cells that are preceded by a U.

Before testing the template, protect it by using /Worksheet Global Protection, and save it to disk. Check that the template works correctly by entering the boat loan numbers in cells B11 through B17 under the heading KNOWN VALUES. The answers will appear under the heading SOLUTIONS.

Tricks, Traps, and Assumptions

Add-on installment loans cost the borrower nearly twice the rate of an amortized loan with the same stated interest rate. Before initiating an add-on installment loan, calculate the annual percentage rate (APR) and compare the amount to other forms of credit.

Installment lenders are required by law to display the APR in boldface numbers on all installment loan contracts. Lenders may use either an exact APR or an approximation method.

For more information on installment loans, see the previous section, "Add-On Interest Installment Loans."

List of Cells 3.4

```
A2: PR [W17] 'REBATE ON PREPAID LOAN - RULE OF 78s
A3: PR [W17] \=
B3: PR [W12] \=
C3: PR [W8] \=
D3: PR [W18] \=
E3: PR [W12] \=
A5: PR [W17] 'Enter all four known values in left column.
A6: PR [W17] 'Answers display in right column.
A7: U [W17] 'This rebate is valid only for add-on interest (installment) loans.
A9: PR [W17] 'KNOWN VALUES
D9: PR [W18] 'SOLUTIONS
A10: PR [W17] \=
B10: PR [W12] \=
D10: PR [W18] \=
E10: PR [W12] \=
A11: PR [W17] "Finance Charge=
B11: (C2) U [W12] 1200
D11: PR [W18] "Rebated Interest=
E11: (C2) PR [W12] +FC*(N-LASTN)*(N-LASTN+1)/(N*(N+1))
A13: PR [W17] "Monthly Payment=
B13: (C2) U [W12] 300
D13: PR [W18] "Balance Owed=
E13: (C2) PR [W12] +PMT*(N-LASTN)-REBATE
A15: PR [W17] "Periods=
B15: (F0) U [W12] 24
A17: PR [W17] "Last Period Paid=
B17: (F0) U [W12] 7
```

Amortized Loan Schedule

The largest financial transactions that most people make are the purchases of homes and rental properties. One advantage of these purchases is the chance to deduct the mortgage interest payments from income. The 1-2-3 Amortized Loan Schedule template can provide the important information you need for these purchases as well as save you time and effort. With other mortgage schedules, you have to wade through reams of paper to find the dates you want. With the Amortized Loan Schedule template, however, you can start the schedule at any date in the mortgage life. Another benefit of the template is that you can print the schedule to help you figure taxes. Also, the template labels the months and years so that you easily can find the increase between different periods.

Calculating Mortgage Schedules from Any Time

Assume that you have just purchased a small rustic cabin on the California coast near Mendocino. For tax purposes, your accountant wants to know what portion of your payments in the third tax year will be toward the interest. Your $250,000 mortgage is for 30 years, and you made the first payment on July 1, 1985. The annual interest rate on the loan is 12.5 percent.

When you enter the loan amount, annual interest, and term (360 months), the Amortized Loan Schedule template calculates the monthly payment. You then enter the month (7) and year (1985) of your first payment and the month and year of the start of your third tax year (10 and 1987, respectively). The upper portion of figure 3.5 shows this entry portion of the 1-2-3 template.

The template calculates the loan balance at the start of the schedule (October 1, 1987) and creates a schedule of payments through September 30, 1990. You can look at the change between 10/87 and 9/88 in the Interest to Date column and see that during this period you will pay $30,941.83 in interest ($100,998.25–$70,056.42). Once the mortgage balance is calculated for a future date, a few simple formulas are used repeatedly to produce the loan schedule shown in the lower part of figure 3.5.

```
     A    B        C         D         E         F         G         H
 1
 2  AMORTIZED LOAN SCHEDULE: MORTGAGE SCHEDULE FROM ANY PERIOD
 3  ==========================================================================
 4
 5  Enter values over highlighted cells.
 6
 7  Initial Loan           250000.00
 8  Annual Interest            0.1250
 9  Total No. Payments           360
10
11  Actual Payment            2668.14              Calc Pmt    2668.144405
12
13  First Payment Month            7
14  First Payment Year          1985
15
16  Start Sched. Month            10
17  Start Sched. Year           1987
18
19  Payments Past                 27
20  Payments Remaining           333
21
22  Starting Balance       248016.64
23  ==========================================================================
24
25                        LOAN SCHEDULE
26
27  End of        Balance   Principal  Principal   Interest   Interest
28  Mo.   Yr.     of Loan    Payment   to Date     Payment    to Date
29  ------------------------------------------------------------------------
30             248016.64                1983.36               70056.42
31  10  1987   247932.01      84.63     2067.99    2583.51    72639.93
32  11  1987   247846.50      85.51     2153.50    2582.63    75222.56
33  12  1987   247760.09      86.41     2239.91    2581.73    77804.29
34   1  1988   247672.78      87.31     2327.22    2580.83    80385.12
35   2  1988   247584.56      88.22     2415.44    2579.92    82965.04
36   3  1988   247495.43      89.13     2504.57    2579.01    85544.05
37   4  1988   247405.37      90.06     2594.63    2578.08    88122.13
38   5  1988   247314.37      91.00     2685.63    2577.14    90699.27
39   6  1988   247222.42      91.95     2777.58    2576.19    93275.46
40   7  1988   247129.51      92.91     2870.49    2575.23    95850.69
41   8  1988   247035.64      93.87     2964.36    2574.27    98424.96
42   9  1988   246940.79      94.85     3059.21    2573.29   100998.25
43  10  1988   246844.95      95.84     3155.05    2572.30   103570.55
44  11  1988   246748.11      96.84     3251.89    2571.30   106141.85
45  12  1988   246650.26      97.85     3349.74    2570.29   108712.14
46   1  1989   246551.39      98.87     3448.61    2569.27   111281.41
47   2  1989   246451.49      99.90     3548.51    2568.24   113849.65
48   3  1989   246350.55     100.94     3649.45    2567.20   116416.85
49   4  1989   246248.56     101.99     3751.44    2566.15   118983.00
50   5  1989   246145.51     103.05     3854.49    2565.09   121548.09
51   6  1989   246041.39     104.12     3958.61    2564.02   124112.11
52   7  1989   245936.18     105.21     4063.82    2562.93   126675.04
53   8  1989   245829.88     106.30     4170.12    2561.84   129236.88
54   9  1989   245722.47     107.41     4277.53    2560.73   131797.61
55  10  1989   245613.94     108.53     4386.06    2559.61   134357.22
56  11  1989   245504.28     109.66     4495.72    2558.48   136915.70
57  12  1989   245393.48     110.80     4606.52    2557.34   139473.04
58   1  1990   245281.52     111.96     4718.48    2556.18   142029.22
59   2  1990   245168.40     113.12     4831.60    2555.02   144584.24
60   3  1990   245054.10     114.30     4945.90    2553.84   147138.08
61   4  1990   244938.61     115.49     5061.39    2552.65   149690.73
62   5  1990   244821.91     116.70     5178.09    2551.44   152242.17
63   6  1990   244704.00     117.91     5296.00    2550.23   154792.40
64   7  1990   244584.86     119.14     5415.14    2549.00   157341.40
65   8  1990   244464.48     120.38     5535.52    2547.76   159889.16
66   9  1990   244342.85     121.63     5657.15    2546.51   162435.67
67
68
69
70
71
```

*Fig. 3.5. Amortized Loan
Schedule: Mortgage Schedule from
Any Period template.*

Financial Formulas

The Amortized Loan Schedule template uses the mortgage payment as a starting point for other calculations. 1-2-3's @PMT function calculates the monthly loan payment from the loan amount, interest, and period. The program then uses the mortgage balance (the unpaid loan amount) as the starting point for the schedule.

The mortgage balance is calculated as the present value of the remaining monthly payments at the mortgage lending rate. You can use the 1-2-3 @PV function for this calculation if you first find the number of months remaining in the loan (NREMAIN). The loan balance at any time is equal to @PV(PMT,INT,NREMAIN).

Amortized loans pay the principal and interest of the loan from a constant periodic payment calculated with @PMT. The interest owed each period is calculated on the remaining balance of the loan. The remainder of the monthly payment pays off a portion of the loan's remaining balance. The three formulas that produce the schedule are

$$PMT_{int}=INT*BALANCE_{old}$$

$$PMT_{princ}=PMT- PMT_{int}$$

$$BALANCE_{new}=BALANCE_{old}-PMT_{princ}$$

PMT is the total monthly payment, PMT_{int} is the monthly interest payment, and PMT_{princ} is the monthly principal payment. The interest (INT) is the monthly interest (annual interest divided by 12) expressed as a decimal. $BALANCE_{old}$ is the loan balance before the monthly payment, and $BALANCE_{new}$ is the balance after the monthly payment. Relative cell references are used in the spreadsheet for most of the terms in the schedule, because these three formulas are copied over 36 rows.

Creating the Template

The formulas use range names for the cells containing information such as the payment (PMT) or the number of periods in the term (N). The range names also make the formulas easier to understand. Create the range names before you enter the formulas. The range names and their addresses are

Address	*Range Name*
D7	LOAN
D8	INT
D9	N
D11	PMT
D20	NREMAIN

LOAN is the loan amount, INT names the annual interest, and N is the term. The rounded payment, with the range name PMT, is used to calculate the principal payment. NREMAIN is the number of months remaining in the loan.

Four 1-2-3 formulas are used. The first formula, in cell G11, calculates the mortgage payment by using the @PMT function. A second formula (in cell D22) calculates the remaining loan balance at any time during the loan. The third and fourth formulas, in row 32, determine how much of each payment goes to interest and how much to loan repayment. The formulas in row 32 are copied down the spreadsheet to produce the schedule. The essential formulas are

Term	*Address*	*Formula*
Calc Payment	G11	@PMT(LOAN,INT/12,N)
Start Balance	D22	@ROUND(@PV(PMT,INT/12,NREMAIN),2)
Loan Balance	C32	+C31−D32
Princ Payment	D32	+$PMT−F32
Princ to Date	E32	+E31+D32
Int Payment	F32	@ROUND(C31*$INT/12,2)
Int to Date	G32	+G31+F32

The rounded value of PMT, displayed in cell D11, is the amount paid on the loan each month. The unrounded value in G11 is used to calculate the loan balance at any point. Dates are automatically generated from the starting date of the schedule by using the @MOD function beginning in cell A32.

You build the 1-2-3 Amortized Loan Schedule template by entering list of cells 3.5. Before entering the listing, change the column widths so that column A is 4 and column B is 5. Using figure 3.5 as a reference, enter the labels and numbers from the listing. Then create the range names used by the formulas and enter the formulas. Unprotect the data entry cells that are preceded by U in the listing. To protect the entire worksheet, use /Worksheet Global Protection. After you have entered the cell listings, save the template to disk before testing.

To test the template, enter the loan amount, annual interest, and total number of payments (next to the appropriate labels) in cells D7, D8, and D9, respectively. 1-2-3 calculates the monthly payment from these values. Enter the first month and year of the loan and of the schedule in cells D13 through D17. The template uses these entries to calculate past payments, payments remaining, and starting balance of the schedule.

The lower portion of the screen displays the loan payment schedule. The first amount under Balance of Loan is the balance for the first day of the schedule. The amounts listed in the schedule are effective after the payment is made for the month given in the first column.

If data entry seems slow, you can turn off the automatic recalculation by invoking /Worksheet Global Recalculation Manual. To calculate the schedule when manual recalculation is activated, you will have to press the F9 key (CALC).

The schedule displays 36 months of information. To add more months to the schedule, copy the formulas in row 66 (columns A through G) down as many rows as you need.

Tricks, Traps, and Assumptions

This schedule is designed for amortized loans. If your loan is an add-on interest installment loan, also known as a consumer or installment loan, this schedule does not apply. For those cases, refer to previous sections in this chapter, "Add-On Installment Loans" and "Rule of 78s: Interest Rebates."

The last payment of the loan may be slightly different from the constant payment. This difference is usually added to the final payment.

Because of differences in rounding, this template may have small discrepancies when compared with schedules produced by lending institutions. If your schedules must be exact, check the procedure that the lending institution uses and modify the template so that the two agree.

List of Cells 3.5

```
A2:  PR [W4] 'AMORTIZED LOAN SCHEDULE: MORTGAGE SCHEDULE FROM ANY PERIOD
A3:  PR [W4] \=
B3:  PR [W5] \=
C3:  PR [W14] \=
D3:  PR [W12] \=
E3:  PR [W12] \=
F3:  PR [W12] \=
G3:  PR [W12] \=
A5:  PR [W4] 'Enter values over highlighted cells.
A7:  PR [W4] 'Initial Loan
D7:  (F2) U [W12] 250000
A8:  PR [W4] 'Annual Interest
D8:  (F4) U [W12] 0.125
A9:  PR [W4] 'Total No. Payments
D9:  (F0) U [W12] 360
A11: PR [W4] 'Actual Payment
D11: (F2) PR [W12] @ROUND(G11,2)
F11: PR [W12] 'Calc Pmt
G11: PR [W12] @PMT(LOAN,INT/12,N)
A13: PR [W4] 'First Payment Month
D13: (F0) U [W12] 7
A14: PR [W4] 'First Payment Year
D14: (F0) U [W12] 1985
A16: PR [W4] 'Start Sched. Month
D16: (F0) U [W12] 10
A17: PR [W4] 'Start Sched. Year
D17: (F0) U [W12] 1987
A19: PR [W4] 'Payments Past
D19: (F0) PR [W12] (D17*12+D16)-(D14*12+D13)
A20: PR [W4] 'Payments Remaining
D20: (F0) PR [W12] +N-D19
A22: PR [W4] 'Starting Balance
D22: (F2) PR [W12] @ROUND(@PV(PMT,INT/12,NREMAIN),2)
A23: PR [W4] \=
B23: PR [W5] \=
C23: PR [W14] \=
D23: PR [W12] \=
E23: PR [W12] \=
F23: PR [W12] \=
G23: PR [W12] \=
D25: PR [W12] '    LOAN SCHEDULE
A27: PR [W4] ' End of
C27: PR [W14] "Balance
D27: PR [W12] "Principal
E27: PR [W12] "Principal
F27: PR [W12] "Interest
G27: PR [W12] "Interest
A28: PR [W4] "Mo.
B28: PR [W5] "Yr.
C28: PR [W14] "of Loan
D28: PR [W12] "Payment
E28: PR [W12] "to Date
F28: PR [W12] "Payment
G28: PR [W12] "to Date
A29: PR [W4] \-
B29: PR [W5] \-
C29: PR [W14] \-
D29: PR [W12] \-
E29: PR [W12] \-
F29: PR [W12] \-
G29: PR [W12] \-
C30: (F2) PR [W14] +D22
E30: (F2) PR [W12] +LOAN-C30
```

```
G30: (F2) PR [W12] @ROUND($D$19*$PMT-E30,2)
A31: PR [W4] +D16
B31: PR [W5] +D17
C31: (F2) PR [W14] +C30-D31
D31: (F2) PR [W12] +$PMT-F31
E31: (F2) PR [W12] +E30+D31
F31: (F2) PR [W12] @ROUND(C30*$INT/12,2)
G31: (F2) PR [W12] +G30+F31
A32: PR [W4] @MOD(A31,12)+1
B32: PR [W5] @IF(A32=1,B31+1,B31)
C32: (F2) PR [W14] +C31-D32
D32: (F2) PR [W12] +$PMT-F32
E32: (F2) PR [W12] +E31+D32
F32: (F2) PR [W12] @ROUND(C31*$INT/12,2)
G32: (F2) PR [W12] +G31+F32
A33: PR [W4] @MOD(A32,12)+1
B33: PR [W5] @IF(A33=1,B32+1,B32)
C33: (F2) PR [W14] +C32-D33
D33: (F2) PR [W12] +$PMT-F33
E33: (F2) PR [W12] +E32+D33
F33: (F2) PR [W12] @ROUND(C32*$INT/12,2)
G33: (F2) PR [W12] +G32+F33
A34: PR [W4] @MOD(A33,12)+1
B34: PR [W5] @IF(A34=1,B33+1,B33)
C34: (F2) PR [W14] +C33-D34
D34: (F2) PR [W12] +$PMT-F34
E34: (F2) PR [W12] +E33+D34
F34: (F2) PR [W12] @ROUND(C33*$INT/12,2)
G34: (F2) PR [W12] +G33+F34
A35: PR [W4] @MOD(A34,12)+1
B35: PR [W5] @IF(A35=1,B34+1,B34)
C35: (F2) PR [W14] +C34-D35
D35: (F2) PR [W12] +$PMT-F35
E35: (F2) PR [W12] +E34+D35
F35: (F2) PR [W12] @ROUND(C34*$INT/12,2)
G35: (F2) PR [W12] +G34+F35
A36: PR [W4] @MOD(A35,12)+1
B36: PR [W5] @IF(A36=1,B35+1,B35)
C36: (F2) PR [W14] +C35-D36
D36: (F2) PR [W12] +$PMT-F36
E36: (F2) PR [W12] +E35+D36
F36: (F2) PR [W12] @ROUND(C35*$INT/12,2)
G36: (F2) PR [W12] +G35+F36
A37: PR [W4] @MOD(A36,12)+1
B37: PR [W5] @IF(A37=1,B36+1,B36)
C37: (F2) PR [W14] +C36-D37
D37: (F2) PR [W12] +$PMT-F37
E37: (F2) PR [W12] +E36+D37
F37: (F2) PR [W12] @ROUND(C36*$INT/12,2)
G37: (F2) PR [W12] +G36+F37
A38: PR [W4] @MOD(A37,12)+1
B38: PR [W5] @IF(A38=1,B37+1,B37)
C38: (F2) PR [W14] +C37-D38
D38: (F2) PR [W12] +$PMT-F38
E38: (F2) PR [W12] +E37+D38
F38: (F2) PR [W12] @ROUND(C37*$INT/12,2)
G38: (F2) PR [W12] +G37+F38
A39: PR [W4] @MOD(A38,12)+1
B39: PR [W5] @IF(A39=1,B38+1,B38)
C39: (F2) PR [W14] +C38-D39
D39: (F2) PR [W12] +$PMT-F39
E39: (F2) PR [W12] +E38+D39
F39: (F2) PR [W12] @ROUND(C38*$INT/12,2)
G39: (F2) PR [W12] +G38+F39
A40: PR [W4] @MOD(A39,12)+1
B40: PR [W5] @IF(A40=1,B39+1,B39)
```

```
C40: (F2) PR [W14] +C39-D40
D40: (F2) PR [W12] +$PMT-F40
E40: (F2) PR [W12] +E39+D40
F40: (F2) PR [W12] @ROUND(C39*$INT/12,2)
G40: (F2) PR [W12] +G39+F40
A41: PR [W4] @MOD(A40,12)+1
B41: PR [W5] @IF(A41=1,B40+1,B40)
C41: (F2) PR [W14] +C40-D41
D41: (F2) PR [W12] +$PMT-F41
E41: (F2) PR [W12] +E40+D41
F41: (F2) PR [W12] @ROUND(G40*$INT/12,2)
G41: (F2) PR [W12] +G40+F41
A42: PR [W4] @MOD(A41,12)+1
B42: PR [W5] @IF(A42=1,B41+1,B41)
C42: (F2) PR [W14] +C41-D42
D42: (F2) PR [W12] +$PMT-F42
E42: (F2) PR [W12] +E41+D42
F42: (F2) PR [W12] @ROUND(C41*$INT/12,2)
G42: (F2) PR [W12] +G41+F42
A43: PR [W4] @MOD(A42,12)+1
B43: PR [W5] @IF(A43=1,B42+1,B42)
C43: (F2) PR [W14] +C42-D43
D43: (F2) PR [W12] +$PMT-F43
E43: (F2) PR [W12] +E42+D43
F43: (F2) PR [W12] @ROUND(C42*$INT/12,2)
G43: (F2) PR [W12] +G42+F43
A44: PR [W4] @MOD(A43,12)+1
B44: PR [W5] @IF(A44=1,B43+1,B43)
C44: (F2) PR [W14] +C43-D44
D44: (F2) PR [W12] +$PMT-F44
E44: (F2) PR [W12] +E43+D44
F44: (F2) PR [W12] @ROUND(C43*$INT/12,2)
G44: (F2) PR [W12] +G43+F44
A45: PR [W4] @MOD(A44,12)+1
B45: PR [W5] @IF(A45=1,B44+1,B44)
C45: (F2) PR [W14] +C44-D45
D45: (F2) PR [W12] +$PMT-F45
E45: (F2) PR [W12] +E44+D45
F45: (F2) PR [W12] @ROUND(C44*$INT/12,2)
G45: (F2) PR [W12] +G44+F45
A46: PR [W4] @MOD(A45,12)+1
B46: PR [W5] @IF(A46=1,B45+1,B45)
C46: (F2) PR [W14] +C45-D46
D46: (F2) PR [W12] +$PMT-F46
E46: (F2) PR [W12] +E45+D46
F46: (F2) PR [W12] @ROUND(C45*$INT/12,2)
G46: (F2) PR [W12] +G45+F46
A47: PR [W4] @MOD(A46,12)+1
B47: PR [W5] @IF(A47=1,B46+1,B46)
C47: (F2) PR [W14] +C46-D47
D47: (F2) PR [W12] +$PMT-F47
E47: (F2) PR [W12] +E46+D47
F47: (F2) PR [W12] @ROUND(C46*$INT/12,2)
G47: (F2) PR [W12] +G46+F47
A48: PR [W4] @MOD(A47,12)+1
B48: PR [W5] @IF(A48=1,B47+1,B47)
C48: (F2) PR [W14] +C47-D48
D48: (F2) PR [W12] +$PMT-F48
E48: (F2) PR [W12] +E47+D48
F48: (F2) PR [W12] @ROUND(C47*$INT/12,2)
G48: (F2) PR [W12] +G47+F48
A49: PR [W4] @MOD(A48,12)+1
B49: PR [W5] @IF(A49=1,B48+1,B48)
C49: (F2) PR [W14] +C48-D49
D49: (F2) PR [W12] +$PMT-F49
E49: (F2) PR [W12] +E48+D49
```

```
F49: (F2) PR [W12] @ROUND(C48*$INT/12,2)
G49: (F2) PR [W12] +G48+F49
A50: PR [W4] @MOD(A49,12)+1
B50: PR [W5] @IF(A50=1,B49+1,B49)
C50: (F2) PR [W14] +C49-D50
D50: (F2) PR [W12] +$PMT-F50
E50: (F2) PR [W12] +E49+D50
F50: (F2) PR [W12] @ROUND(C49*$INT/12,2)
G50: (F2) PR [W12] +G49+F50
A51: PR [W4] @MOD(A50,12)+1
B51: PR [W5] @IF(A51=1,B50+1,B50)
C51: (F2) PR [W14] +C50-D51
D51: (F2) PR [W12] +$PMT-F51
E51: (F2) PR [W12] +E50+D51
F51: (F2) PR [W12] @ROUND(C50*$INT/12,2)
G51: (F2) PR [W12] +G50+F51
A52: PR [W4] @MOD(A51,12)+1
B52: PR [W5] @IF(A52=1,B51+1,B51)
C52: (F2) PR [W14] +C51-D52
D52: (F2) PR [W12] +$PMT-F52
E52: (F2) PR [W12] +E51+D52
F52: (F2) PR [W12] @ROUND(C51*$INT/12,2)
G52: (F2) PR [W12] +G51+F52
A53: PR [W4] @MOD(A52,12)+1
B53: PR [W5] @IF(A53=1,B52+1,B52)
C53: (F2) PR [W14] +C52-D53
D53: (F2) PR [W12] +$PMT-F53
E53: (F2) PR [W12] +E52+D53
F53: (F2) PR [W12] @ROUND(C52*$INT/12,2)
G53: (F2) PR [W12] +G52+F53
A54: PR [W4] @MOD(A53,12)+1
B54: PR [W5] @IF(A54=1,B53+1,B53)
C54: (F2) PR [W14] +C53-D54
D54: (F2) PR [W12] +$PMT-F54
E54: (F2) PR [W12] +E53+D54
F54: (F2) PR [W12] @ROUND(C53*$INT/12,2)
G54: (F2) PR [W12] +G53+F54
A55: PR [W4] @MOD(A54,12)+1
B55: PR [W5] @IF(A55=1,B54+1,B54)
C55: (F2) PR [W14] +C54-D55
D55: (F2) PR [W12] +$PMT-F55
E55: (F2) PR [W12] +E54+D55
F55: (F2) PR [W12] @ROUND(C54*$INT/12,2)
G55: (F2) PR [W12] +G54+F55
A56: PR [W4] @MOD(A55,12)+1
B56: PR [W5] @IF(A56=1,B55+1,B55)
C56: (F2) PR [W14] +C55-D56
D56: (F2) PR [W12] +$PMT-F56
E56: (F2) PR [W12] +E55+D56
F56: (F2) PR [W12] @ROUND(C55*$INT/12,2)
G56: (F2) PR [W12] +G55+F56
A57: PR [W4] @MOD(A56,12)+1
B57: PR [W5] @IF(A57=1,B56+1,B56)
C57: (F2) PR [W14] +C56-D57
D57: (F2) PR [W12] +$PMT-F57
E57: (F2) PR [W12] +E56+D57
F57: (F2) PR [W12] @ROUND(C56*$INT/12,2)
G57: (F2) PR [W12] +G56+F57
A58: PR [W4] @MOD(A57,12)+1
B58: PR [W5] @IF(A58=1,B57+1,B57)
C58: (F2) PR [W14] +C57-D58
D58: (F2) PR [W12] +$PMT-F58
E58: (F2) PR [W12] +E57+D58
F58: (F2) PR [W12] @ROUND(C57*$INT/12,2)
G58: (F2) PR [W12] +G57+F58
A59: PR [W4] @MOD(A58,12)+1
```

```
B59: PR [W5] @IF(A59=1,B58+1,B58)
C59: (F2) PR [W14] +C58-D59
D59: (F2) PR [W12] +$PMT-F59
E59: (F2) PR [W12] +E58+D59
F59: (F2) PR [W12] @ROUND(C58*$INT/12,2)
G59: (F2) PR [W12] +G58+F59
A60: PR [W4] @MOD(A59,12)+1
B60: PR [W5] @IF(A60=1,B59+1,B59)
C60: (F2) PR [W14] +C59-D60
D60: (F2) PR [W12] +$PMT-F60
E60: (F2) PR [W12] +E59+D60
F60: (F2) PR [W12] @ROUND(C59*$INT/12,2)
G60: (F2) PR [W12] +G59+F60
A61: PR [W4] @MOD(A60,12)+1
B61: PR [W5] @IF(A61=1,B60+1,B60)
C61: (F2) PR [W14] +C60-D61
D61: (F2) PR [W12] +$PMT-F61
E61: (F2) PR [W12] +E60+D61
F61: (F2) PR [W12] @ROUND(C60*$INT/12,2)
G61: (F2) PR [W12] +G60+F61
A62: PR [W4] @MOD(A61,12)+1
B62: PR [W5] @IF(A62=1,B61+1,B61)
C62: (F2) PR [W14] +C61-D62
D62: (F2) PR [W12] +$PMT-F62
E62: (F2) PR [W12] +E61+D62
F62: (F2) PR [W12] @ROUND(C61*$INT/12,2)
G62: (F2) PR [W12] +G61+F62
A63: PR [W4] @MOD(A62,12)+1
B63: PR [W5] @IF(A63=1,B62+1,B62)
C63: (F2) PR [W14] +C62-D63
D63: (F2) PR [W12] +$PMT-F63
E63: (F2) PR [W12] +E62+D63
F63: (F2) PR [W12] @ROUND(C62*$INT/12,2)
G63: (F2) PR [W12] +G62+F63
A64: PR [W4] @MOD(A63,12)+1
B64: PR [W5] @IF(A64=1,B63+1,B63)
C64: (F2) PR [W14] +C63-D64
D64: (F2) PR [W12] +$PMT-F64
E64: (F2) PR [W12] +E63+D64
F64: (F2) PR [W12] @ROUND(C63*$INT/12,2)
G64: (F2) PR [W12] +G63+F64
A65: PR [W4] @MOD(A64,12)+1
B65: PR [W5] @IF(A65=1,B64+1,B64)
C65: (F2) PR [W14] +C64-D65
D65: (F2) PR [W12] +$PMT-F65
E65: (F2) PR [W12] +E64+D65
F65: (F2) PR [W12] @ROUND(C64*$INT/12,2)
G65: (F2) PR [W12] +G64+F65
A66: PR [W4] @MOD(A65,12)+1
B66: PR [W5] @IF(A66=1,B65+1,B65)
C66: (F2) PR [W14] +C65-D66
D66: (F2) PR [W12] +$PMT-F66
E66: (F2) PR [W12] +E65+D66
F66: (F2) PR [W12] @ROUND(C65*$INT/12,2)
G66: (F2) PR [W12] +G65+F66
```

Financial Management Rate of Return

Most major investment and purchase decisions are choices between alternatives. If you make the wrong choice, you may have an investment with a poor return. Even worse, your decision may burden you with unexpected cash outlays (out-of-pocket expenses not paid for by current cash flow). The Financial Management Rate of Return (FMRR) template finds the yield from complex positive and negative cash flows.[1] The template also calculates your initial and future cash requirements.

Although the Internal Rate of Return (IRR) method is frequently used to analyze cash flow problems, the IRR method doesn't accurately reflect how cash flows are handled in the real world. The IRR method also causes problems when used on complex cash flows.

The IRR method assumes that positive cash flows are reinvested at the same rate as the Internal Rate of Return. Because the cash flows usually are smaller than the initial investment and therefore don't earn as much, this rarely is possible. Also, in many cases, positive cash flow must be kept liquid so that cash is available to cover future expenses. The IRR method discounts negative cash flows at the same rate as the Internal Rate of Return. In reality, cash outlays should be discounted at a safer, and therefore lower, investment rate.

Another problem with the IRR method is that it may give investors an inaccurate picture of the initial investment required. In the IRR method, the initial investment appears to be the only consideration. Actually, additional funds may need to be set aside at the safe rate to cover future outlays. A final problem is that the IRR method produces more than one solution when you have more than one sign change in the cash flow. In those cases, determining which of the multiple IRR solutions is correct is left up to you.

The FMRR template solves many problems inherent to the IRR method. For example, using the FMRR template on the following real estate project produces a more accurate rate of return and estimate of cash outlays.

---

[1] The Financial Management Rate of Return model was developed in 1973 by M. Chapman Findlay and Stephen D. Messner of the School of Business Administration, University of Connecticut, Storrs, Conn.

Analyzing Complex Cash Flows on a Real Estate Investment

Suppose that you own a company that moves Victorian houses from outlying farm areas to suburban lots. In their new settings, the houses are renovated and leased as private offices. You plan to build a large Victorian office park in stages. As each house is completed, its offices will be leased. This procedure will create a complex schedule of renovation expenses and lease income. After six years, you plan to sell the completed, fully occupied office park.

You can reinvest positive after-tax cash flows at 10 percent, and you expect to save for outlays at a safe and liquid rate of 5 percent. What is the return on your project and how much do you need at the start of the project to cover your investment and expenses? Your forecasted cash flows for the project (after tax and debt service) are

Year	Cash Flow
0	(320,000)
1	25,000
2	(335,000)
3	45,000
4	(450,000)
5	60,000
6	3,534,000

If you can meet this schedule of after-tax cash flows without resorting to assistance from other leases or financing, the project will yield an FMRR of 25.27 percent (see fig. 3.6). Although the cash needed at the start of the project appears to be $320,000, additional funds are needed at startup to cover negative cash flows in the second and fourth years. These expenses can be covered partially by reinvesting lease earnings after the first and third years. The total amount needed at the start of the project is $931,388.

You can see from figure 3.6 that the IRR method shows an investment yield of 34.74 percent and a starting cash requirement of only $320,000. This overstatement of return and understatement of required capital can make the IRR method dangerous to use.

Financial Formulas and Macros

The FMRR template uses a master macro, \s, that controls two other macros, \d and \c. The master macro prepares the screen and then calls the \d macro to discount negative cash flows out of the cash flow schedule.

The \d macro, starting at cell A55, discounts cash outlays to find how much initial investment and positive cash flow must be saved to cover the future outlays. Future positive cash flows are used to offset some future expenses. What cannot be offset must be saved for from the initial investment. Any positive cash flows that remain after offsetting outlays are moved into cells F31..F37 in the COMPOUND POSITIVES column.

The \d macro copies the entire series of cash flows from the ENTER CASH FLOW column into the DISCOUNT NEGATIVES column. The macro then moves the cursor to the bottom of the DISCOUNT NEGATIVES column (the most future date) and begins working up the column.

As the cursor moves up the DISCOUNT NEGATIVES column, the macro checks whether a cash flow is positive or negative. If a cash flow is positive, it is copied to the same row under the COMPOUND POSITIVE column and deleted from the DISCOUNT NEGATIVES column. If a cash flow is negative, the macros in cells B59 and B60 discount the negative cash flow at the safe rate and add this discounted amount to the previous year. This has the same effect as setting aside cash at the safe rate to cover next year's oulays. The discount formula used is

$$\text{Cash Flow}_{Year}=\text{Cash Flow}_{Year+1}/(1+\text{SAFERATE})$$

This process of moving up the column and discounting negative cash flows continues until all positive cash flows are in the COMPOUND POSITIVES column and all negative cash flows have been discounted into a single initial investment.

When discounting is complete, the compounding macro, \c (beginning in A69), takes over. The compounding macro invests all the positive cash flows (in the COMPOUND POSITIVES column) that remain after future outlays have been paid off. The compounding formula, in cells B71 and B72, invests a positive cash flow for one year at the REINVEST RATE and adds the amount to the next year's positive cash flow. The compounding formula is

$$\text{Cash Flow}_{Year+1}=\text{Cash Flow}_{Year}*(1+\text{REINVESTRATE})$$

FINANCIAL MANAGEMENT RATE OF RETURN
===

Enter the rate for investments that cover future negative cash flows.
SAFE RATE   0.0500

Enter the rate at which positive cash flows are reinvested.
REINVEST RATE   0.1000

Use a decimal rate covering the same period as the cash flow.
Enter the cash flow below and press Alt-s to start.
===
RATES OF RETURN

IRR   0.3474

FMRR   0.2527

===
CASH FLOW DATA AND CALCULATIONS
===

Enter positive, negative, or zero cash flow for each period.
Insert additional rows in the middle. Do not insert or delete on the
first or last row.

PERIOD	ENTER CASH FLOW	DISCOUNT NEGATIVES	COMPOUND POSITIVES	RESULT
0	-320000	-931388.		-931388.
1	25000			
2	-335000			
3	45000			
4	-450000			
5	60000			
6	3534000		3600000	3600000

```
40 |==========================================================
41 |MACROS
42 |----------------------------------------------------------
43
44        START (Master macro, others are subroutines)
         {HOME}{GOTO}A21~                        Position screen
45  \s   /wgrm                                   Manual calc
46       /dfDISCNT~0~0~~                          Fill areas with 0
47       /dfCOMPOUND~0~0~~                        Fill areas with 0
48       /xc\D~                                   Discount subroutine
49       /xc\C~                                   Compound subroutine
50       /wgra                                    Automatic calc
51       {CALC}{HOME}{BEEP}                       Show results
52
53       DISCOUNT NEGATIVE CASH FLOWS AND COVER WITH POSITIVE CASH FLOWS
54  \d   /cCASH FLOW~DISCNT~                      Copy data into discount area
55       {GOTO}DISCNT~
56       {END}{DOWN}
57                                                Start at bottom, work up
58 DAGAIN /rncHERE~~/rndHERE~/rncHERE~~           Name cell being worked on
59       {IF HERE<0}{EDIT}/(1+SAFERATE)~          If cell<0, discount at safe rate
60       {IF HERE<0}{UP}{EDIT}+{DOWN}~{EDIT}{CALC}~  If cell<0, add discnt value to cell above
61       {IF HERE>0}/cHERE~{RIGHT}{RIGHT}~        If cell>0, copy two cells right
62       {GOTO}HERE~{BLANK HERE}~                 Erase cell when work complete
63       {UP}{UP}                                 Move up two to check for blank
64       {IF @CELLPOINTER("type")="b"}/xr         Return to \s when cell at top is blank
65       {DOWN}                                   Move down to next cell checked
66       /xgDAGAIN~                               Repeat again
67
68       COMPOUND POSITIVE CASH FLOWS FORWARD
69  \c   {GOTO}COMPOUND~                          Start at top of compound area
70 CAGAIN /rncHERE~~/rndHERE~/rncHERE~~           Name current cell
71       {EDIT}*(1+REINVESTRATE)~                 Compound interest current cell
72       {DOWN}{EDIT}+{UP}~{EDIT}{CALC}~          Add current cell to one below
73       {BLANK HERE}~                            Erase current cell
74       {DOWN}                                   Position to check for blank
75       {IF @CELLPOINTER("type")="b"}{RETURN}    Return to \d when bottom cell is blank
76       {UP}                                     Reposition for next calculation
77       /xgCAGAIN~                               Repeat again
78
79
```

Fig. 3.6. *Financial Management Rate of Return template.*

The result is a single positive amount at the end of the investment (cells F37 and H37). The FMRR is calculated using the 1-2-3 function @IRR in cell B19 on the range named RESULT, cells H31 to H37. This range contains only two nonzero numbers: the initial investment and the final return. Because only one sign change between these two values is possible, @IRR produces only one valid answer.

Creating the Template

Most of the calculations used in the FMRR template are performed by the macros. These macros use range names that name the cash flow and result areas, the safe and reinvestment rates, and the macro names. The range names and their locations are

Address	Range Name
B31..B37	CASH FLOW
B45	\S
B55	\D
B58	DAGAIN
B69	\C
B70	CAGAIN
C6	SAFERATE
C9	REINVESTRATE
D31..D37	DISCNT
F31..F37	COMPOUND
F36	HERE
H31..H37	RESULT

Two @IRR functions calculate the IRR and FMRR answers, but each function operates on a different range of cash flows. Consider the following formulas:

Term	Address	Formula
IRR	B17	@IRR(0.1,CASH FLOW)
FMRR	B19	@IRR(0.1,RESULT)

You can see that the IRR rate uses the original schedule of cash flows. When cash flows change from positive to negative and back many times, the @IRR function can produce more than one answer. Only by testing different estimates (shown in the sample formula as 0.1) can you find a valid solution. FMRR also uses the @IRR function, but the RESULT range contains a single investment and a single result. FMRR can have only one answer.

You can enter list of cells 3.6 without changing any column widths. Do not use /Worksheet Global Protection when operating this template. Although global protection is not used, unprotecting the cells preceded by U in the listing will highlight them as data entry cells. 1-2-3 must be set with Automatic recalculation in natural order. After you have created the template, save it to disk.

Test the template by entering the safe rate and reinvestment rate in the upper section of the template, as shown in figure 3.6. Then enter the cash flow values in cells B31 through B37. When these amounts are entered, invoke the master macro by holding down the Alt key and pressing S.

Insert or delete rows in the cash flow area to fit the size of your schedule. Inserting or deleting on the top or bottom row of the CASH FLOW range destroys the range names CASH FLOW and RESULT. Insert rows by moving the cursor to a middle row and selecting /Worksheet Insert Row. Then highlight the number of additional rows you want. Delete rows by moving the cursor to the middle of the schedule, selecting /Worksheet Delete Row, and highlighting the rows to be deleted.

The safe rate (SAFE RATE) is the rate at which you can invest money to cover future outlays. The template calculates exactly how much must be invested to meet the forecasted outlays in the example. Actually, you rarely will know exactly how much your future expenses will be.

The reinvestment rate (REINVEST RATE) normally is higher than the safe rate, but lower than the expected FMRR. This is because reinvestments usually can be invested for a longer period of time than monies invested at the safe rate that must later be withdrawn to cover outlays. Because the amount reinvested is smaller than the initial investment, the reinvestment rate usually will be less than the expected FMRR.

Enter your cash flow amounts under the column labeled ENTER CASH FLOW. Enter outlays as negative numbers. The amount of the initial investment should be entered in PERIOD 0. Consider the initial investment to be at Period 0. All other cash flows are at the end of each period.

To calculate the new FMRR, hold down the Alt key and press S to start the calculation. The cursor moves to cell A1, and the macro sounds the bell when the FMRR is complete.

Tricks, Traps, and Assumptions

The FMRR method used in the template assumes that all cash flows are after taxes and that the initial funding is from outside sources. The rest of the investment or project is self-funding. If you plan to offset expenses and outlays with funding from outside financing, you must modify the template.

Cash flows in this model are after-debt and after-tax payments, so you will have a more accurate picture of your true rate of return. After-tax cash flow is used because not all of the before-tax cash flow is available for reinvestment; the only monies available for reinvestment are those remaining after taxes. Another reason for using after-tax cash flows is that the cash flows will vary depending on the tax rate of the business or investor involved. Tax advantages that shield income will affect different investors by different amounts. What may appear to be an excellent investment for one business may be a poor investment for another, simply because of their different tax positions. To forecast your future tax position, you should consult with a CPA familiar with your investment or business plans.

List of Cells 3.6

```
A2: 'FINANCIAL MANAGEMENT RATE OF RETURN
A3: \=
B3: \=
C3: \=
D3: \=
E3: \=
F3: \=
G3: \=
H3: \=
A5: 'Enter the rate for investments that cover future negative cash flows.
A6: 'SAFE RATE
C6: (F4) U 0.05
A8: 'Enter the rate at which positive cash flows are reinvested.
A9: 'REINVEST RATE
C9: (F4) U 0.1
A11: 'Use a decimal rate covering the same period as the cash flow.
A12: 'Enter the cash flow below and press Alt-s to start.
A13: \=
B13: \=
C13: \=
D13: \=
E13: \=
F13: \=
G13: \=
H13: \=
A14: 'RATES OF RETURN
A15: \-
B15: \-
C15: \-
D15: \-
```

```
E15: \-
F15: \-
G15: \-
H15: \-
A17: 'IRR
B17: (F4) @IRR(0.1,CASH FLOW)
A19: 'FMRR
B19: (F4) @IRR(0.1,RESULT)
A21: \=
B21: \=
C21: \=
D21: \=
E21: \=
F21: \=
G21: \=
H21: \=
A22: 'CASH FLOW DATA AND CALCULATIONS
A23: \-
B23: \-
C23: \-
D23: \-
E23: \-
F23: \-
G23: \-
H23: \-
A24: 'Enter positive, negative, or zero cash flow for each period.
A25: 'Insert additional rows in the middle. Do not insert or delete on the
A26: 'first or last row.
B28: "ENTER
D28: "DISCOUNT
F28: "COMPOUND
B29: "CASH
D29: "NEGATIVES
F29: "POSITIVES
H29: "RESULT
A30: "PERIOD
B30: "FLOW
A31: 0
B31: U -320000
D31: U -931388.7732
H31: +D31
A32: 1
B32: U 25000
A33: 2
B33: U -335000
A34: 3
B34: U 45000
A35: 4
B35: U -450000
A36: 5
B36: U 60000
A37: 6
B37: U 3534000
F37: U 3600000
H37: +F37
A40: \=
B40: \=
C40: \=
D40: \=
E40: \=
F40: \=
G40: \=
H40: \=
A41: 'MACROS
A42: \-
B42: \-
C42: \-
```

```
D42: \-
E42: \-
F42: \-
G42: \-
H42: \-
B44: 'START (Master macro, others are subroutines)
A45: '\s
B45: '{HOME}{GOTO}A21~
F45: 'Position screen
B46: '/wgrm
F46: 'Manual calc
B47: '/dfDISCNT~0~0~~
F47: 'Fill areas with 0
B48: '/dfCOMPOUND~0~0~~
F48: 'Fill areas with 0
B49: '/xc\D~
F49: 'Discount subroutine
B50: '/xc\C~
F50: 'Compound subroutine
B51: '/wgra
F51: 'Automatic calc
B52: '{CALC}{HOME}{BEEP}
F52: 'Show results
B54: 'DISCOUNT NEGATIVE CASH FLOWS AND COVER WITH POSITIVE CASH FLOWS
A55: '\d
B55: '/cCASH FLOW~DISCNT~
G55: 'Copy data into discount area
B56: '{GOTO}DISCNT~
B57: '{END}{DOWN}
G57: 'Start at bottom, work up
A58: 'DAGAIN
B58: '/rncHERE~~/rndHERE~/rncHERE~~
G58: 'Name cell being worked on
B59: '{IF HERE<0}{EDIT}/(1+SAFERATE)~
G59: 'If cell<0, discount at safe rate
B60: '{IF HERE<0}{UP}{EDIT}+{DOWN}~{EDIT}{CALC}~
G60: 'If cell<0, add discnt value to cell above
B61: '{IF HERE>0}/cHERE~{RIGHT}{RIGHT}~
G61: 'If cell>0, copy two cells right
B62: '{GOTO}HERE~{BLANK HERE}~
G62: 'Erase cell when work complete
B63: '{UP}{UP}
G63: 'Move up two to check for blank
B64: '{IF @CELLPOINTER("type")="b"}/xr
G64: 'Return to \s when cell at top is blank
B65: '{DOWN}
G65: 'Move down to next cell checked
B66: '/xgDAGAIN~
G66: 'Repeat again
B68: 'COMPOUND POSITIVE CASH FLOWS FORWARD
A69: '\c
B69: '{GOTO}COMPOUND~
G69: 'Start at top of compound area
A70: 'CAGAIN
B70: '/rncHERE~~/rndHERE~/rncHERE~~
G70: 'Name current cell
B71: '{EDIT}*(1+REINVESTRATE)~
G71: 'Compound interest current cell
B72: '{DOWN}{EDIT}+{UP}~{EDIT}{CALC}~
G72: 'Add current cell to one below
B73: '{BLANK HERE}~
G73: 'Erase current cell
B74: '{DOWN}
G74: 'Position to check for blank
B75: '{IF @CELLPOINTER("type")="b"}{RETURN}
```

```
G75: 'Return to \d when bottom cell is blank
B76: '{UP}
G76: 'Reposition for next calculation
B77: '/xgCAGAIN~
G77: 'Repeat again
```

Present Value of an Annuity (Interest Rate Known)

Present value annuities are of two types: ordinary annuities and annuities due. The type is determined by when the payments are made or received. Payments in an *ordinary annuity*, such as a mortgage, are made or received at the end of each period. Annuities that make or receive payments at the beginning of each period, such as a savings plan, are known as *annuities due*. This section explains and builds templates for both types of present value annuities.

Finding the present value of an annuity has many uses beyond calculating amortized loans. The present value of an annuity can help you in calculating your own loan terms, deciding whether to accept up-front payment in place of a stream of payments, and comparing investments and purchases that return or require a constant cash flow.

Calculating Your Own Mortgage Terms

Most people are more familiar with the word *mortgage* than they are with the term *present value of an ordinary annuity*. The present value of an ordinary annuity is the value to you today of a series of constant payments in the future. The series of payments may end with a final large payment, known as a *balloon payment*.

One of the most common present value ordinary annuities is a mortgage. With the Ordinary Annuity/Present Value (Interest Rate Known) template, you can do "what if" analysis and calculate different combinations of any of the four terms used in flat-rate mortgages. For example, you could determine the amount of the monthly payments on a house with a 20-year mortgage at 13.5 percent, an initial value of $120,000, and a balloon payment of $30,000. Because mortgage payments are made at the end of each period, the template for ordinary annuities is used. The periodic interest on the loan is .01125 (13.5 divided by 12 months). The 240 monthly payments will be $1,424.14 each. Figure 3.7 shows the answer displayed.

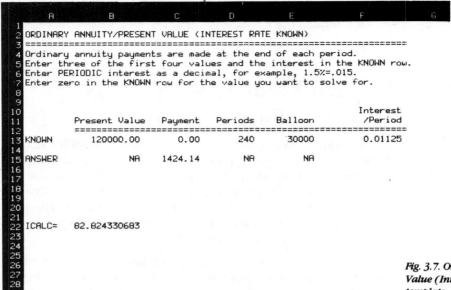

```
     A         B          C        D        E        F        G
 1
 2 ORDINARY ANNUITY/PRESENT VALUE (INTEREST RATE KNOWN)
 3 =================================================================
 4 Ordinary annuity payments are made at the end of each period.
 5 Enter three of the first four values and the interest in the KNOWN row.
 6 Enter PERIODIC interest as a decimal, for example, 1.5%=.015.
 7 Enter zero in the KNOWN row for the value you want to solve for.
 8
 9
10                                                         Interest
11         Present Value   Payment   Periods   Balloon     /Period
12         =================================================================
13 KNOWN      120000.00      0.00      240      30000       0.01125
14
15 ANSWER          NA      1424.14       NA        NA
16
17
18
19
20
21
22 ICALC=   82.824330683
23
24
25
26
27
28
```

Fig. 3.7. Ordinary Annuity/Present Value (Interest Rate Known) template.

By making certain changes to the ordinary annuity template, you can create a template for solving the annuity due problems required to make many investment and purchase decisions. For example, suppose that you want to add $25,000 worth of enhancements to a leased machine. With the improvements, the machine should bring an extra $4,300 at the beginning of each year for the next 5 years. At the end of that time, the machine's resale value will be increased by $3,500, directly attributable to the improvements. If you require a minimum of 13 percent return, will the improvements be worth making?

Because the $4,300 annual lease increase is received at the beginning of the year, you should use the annuity due template to perform the calculations. The present value of the $4,300 per year and the final value of $3,500 (balloon) taken at 13 percent produces a present value of the investment of $36,086.82—well above the $25,000 cost of the improvements. The result suggests that you should make the improvements. If you actually were making this decision, you also would want to weigh this financial result along with other factors such as competitive pressure and new equipment designs.

Financial Formulas

Present value annuity formulas convert a series of payments to their present value, or "cash in hand" value, based on the current investment or loan interest rate. Payments for ordinary annuities are made at the end of each period, and payments for annuities due are made at the beginning of each period. Annuities of both types may have a balloon payment.

The formulas for the present value of an ordinary annuity are given first, followed by the annuity due formulas. The formulas for the present value of an ordinary annuity with balloon payments are

$$PV=PMT*(1-(1+INT)^{-N})/INT+BLN*(1+INT)^{-N}$$
$$PMT=INT*(PV-BLN*(1+INT)^{-N})/(1-(1+INT)^{-N})$$
$$BLN=(PV-PMT*((1-(1+INT)^{-N})/INT))/(1+INT)^{-N}$$
$$N=-(\ln((INT*PV-PMT)/(INT*BLN-PMT)))/\ln(1+INT)$$

PV is the present value of the annuity (the price of the investment), PMT is the payment at the end of each period, BLN is the balloon payment, and N is the number of periodic payments. The periodic interest, INT, is entered as a decimal.

Two of these ordinary annuity formulas can be rewritten easily so that they use 1-2-3 functions.

$$PV=@PV(PMT,INT,N)+BLN*(1+INT)^{-N}$$
$$PMT=@PMT(PV,INT,N)-INT*BLN*(1+INT)^{-N}/(1-(1+INT)^{-N})$$

The formulas for the present value of an annuity due are

$$PV=PMT*((1+INT)-(1+INT)^{1-N})/INT+(BLN*(1+INT)^{-N})$$
$$PMT=INT*(PV-BLN*(1+INT)^{-N})/((1+INT)-(1+INT)^{1-N})$$
$$BLN=(PV-PMT*(((1+INT)-(1+INT)^{1-N})/INT))/(1+INT)^{-N}$$
$$N=\ln((BLN-PMT*(1+INT)/INT)/(PV-PMT*(1+INT)/INT))/\ln(1+INT)$$

The present value form of the annuity due equation can be rewritten easily using the @PV function.

$$PV=@PV(PMT,INT,N)*(1+INT)+BLN*(1+INT)^{-N}$$

Creating the Templates

The formulas are easier to enter in your spreadsheet if you assign range names to the cells that contain the needed information. To reduce the amount of typing and number of possible errors, one segment from several formulas has been broken out and used many times. This segment, ICALC, contains $(1-(1+INT)^{-N})$ in cell B22 on the ordinary annuity template.

The range names are the same as the variable names used in the formulas. Both the ordinary annuity and annuity due templates use the following range names and addresses:

Address	Range Name
B13	PV
B22	ICALC
C13	PMT
D13	N
E13	BLN
F13	INT

The formulas in the present value of an ordinary annuity template use the @IF function to determine which formula should display a solution. For example, the formula solves only for PV when PV in the KNOWN row contains zero; otherwise, the row displays NA for PV. The formulas and their locations are

Term	Address	Formulas
PV	B15	@IF(PV=0,@PV(PMT,INT,N) +BLN*(1+INT)^-N,@NA)
PMT	C15	@IF(PMT=0,(PV−BLN*(1+INT)^-N)/ICALC, @NA)
N	D15	@IF(N=0,−@LN((INT*PV−PMT)/ (INT*BLN−PMT))/@LN(1+INT),@NA)
BLN	E15	@IF(BLN=0#AND#PV<>0#AND#PMT<>0 #AND#N<>0,(PV−PMT*ICALC)/(1+INT)^-N, @NA)
ICALC	B22	(1−(1+INT)^-N)/INT

Before entering the formulas from the cell listings, adjust the column widths as follows: column B to 13, C and E to 11, D to 10, and F to 16. Enter the labels and then create the range names. All the cell listings are given in list of cells 3.7. After entering the listing, unprotect the cells preceded by U in the listing, then use /Worksheet Global Protection to protect the template.

You can change the ordinary annuity present value template to an annuity due template by changing the formulas as shown in the following listings. The annuity due template calculates annuities for which payments are made at the beginning of each period. The formula in cell C15 is the same in both templates, but the ICALC segment that the formula uses is changed.

Term	Address	Formula
PV	B15	@IF(PV=0,@PV(PMT,INT,N)*(1+INT)+BLN*(1+INT)^−N,@NA)
PMT	C15	@IF(PMT=0,(PV−BLN*(1+INT)^−N)/ICALC,@NA)
N	D15	@IF(N=0,@LN((BLN−PMT*(1+INT)/INT)/(PV−PMT*(1+INT)/INT))/@LN(1+INT),@NA)
BLN	E15	@IF(BLN=0#AND#PV<>0#AND#PMT<>0#AND#N<>0,(PV−PMT*ICALC)/(1+INT)^−N,@NA)
ICALC	B22	((1+INT)−(1+INT)^(1−N))/INT

You also need to change the following cells:

Term	Address	Change
label	A2	ANNUITY DUE/PRESENT VALUE (INTEREST RATE KNOWN)
label	A4	Annuity due payments are made at the beginning of each period.

To make these changes to the ordinary annuity template, you first must unprotect the spreadsheet with /Worksheet Global Protection Disable. After making the changes, protect the spreadsheet again.

Before testing the template, save it to disk. Then use the sample problems to determine whether the formulas work correctly. Use the mortgage problem to test the ordinary annuity template and use the machine enhancement problem to test the annuity due template. Test all the formulas by entering a zero in the KNOWN row for the value you want calculated. You cannot solve for interest with these templates. You must use the template shown in figure 3.8 to calculate unknown interest.

Figure 3.7 shows both the data-entry and solution areas for the Ordinary Annuity/Present Value (Interest Rate Known) template. Known values are entered under the appropriate label in the KNOWN row. The periodic interest always must be entered. Enter the interest per period as a decimal. The easiest way to enter the interest per period is as annual interest divided by the number of periods. For example, 13 percent annual interest with monthly payments can be entered as *.13/12*. Enter the unknown value as a zero in the KNOWN row. The answer appears below the zero in the ANSWER row.

Tricks, Traps, and Assumptions

The ordinary annuity template assumes that payments (or receipts) are made at the end of each period. The annuity due template assumes that payments (or receipts) are made at the beginning of each period. In both cases, the balloon payment comes at the end of the final period.

The balloon payment and number of periods must be equal to or greater than zero. For mortgages or annuities without balloon payments, enter zero as the amount of the balloon payment.

When the annuity is a loan, the balloon payments reduce the monthly payments; but balloon payments put a heavy burden on the borrower when the balloon comes due. In an investment, the balloon payment may be a final receipt or the final market value of the investment.

If you need to find the interest returned by an annuity, use the Ordinary Annuity/Present Value (Interest Rate Unknown) template in this chapter (see fig. 3.8).

List of Cells 3.7

```
A2: PR 'ORDINARY ANNUITY/PRESENT VALUE (INTEREST RATE KNOWN)
A3: PR \=
B3: PR [W13] \=
C3: PR [W11] \=
D3: PR [W10] \=
E3: PR [W11] \=
F3: PR [W16] \=
A4: U 'Ordinary annuity payments are made at the end of each period.
A5: PR 'Enter three of the first four values and the interest in the KNOWN row.
A6: PR 'Enter PERIODIC interest as a decimal, for example, 1.5%=.015.
A7: PR 'Enter zero in the KNOWN row for the value you want to solve for.
F10: PR [W16] "Interest
A11: PR '
B11: PR [W13] "Present Value
C11: PR [W11] "Payment
D11: PR [W10] "Periods
E11: PR [W11] "Balloon
F11: PR [W16] "/Period
B12: PR [W13] \=
C12: PR [W11] \=
D12: PR [W10] \=
```

```
E12: PR [W11] \=
F12: PR [W16] \=
A13: PR 'KNOWN
B13: (F2) U [W13] 120000
C13: (F2) U [W11] 0
D13: (F0) U [W10] 240
E13: U [W11] 30000
F13: (F5) U [W16] 0.135/12
A15: PR 'ANSWER
B15: (F2) PR [W13] @IF(PV=0,@PV(PMT,INT,N)+BLN*(1+INT)^-N,@NA)
C15: (F2) PR [W11] @IF(PMT=0,(PV-BLN*(1+INT)^-N)/ICALC,@NA)
D15: (F2) PR [W10] @IF(N=0,-@LN((INT*PV-PMT)/(INT*BLN-PMT))/@LN(1+INT),@NA)
E15: (F2) PR [W11] @IF(BLN=0#AND#PV<>0#AND#PMT<>0#AND#N<>0,(PV-PMT*ICALC)/(1+INT)^-N,@NA)
A22: PR 'ICALC=
B22: PR [W13] (1-(1+INT)^-N)/INT
```

Present Value of an Annuity (Interest Rate Unknown)

The previous section explained that the present value of an annuity can take many forms, such as amortized loans, mortgages, equipment purchases, and leases. In this section, you will learn how to use the rate of return from an annuity to compare different leases, investments, and loans. By experimenting with different periodic payments, initial investments, and balloon payments, you can create a wider range of alternatives.

Often, you know the dollar amounts involved in the series of payments, but you do not know the interest rate of the loan or investment. The two templates described in this section solve for the interest rate. The first finds the interest rate for an ordinary annuity, an annuity where payments are made at the end of the period. The second template finds the interest rate for an annuity due, where payments are made at the beginning of each period.

Finding the Rate of Return from a Lease

Assume that your leasing company is about to purchase a piece of heavy equipment for $45,000. The lease for the equipment is expected to return $1,000 at the end of each month for 5 years. At the end of the lease, the user will purchase the equipment for $3,000. Disregarding taxes, what return will you make on your initial investment?

Because these lease payments are made at the end of each period, you use the ordinary annuity template shown in figure 3.8. The present

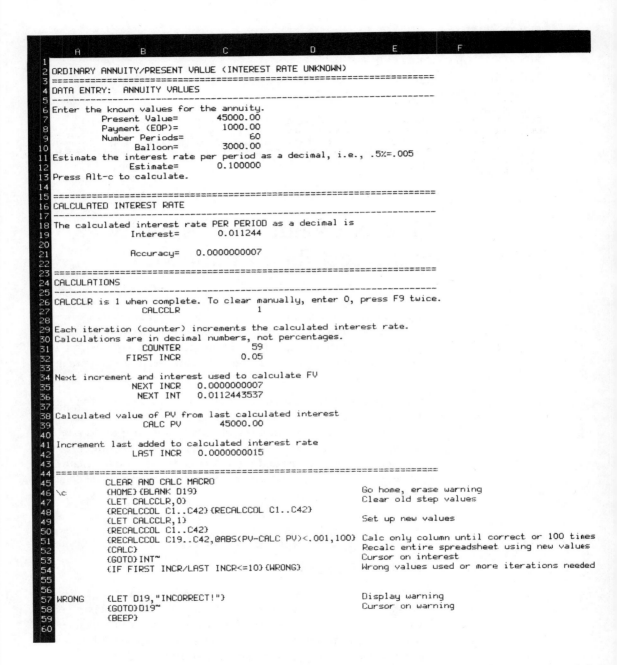

```
          A              B              C              D              E         F
1
2  ORDINARY ANNUITY/PRESENT VALUE (INTEREST RATE UNKNOWN)
3  ===================================================================
4  DATA ENTRY:   ANNUITY VALUES
5  -------------------------------------------------------------------
6  Enter the known values for the annuity.
7            Present Value=        45000.00
8           Payment (EOP)=         1000.00
9          Number Periods=             60
10               Balloon=          3000.00
11 Estimate the interest rate per period as a decimal, i.e., .5%=.005
12               Estimate=        0.100000
13 Press Alt-c to calculate.
14
15 ===================================================================
16 CALCULATED INTEREST RATE
17 -------------------------------------------------------------------
18 The calculated interest rate PER PERIOD as a decimal is
19               Interest=        0.011244
20
21               Accuracy=    0.0000000007
22
23 ===================================================================
24 CALCULATIONS
25 -------------------------------------------------------------------
26 CALCCLR is 1 when complete. To clear manually, enter 0, press F9 twice.
27               CALCCLR              1
28
29 Each iteration (counter) increments the calculated interest rate.
30 Calculations are in decimal numbers, not percentages.
31               COUNTER             59
32            FIRST INCR           0.05
33
34 Next increment and interest used to calculate FV
35            NEXT INCR    0.0000000007
36             NEXT INT    0.0112443537
37
38 Calculated value of PV from last calculated interest
39              CALC PV        45000.00
40
41 Increment last added to calculated interest rate
42             LAST INCR    0.0000000015
43
44 ===================================================================
45          CLEAR AND CALC MACRO
46 \c       {HOME} {BLANK D19}                       Go home, erase warning
47          {LET CALCCLR,0}                          Clear old step values
48          {RECALCCOL C1..C42} {RECALCCOL C1..C42}
49          {LET CALCCLR,1}                          Set up new values
50          {RECALCCOL C1..C42}
51          {RECALCCOL C19..C42,@ABS(PV-CALC PV)<.001,100} Calc only column until correct or 100 times
52          {CALC}                                   Recalc entire spreadsheet using new values
53          {GOTO}INT~                               Cursor on interest
54          {IF FIRST INCR/LAST INCR<=10}{WRONG}     Wrong values used or more iterations needed
55
56
57 WRONG    {LET D19,"INCORRECT!"}                   Display warning
58          {GOTO}D19~                               Cursor on warning
59          {BEEP}
60
```

Fig. 3.8. Ordinary Annuity/Present Value (Interest Rate Unknown) template.

value of the equipment is $45,000. The lease returns $1,000 at the end of each of the 60 periods and then returns $3,000 in a final balloon payment. These conditions provide a monthly return of .011244 percent, or 13.5 percent annually.

For investments that make payments at the beginning of each period, such as deposits to savings accounts, you should use the annuity due template. (The next sections include explanations on how to convert the ordinary annuity template to the annuity due template.)

Financial Formulas

Unknown annuity interest rates cannot be calculated directly in 1-2-3. Instead, 1-2-3 must use multiple estimates adjusted so that each estimate becomes increasingly more accurate. You supply a beginning estimated interest rate, which is used to calculate a known value, the present value. If the calculated present value is higher or lower than the true present value, 1-2-3 adjusts the estimated interest. These adjustments bring the estimated interest figure closer and closer to the rate that produced the known present value. The more times the estimation process is repeated, the more accurate the estimated interest becomes. This process of iteration is explained in detail in Chapter 1. The iteration process is used in the present value formula.

The formula used to calculate present value in an ordinary annuity is

$$PV=PMT*(1-(1+INT)^{-N})/INT+BLN*(1+INT)^{-N}$$

This formula can be rewritten to use the 1-2-3 @PV function, as follows:

$$PV=@PV(PMT,INT,N)+BLN*(1+INT)^{-N}$$

PV is the present value of the annuity, PMT is the payment at the end of each period, BLN is the balloon payment, and N is the number of periodic payments. INT, the periodic interest, begins with your first estimate and is adjusted toward the true periodic interest.

The annuity due interest problem is solved in the same way, but the formula for the present value of the annuity due is used. The formula for annuity due present value is

$$PV=PMT*(1+INT)*(1-(1+INT)^{-N})/INT+BLN*(1+INT)^{-N}$$

In 1-2-3, this formula is

$$PV=@PV(PMT,INT,N)*(1+INT)+BLN*(1+INT)^{\wedge}-N$$

Creating the Templates

All the variables used in these formulas are easier to enter in spread-sheets if the appropriate cells are given range names that are the same as the variable names. Both templates use the same range names and addresses.

Address	*Range Name*
B46	\C
B57	WRONG
C7	PV
C8	PMT
C9	N
C10	BLN
C12	ESTINT
C19	INT
C27	CALCCLR
C31	COUNTER
C32	FIRST INCR
C35	NEXT INCR
C36	NEXT INT
C39	CALC PV
C42	LAST INCR

The financial formulas used in this template are the same as those used in the previous section. The iteration formulas are discussed in greater detail at the end of Chapter 1.

The primary financial formula, CALC PV, is calculated in cell C39 with the following ordinary annuity formula:

@IF(CALCCLR=0,0.001,@PV(PMT,INT,N)+BLN*(1+INT)^–N)

The \c macro is used to calculate the PV formula. This macro, begin-ning at cell B46, first erases old estimates by setting the cell CALCCLR to zero and recalculating twice with {RECALCCOL C1..C42}. This clearing action causes the macro to begin with your estimate of the interest.

The {RECALCCOL} command in cell B51 recalculates the spreadsheet area between C19 and C42 until one of two conditions is satisfied: either the true and estimated values of PV are within one-tenth of a cent of each other, or the area has been recalculated 100 times.

The macro ends by determining whether the last increment added to the interest is at least 10 times smaller than the first increment. If this condition isn't true, your initial estimate of the interest is probably too small. When the estimate is too small, the macro prints a warning in cell D19.

Appendix D contains the macros that run these templates in 1-2-3 Release 1A. Chapter 1 describes in more detail how the macro and cells C27 to C42 work together to find the interest rate.

Enter the ordinary annuity template from list of cells 3.8. Note: Before you enter the cell listings, be sure to enter the CALCCLR value in cell C27 as zero. This entry causes the circular reference formulas initially to display constant values and prevents an ERR condition. All the labels, values, and formulas that create this template are given in the cell listings.

You can change a few lines in this template so that it will solve annuity due problems. For the present value of an annuity due template, make the following changes:

Term	Address	Change
label	A2	ANNUITY DUE/PRESENT VALUE (INTEREST RATE UNKNOWN)
label	A6	Annuity due payments are made at the beginning of each period.
PV CALC	C39	@IF(CALCCLR=0,0.001,@PV(PMT,INT,N)*(1+INT)+BLN*(1+INT)^-N)

Before entering the listing for either template, change columns B and C to a width of 15, column D to a width of 17, and E to a width of 14. After entering the listing, unprotect the cells preceded by U, then protect the entire worksheet. After entering the cell listings and before running the macro, save your work to disk.

Next, check the template. Enter the known amounts for the annuity in the top portion of the template (see fig. 3.8). You must enter the present value, periodic payment, and number of periods as positive numbers. The balloon may be zero. The estimated interest per period, as a decimal, is the last line entered in the DATA ENTRY section. Estimates between .01 and 1.0 supply a correct answer for most rates of return.

After entering the data, hold down the Alt key and press C. When calculations are completed, the cursor highlights the answer. The answer and its accuracy are shown in the CALCULATED INTEREST RATE section of the template. The answer is the periodic interest rate, in this case, for monthly periods. To find the annual interest, you multiply by 12 the monthly rate and accuracy shown.

Tricks, Traps, and Assumptions

The ordinary annuity template assumes that payments (or receipts) are made at the end of each period. The annuity due template assumes that payments (or receipts) are made at the beginning of each period. In both cases, the balloon payment is at the end of the final period.

The interest rate calculated is for the period. Annual interest equals this rate times the number of periods per year.

The leading zeros in the Accuracy cell (C20) indicate the accuracy for the estimated periodic interest. To recalculate for more accuracy, enter the calculated interest as the estimated interest and press Alt-c again.

The message INCORRECT! displayed next to the solution means either that additional calculations are necessary or that the input is wrong. If this happens, check the data you entered. If you find no errors, the estimated interest may be too low. Use the calculated interest as the new estimate and press Alt-c again.

The present value, payment amount, number of periods, and balloon payment must be positive numbers. The balloon payment can be zero.

List of Cells 3.8

```
A2:  PR 'ORDINARY ANNUITY/PRESENT VALUE (INTEREST RATE UNKNOWN)
A3:  PR \=
B3:  PR [W15] \=
C3:  PR [W15] \=
D3:  PR [W17] \=
E3:  PR [W14] \=
A4:  PR 'DATA ENTRY:   ANNUITY VALUES
A5:  PR \-
B5:  PR [W15] \-
C5:  PR [W15] \-
D5:  PR [W17] \-
E5:  PR [W14] \-
A6:  PR 'Enter the known values for the annuity.
B7:  PR [W15] "Present Value=
C7:  (F2) U [W15] 45000
B8:  PR [W15] "Payment (EOP)=
C8:  (F2) U [W15] 1000
B9:  PR [W15] 'Number Periods=
C9:  (F0) U [W15] 60
B10: PR [W15] "Balloon=
C10: (F2) U [W15] 3000
A11: PR 'Estimate the interest rate per period as a decimal, i.e., .5%=.005
```

```
B12: PR [W15] "Estimate=
C12: (F6) U [W15] 0.1
A13: U 'Press Alt-c to calculate.
A15: PR \=
B15: PR [W15] \=
C15: PR [W15] \=
D15: PR [W17] \=
E15: PR [W14] \=
A16: PR 'CALCULATED INTEREST RATE
A17: PR \-
B17: PR [W15] \-
C17: PR [W15] \-
D17: PR [W17] \-
E17: PR [W14] \-
A18: PR 'The calculated interest rate PER PERIOD as a decimal is
B19: PR [W15] "Interest=
C19: (F6) PR [W15] @IF(COUNTER<2,ESTINT,NEXT INT)
B21: PR [W15] "Accuracy=
C21: PR [W15] +NEXT INCR
A23: PR \=
B23: PR [W15] \=
C23: PR [W15] \=
D23: PR [W17] \=
E23: PR [W14] \=
A24: PR 'CALCULATIONS
A25: PR \-
B25: PR [W15] \-
C25: PR [W15] \-
D25: PR [W17] \-
E25: PR [W14] \-
A26: PR 'CALCCLR is 1 when complete. To clear manually, enter 0, press F9 twice.
B27: PR [W15] "CALCCLR
C27: U [W15] 0
A29: PR 'Each iteration (counter) increments the calculated interest rate.
A30: PR 'Calculations are in decimal numbers, not percentages.
B31: PR [W15] "COUNTER
C31: PR [W15] @IF(CALCCLR=1,COUNTER+1,0)
B32: PR [W15] "FIRST INCR
C32: PR [W15] +ESTINT/2
A34: PR 'Next increment and interest used to calculate FV
B35: PR [W15] "NEXT INCR
C35: PR [W15] @IF(CALCCLR=0,ESTINT,@IF(PV<CALC PV,LAST INCR,LAST INCR/2))
B36: PR [W15] "NEXT INT
C36: PR [W15] @IF(PV<CALC PV,INT+LAST INCR,INT-LAST INCR)
A38: PR 'Calculated value of PV from last calculated interest
B39: PR [W15] "CALC PV
C39: (F2) PR [W15] @IF(CALCCLR=0,0.001,@PV(PMT,INT,N)+BLN*(1+INT)^-N)
A41: PR 'Increment last added to calculated interest rate
B42: PR [W15] "LAST INCR
C42: PR [W15] @IF(COUNTER<2,FIRST INCR,NEXT INCR)
A44: PR \=
B44: PR [W15] \=
C44: PR [W15] \=
D44: PR [W17] \=
E44: PR [W14] \=
B45: PR [W15] 'CLEAR AND CALC MACRO
A46: PR '\c
B46: PR [W15] '{HOME}{BLANK D19}
E46: PR [W14] 'Go home, erase warning
B47: PR [W15] '{LET CALCCLR,0}
E47: PR [W14] 'Clear old step values
B48: PR [W15] '{RECALCCOL C1..C42}{RECALCCOL C1..C42}
B49: PR [W15] '{LET CALCCLR,1}
E49: PR [W14] 'Set up new values
B50: PR [W15] '{RECALCCOL C1..C42}
B51: PR [W15] '{RECALCCOL C19..C42,@ABS(PV-CALC PV)<.001,100}
```

```
E51: PR [W14] 'Calc only column until correct or 100 times
B52: PR [W15] '{CALC}
E52: PR [W14] 'Recalc entire spreadsheet using new values
B53: PR [W15] '{GOTO}INT~
E53: PR [W14] 'Cursor on interest
B54: PR [W15] '{IF FIRST INCR/LAST INCR<=10}{WRONG}
E54: PR [W14] 'Wrong values used or more iterations needed
A57: PR 'WRONG
B57: PR [W15] '{LET D19,"INCORRECT!"}
E57: PR [W14] 'Display warning
B58: PR [W15] '{GOTO}D19~
E58: PR [W14] 'Cursor on warning
B59: PR [W15] '{BEEP}
```

Future Value of an Annuity (Interest Rate Known)

When you save a fixed amount of money every month to meet a future obligation, you are setting up a future value annuity. Most people are familiar with Christmas savings plans, where you save a set amount every month so that you reach a savings goal in time for Christmas. Businesses design similar savings plans, known as *sinking funds*, to meet future cash needs.

Like present value annuities, future value annuities can be of two types: ordinary annuity or annuity due. Ordinary annuities, or sinking funds, make payments or deposits at the end of each period. Annuities due make payments or deposits at the beginning of each period. With the templates in this section, you can calculate the future value, payment, or number of periods for both types of future value annuities. You must know two of the three values and the interest rate in order to make the templates work.

Saving for a Rainy Day

Everyone should consider retirement plans. Assume that you are self-employed and you plan to put $200 a month into a savings account toward your retirement. If the savings account compounds monthly at 6.25 percent annually, how much will the account be worth in 25 years? Although you made the decision to start your savings plan today, you know that you will have to wait until the end of the month to make the first deposit.

The problem involves the future value of an ordinary annuity, also known as a sinking fund. The annual interest (6.25 percent) must be divided by 12 months and entered as a decimal (.005208). After 25 years, your account will be worth $144,054.81 (see fig. 3.9).

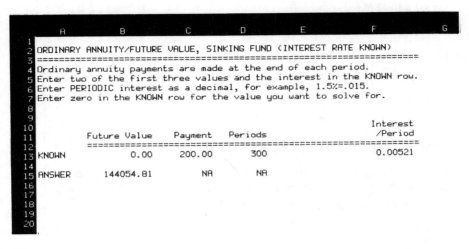

Fig. 3.9. Ordinary Annuity/Future Value, Sinking Fund (Interest Rate Known) template.

Financial Formulas

The three financial formulas used to calculate the future value of ordinary annuities are

$$FV = PMT*((1+INT)^N - 1)/INT$$
$$PMT = FV*INT/((1+INT)^N - 1)$$
$$N = \ln(FV*INT/PMT + 1)/\ln(1+INT)$$

These same formulas for the future value of an annuity due are

$$FV = PMT*((1+INT)^{N+1} - (1+INT))/INT$$
$$PMT = FV*INT/((1+INT)^{N+1} - (1+INT))$$
$$N = (\ln((FV*INT/PMT) + (1+INT))/\ln(1+INT)) - 1$$

FV is the future value of the annuity, PMT is the payment each period, and N is the number of total periods. INT, the periodic interest rate, is entered as a decimal.

The 1-2-3 functions @FV and @TERM can be used in place of the FV and N formulas. For an ordinary annuity, use the following formulas:

FV=@FV(PMT,INT,N)

N=@TERM(PMT,INT,FV)

For an annuity due, use these formulas:

FV=@FV(PMT,INT,N)*(1+INT)

N=@TERM(PMT,INT,FV/(1+INT))

Creating the Templates

The ordinary annuity and annuity due templates are nearly the same. Only their formulas are different. The formulas are easiest to enter if you name the variables with the following range names:

Address	Range Name
B13	FV
C13	PMT
D13	N
E13	INT

After these range names are created, you can enter the following formulas for the future value of an ordinary annuity:

Term	Address	Formula
FV	B15	@IF(FV=0,@FV(PMT,INT,N),@NA)
PMT	C15	@IF(PMT=0,(FV*INT)/((1+INT)^N−1), @NA)
N	D15	@IF(N=0,@TERM(PMT,INT,FV),@NA)

If you are using 1-2-3 Release 1A, you won't have the @TERM function used to find N. Instead, substitute the full N formula for the future value of an ordinary annuity.

The formulas in 1-2-3 use the @IF function to test for a zero in the KNOWN row above the formula. The formula executes only when the zero is found; otherwise, an NA appears in the SOLUTION column for that formula.

The entire listing for the ordinary annuity template is given in list of cells 3.9.

With the following changes, you can modify the listing so that the template solves future value of annuity due problems.

Term	Address	Formula
label	A2	ANNUITY DUE/FUTURE VALUE (INTEREST RATE KNOWN)
label	A4	Annuity due payments are made at the beginning of each period.
FV	B15	@IF(FV=0,@FV(PMT,INT,N)*(1+INT),@NA)
PMT	C15	@IF(PMT=0,(FV*INT)/((1+INT)^(N+1) –(1+INT)),@NA)
N	D15	@IF(N=0,@TERM(PMT,INT,FV/(1+INT)),@NA)

Unprotect the ranges listed with a U. After entering the cell listings for the templates, protect the templates with /Worksheet Global Protection Enable and save them to disk. After saving a copy, test the templates.

You can use the savings plan to test the ordinary annuity template. You must enter two of the three values in the KNOWN rows as well as the interest rate. Enter the interest per period as a decimal. Enter a zero in the KNOWN row for the value for which you are solving. The answer will appear in the ANSWER row.

Tricks, Traps, and Assumptions

The ordinary annuity template assumes that payments (or receipts) are made at the end of each period. The annuity due template assumes that payments (or receipts) are made at the beginning of each period. The future value of the annuity is calculated at the end of the last period.

To find the interest returned on the future value of an annuity, use the Annuity Due/Future Value (Interest Rate Unknown) template in this chapter (see fig. 3.10).

List of Cells 3.9

```
A2: PR 'ORDINARY ANNUITY/FUTURE VALUE, SINKING FUND (INTEREST RATE KNOWN)
A3: PR \=
B3: PR [W13] \=
C3: PR [W11] \=
D3: PR [W10] \=
E3: PR [W11] \=
F3: PR [W16] \=
A4: U 'Ordinary annuity payments are made at the end of each period.
A5: PR 'Enter two of the first three values and the interest in the KNOWN row.
A6: PR 'Enter PERIODIC interest as a decimal, for example, 1.5%=.015.
A7: PR 'Enter zero in the KNOWN row for the value you want to solve for.
F10: PR [W16] "Interest
A11: PR '
B11: PR [W13] "Future Value
C11: PR [W11] "Payment
D11: PR [W10] "Periods
F11: PR [W16] "/Period
B12: PR [W13] \=
C12: PR [W11] \=
D12: PR [W10] \=
E12: PR [W11] \=
F12: PR [W16] \=
A13: PR 'KNOWN
B13: (F2) U [W13] 0
C13: (F2) U [W11] 200
D13: (F0) U [W10] 300
F13: (F5) U [W16] 0.0625/12
A15: PR 'ANSWER
B15: (F2) PR [W13] @IF(FV=0,@FV(PMT,INT,N),@NA)
C15: (F2) PR [W11] @IF(PMT=0,(FV*INT)/((1+INT)^N-1),@NA)
D15: (F2) PR [W10] @IF(N=0,@TERM(PMT,INT,FV),@NA)
```

Future Value of an Annuity (Interest Rate Unknown)

When you have a financial goal to reach, you usually know how much you have to invest periodically and have a certain goal in mind. You want to find out the interest rate that will get you to your goal. The Annuity Due/Future Value (Interest Rate Unknown) template solves for the interest rate necessary to meet your investment goals.

The previous section described a future value of an annuity as the value in the future of a constant investment deposited each period for a specific time. Although the two templates in the previous section solved for three of the four terms in the future value of an annuity, neither template could solve for the interest rate. This section shows you how to use a circular reference to solve "unsolvable" problems like the interest rate of a future value annuity.

As in other types of annuities, deposits can be made at the beginning of each period, an ordinary annuity, or at the end of each period, an annuity due.

Finding the Rate of Return from a Fruitful Investment

Being able to find the interest rate for the future value of an annuity can be useful in several situations. For example, you may have a business that needs to create a sinking fund, and you want to find out what range of interest rates will accomplish your goal. Or, you may be an investor who is putting a constant investment into a project with an estimated future value. Suppose that you plan to spend $2,000 a month for the next 10 years to improve your private vineyard and winery. You pay the $2,000 at the beginning of each month. At the end of the 10 years, you expect the value of your vineyard and winery to have increased by $385,000, directly attributable to your monthly investments. If that is true, what will be the annual interest rate returned by your investment?

You pay $2,000 at the beginning of each month for 120 months. Because payments are made at the beginning of the period, the investment is an annuity due. If your vineyard and winery increase in value by $385,000, you will have made .73 percent per month, which is an annual rate of 8.8 percent (see fig. 3.10).

Financial Formulas

This problem is a type that 1-2-3 can't solve directly. The template, however, can find the answer by making repeated estimates of the interest. The estimated interest is used to solve for the future value of the annuity, even though the future value is already known. The estimated interest is then adjusted according to whether the calculated future value is higher or lower than the real value. After repeated estimates, the estimated interest becomes quite accurate.

The formula used to calculate the future value of an ordinary annuity is the same as the formula given in the previous section.

$$FV=PMT*((1+INT)^N-1)/INT$$

In 1-2-3, the financial formula can be replaced with

$$FV=@FV(PMT,INT,N)$$

```
          A          B          C          D          E        F      G
 1
 2 ANNUITY DUE/FUTURE VALUE (INTEREST RATE UNKNOWN)
 3 ===============================================================================
 4 DATA ENTRY:   ANNUITY VALUES
 5 -------------------------------------------------------------------------------
 6 Annuity due payments are made at the beginning of each period.
 7 Enter the known values for the annuity.
 8          Future Value=       385000.00
 9          Payment (EOP)=        2000.00
10          Number Periods=          120
11
12 Estimate the interest rate per period as a decimal, i.e. .5%=.005
13              Estimate=       0.100000
14 Press Alt-c to calculate.
15 ===============================================================================
16 CALCULATED INTEREST RATE
17 -------------------------------------------------------------------------------
18 The calculated interest rate PER PERIOD as a decimal is
19              Interest=        0.007315
20
21              Accuracy=   2.9103831E-12
22
23 ===============================================================================
24 CALCULATIONS
25 -------------------------------------------------------------------------------
26 CALCCLR is 1 when complete. To clear manually, enter 0, press F9 twice.
27              CALCCLR             1
28
29 Each iteration (counter) increments the calculated interest rate.
30 Calculations are in decimal numbers, not percentages.
31              COUNTER            76
32              FIRST INCR       0.05
33
34 Next increment and interest used to calculate FV
35              NEXT INCR   2.9103831E-12
36              NEXT INT    0.0073148312
37
38 Calculated value of FV from last calculated interest
39              CALC FV        385000.00
40
41 Increment last added to calculated interest rate
42              LAST INCR   5.8207661E-12
43
44 ===============================================================================
45          CLEAR AND CALC MACRO
46 \c       {HOME}{BLANK D19}                          Go home, erase warning
47          {LET CALCCLR,0}                            Clear old step values
48          {RECALCCOL C1..C42}{RECALCCOL C1..C42}
49          {LET CALCCLR,1}                            Set up new values
50          {RECALCCOL C1..C42}
51          {RECALCCOL C19..C42,@ABS(FV-CALC FV)<.001,100}  Calc only column until correct or 100 times
52          {CALC}                                     Recalc entire spreadsheet using new values
53          {GOTO}INT~                                 Cursor on interest
54          {IF FIRST INCR/LAST INCR<=10}{WRONG}       Wrong values used or more iterations needed
55
56
57 WRONG    {LET D19,"INCORRECT!"}                     Display warning
58          {GOTO}D19~                                 Cursor on warning
59          {BEEP}
60
61
62
63
64
65
66
67
68
69
```

Fig. 3.10. Annuity Due/Future Value (Interest Rate Unknown) template.

The future value of an annuity due, described in the sample problem, uses the same formula multiplied by (1+INT).

$$FV=PMT[(1+INT)^{N+1}-(1+INT)]/INT$$

The 1-2-3 formula is

$$FV=@FV(PMT,INT,N)*(1+INT)$$

FV is the future value of the annuity, PMT is the payment, and N is the number of periods. The periodic interest, INT, which is found by iteration, is expressed as a decimal.

Creating the Templates

The formulas used in the templates can be entered just as they appear in the cell listings if you first give range names to the cells containing the variables. The macro that controls the iteration process also uses a number of range names. The range names and their addresses are

Address	Range Name
B46	\C
B57	WRONG
C8	FV
C9	PMT
C10	N
C13	ESTINT
C19	INT
C27	CALCCLR
C31	COUNTER
C32	FIRST INCR
C35	NEXT INCR
C36	NEXT INT
C39	CALC FV
C42	LAST INCR

The \c macro controls the iteration that solves for the interest rate. This macro, beginning at cell B46, first erases old estimates by setting the cell CALCCLR to zero and recalculating twice with {RECALCCOL C1..C42}. This clearing process lets the macro begin with your estimate of the interest.

The {RECALCCOL} command in cell B51 recalculates the spreadsheet area between C19 and C42 until one of two conditions is satisfied:

either the true and calculated values of FV are within one-tenth of a cent of each other, or 100 recalculations have been performed.

The macro ends by determining whether the last adjustment, LAST INCR, added to the interest is at least 10 times smaller than the first adjustment, FIRST INCR. If this condition isn't true, your initial estimate of the interest is probably too small. When the estimate is too small, the macro prints a warning in cell D19.

Chapter 1 describes how the macro and cells C27 to C42 work together to find the interest rate.

From list of cells 3.10, you can create the annuity due template that solved the sample problem. Note: Before you enter the cell listings, be sure to enter the CALCCLR value in C27 as zero. This entry causes the circular reference formulas initially to display constant values and prevents an ERR condition. All the labels, values, and formulas that create this template are given in the cell listing.

Create the template by first entering the labels and section division lines. Change the column widths as shown in the listing. For example, [W15] means a column width of 15. Next, enter all values. Make sure that you enter zero (0) in cell C27. Then create the range names. When the range names have been created, enter the formulas.

After you have made all the entries, unprotect the cells that are preceded by U in the listing. Protect the entire spreadsheet before saving it to disk.

You can change a few lines in this template so that it solves ordinary annuity problems. Make the following changes:

Term	Address	Change
label	A2	ORDINARY ANNUITY/FUTURE VALUE (INTEREST RATE UNKNOWN)
label	A6	Ordinary annuity payments are made at the end of each period.
FV CALC	C39	@IF(CALCCLR=0,0.001,@FV(PMT,INT,N))

After entering either set of listings and before running the macro, save your work to disk.

To test the formulas, enter the known amounts for the annuity in the top portion of the template. You must enter the future value, periodic payment, and number of periods as positive numbers. Your last entry should be the estimated interest per period, entered as a decimal in the DATA ENTRY section. Estimates between .01 and 1.0 supply a correct answer for most rates of return.

After entering the data, hold down the Alt key and press C. When calculations are completed, the cursor highlights the answer. The answer and its accuracy are shown in the CALCULATED INTEREST RATE section of the template. The answer is the periodic interest rate, in this case, for monthly periods. To find the annual interest, you must multiply by 12 the rate and accuracy shown.

Tricks, Traps, and Assumptions

The annuity due template, used to solve the sample problem, assumes that payments (or receipts) are made at the beginning of each period. The ordinary annuity template assumes that payments (or receipts) are made at the end of each period.

The templates solve for the periodic interest rate. To find the annual interest rate, multiply the answer by the number of periods per year.

The leading zeros in the Accuracy cell (C21) indicate the accuracy for the estimated periodic interest. To recalculate for more accuracy, enter the calculated interest as your new estimated interest and press Alt-c.

Appendix D contains the macros that run these templates in 1-2-3 Release 1A.

When INCORRECT! is displayed next to the solution, either additional calculations are necessary or the input is wrong. If this happens, check the data you entered. If you do not find any errors, the estimated interest may be too low. Use the calculated interest as the new estimate and press Alt-c again.

List of Cells 3.10

```
A2:  PR 'ANNUITY DUE/FUTURE VALUE (INTEREST RATE UNKNOWN)
A3:  PR \=
B3:  PR [W15] \=
C3:  PR [W15] \=
D3:  PR [W17] \=
E3:  PR [W14] \=
A4:  PR 'DATA ENTRY:   ANNUITY VALUES
A5:  PR \-
B5:  PR [W15] \-
C5:  PR [W15] \-
D5:  PR [W17] \-
E5:  PR [W14] \-
A6:  U 'Annuity due payments are made at the beginning of each period.
A7:  PR 'Enter the known values for the annuity.
B8:  PR [W15] "Future Value=
C8:  (F2) U [W15] 385000
B9:  PR [W15] "Payment (EOP)=
C9:  (F2) U [W15] 2000
B10: PR [W15] 'Number Periods=
C10: (F0) U [W15] 120
A12: PR 'Estimate the interest rate per period as a decimal, i.e. .5%=.005
B13: PR [W15] "Estimate=
C13: (F6) U [W15] 0.1
A14: U 'Press Alt-c to calculate.
A15: PR \=
B15: PR [W15] \=
C15: PR [W15] \=
D15: PR [W17] \=
E15: PR [W14] \=
A16: PR 'CALCULATED INTEREST RATE
A17: PR \-
B17: PR [W15] \-
C17: PR [W15] \-
D17: PR [W17] \-
E17: PR [W14] \-
A18: PR 'The calculated interest rate PER PERIOD as a decimal is
B19: PR [W15] "Interest=
C19: (F6) PR [W15] @IF(COUNTER<2,ESTINT,NEXT INT)
B21: PR [W15] "Accuracy=
C21: PR [W15] +NEXT INCR
A23: PR \=
B23: PR [W15] \=
C23: PR [W15] \=
D23: PR [W17] \=
E23: PR [W14] \=
A24: PR 'CALCULATIONS
A25: PR \-
B25: PR [W15] \-
C25: PR [W15] \-
D25: PR [W17] \-
E25: PR [W14] \-
A26: PR 'CALCCLR is 1 when complete. To clear manually, enter 0, press F9 twice.
B27: PR [W15] "CALCCLR
C27: U [W15] 0
A29: PR 'Each iteration (counter) increments the calculated interest rate.
A30: PR 'Calculations are in decimal numbers, not percentages.
B31: PR [W15] "COUNTER
C31: PR [W15] @IF(CALCCLR=1,COUNTER+1,0)
B32: PR [W15] "FIRST INCR
C32: PR [W15] +ESTINT/2
A34: PR 'Next increment and interest used to calculate FV
B35: PR [W15] "NEXT INCR
```

```
C35:  PR [W15] @IF(CALCCLR=0,ESTINT,@IF(FV>CALC FV,LAST INCR,LAST INCR/2))
B36:  PR [W15] "NEXT INT
C36:  PR [W15] @IF(FV>CALC FV,INT+LAST INCR,INT-LAST INCR)
A38:  PR 'Calculated value of PV from last calculated interest
B39:  PR [W15] "CALC FV
C39:  (F2) PR [W15] @IF(CALCCLR=0,0.001,@FV(PMT,INT,N)*(1+INT))
A41:  PR 'Increment last added to calculated interest rate
B42:  PR [W15] "LAST INCR
C42:  PR [W15] @IF(COUNTER<2,FIRST INCR,NEXT INCR)
A44:  PR \=
B44:  PR [W15] \=
C44:  PR [W15] \=
D44:  PR [W17] \=
E44:  PR [W14] \=
B45:  PR [W15] 'CLEAR AND CALC MACRO
A46:  PR '\c
B46:  PR [W15] '{HOME}{BLANK D19}
E46:  PR [W14] 'Go home, erase warning
B47:  PR [W15] '{LET CALCCLR,0}
E47:  PR [W14] 'Clear old step values
B48:  PR [W15] '{RECALCCOL C1..C42}{RECALCCOL C1..C42}
B49:  PR [W15] '{LET CALCCLR,1}
E49:  PR [W14] 'Set up new values
B50:  PR [W15] '{RECALCCOL C1..C42}
B51:  PR [W15] '{RECALCCOL C19..C42,@ABS(FV-CALC FV)<.001,100}
E51:  PR [W14] 'Calc only column until correct or 100 times
B52:  PR [W15] '{CALC}
E52:  PR [W14] 'Recalc entire spreadsheet using new values
B53:  PR [W15] '{GOTO}INT~
E53:  PR [W14] 'Cursor on interest
B54:  PR [W15] '{IF FIRST INCR/LAST INCR<=10}{WRONG}
E54:  PR [W14] 'Wrong values used or more iterations needed
A57:  PR 'WRONG
B57:  PR [W15] '{LET D19,"INCORRECT!"}
E57:  PR [W14] 'Display warning
B58:  PR [W15] '{GOTO}D19~
E58:  PR [W14] 'Cursor on warning
B59:  PR [W15] '{BEEP}
```

Financial Ratios that Monitor Your Business

An old adage says that if you don't know where you're going, how you get there doesn't matter. If you're in business, however, you do know where you're going and you have a good idea how to get there. The problem comes in staying on the path to your goal.

One way of staying on the right financial path is to monitor your business with financial ratios. The ratios use information that normally is available from your balance sheet and income statement. Ratios can help you monitor at a glance your business' position in inventory, sales, and investments. Financial ratios also can give you an idea of how your business procedures compare with those of your competitors.

Agencies that monitor business ratios for selected industries are listed in Appendix A. Books published by these agencies can usually be found in the reference section of the library or in the business-loan department at a bank.

Comparing your ratios to your industry's averages can give you a broad picture of how you stand in the industry. However, because of different operating and accounting policies, the ratios may not apply specifically to your business. Also, the balance sheets and income statements of the companies surveyed may not reflect the companies' real situations.

Industry financial ratios are better used as guidelines for your financial path rather than as goals to strive for. With your CPA or financial department, you can define the ratios best suited to serve as guidelines for reaching your business goals. Once you know the important ratios, you can combine 1-2-3's database and graphics capabilities to keep a history of your financial values and to create graphs that show how the ratios change. Your CPA or financial department should be able to help you determine what business factors must change in order to affect the ratios.

Nine of the most important business ratios are given here along with short descriptions of each. Because the ratios are simple formulas that must be considered against your company's total operation, the ratios are not presented in templates. For additional information on business ratios and how they can be used and abused, refer to books on managerial finance. Two suggested books are listed in Appendix A.

Profit Margin. The profit margin, the amount of profit for every dollar of sales, can help you determine whether your prices are high or low with respect to costs. When comparing your profit margin to industry averages, consider that your product and service mix may be different from those measured. You may improve your profit margin by changing your prices, decreasing your costs, or changing the mix of products you sell.

$$\text{Profit Margin} = \frac{\text{net profit after tax}}{\text{sales}}$$

Return on Assets (ROA). The ROA tells you the rate of return you are getting from the total assets you have invested. You can remedy a low return on assets by increasing your net profit after tax through a better profit margin and reducing expenses such as the cost of debt. You also can increase the ROA by increasing the efficient use of your assets or by selling inefficient or unused assets.

$$ROA = \frac{\text{net profit after tax}}{\text{total assets}}$$

Current Ratio. The current ratio measures how well short-term debts are covered by assets that can be converted to cash in the same time frame as the liabilities. Current ratio, which often is used as a measure of a company's short-term solvency, gives creditors an idea of how well their debt is covered by assets that can be converted to cash. A trend toward a decreasing current ratio can signal possible problems.

$$\text{Current Ratio} = \frac{\text{current assets}}{\text{current liabilities}}$$

Quick Ratio or Acid Test. The quick ratio is a more accurate test of how well a company can pay off its short-term debts than the Current Ratio. This is because the following formula does not include liquidating inventory as a means of getting cash.

$$\text{Quick Ratio} = \frac{\text{current assets} - \text{inventories}}{\text{current liabilities}}$$

Total Debt to Total Assets. The debt ratio measures the amount of funds from creditors in a company. If you have a debt ratio that is much higher than your industry's average, you may have difficulty borrowing additional money; this is because you already owe a larger-than-normal portion of the company to creditors.

$$\text{Debt Ratio} = \frac{\text{total debt}}{\text{total assets}}$$

Fixed Charge Coverage. The fixed charge coverage ratio measures how well a company can cover its fixed costs, for instance, interest and lease costs. In most cases, only long-term leases should be considered.

$$\text{Fixed Charge} = \frac{\text{profit before tax} + \text{interest} + \text{lease charges}}{\text{interest} + \text{lease charges}}$$

Inventory Turnover. Inventory turnover can tell you whether you are holding unnecessary inventory. The ratio should be as high as you can achieve while still supplying your sales force with needed products. If your business is highly cyclical or in a rapidly changing business climate, you may need to average or adjust your inventory rather than use inventory for a single point in time. When measuring your inventory against industry averages, be sure to check how the industry inventories were valued.

$$\text{Inventory Turns} = \frac{\text{sales}}{\text{inventory}}$$

Average Collection Period. You can measure how long it takes your company to receive payment after a sale by monitoring the average collection period. Sales per day is calculated as the average from annual sales. You should compare this ratio with your industry segment's average and with your own sales terms and receivables aging schedule. Trends here may indicate that you need to change your trade credit or increase the emphasis you put on collection.

$$\text{Average Collection Period} = \frac{\text{accounts receivable}}{\text{sales per day}}$$

Total Assets Turnover. This ratio measures how well you are using the company's assets to produce revenue. If you are below industry average, your sales may not be high enough, or you may have assets that are not contributing to sales or are being used inefficiently. You may need to increase sales; or, if the assets are not part of future plans, you may want to lease or sell them.

$$\text{Total Assets Turns} = \frac{\text{sales}}{\text{total assets}}$$

4
Trends Analysis

Casey Stengel said, "Don't never predict nothin', especially the future." Being able to stick to Casey's adage would be great, but the "game" often goes to those who make the best forecasts. The tools in this chapter can help you improve your forecasts.

Determining past trends, predicting future results, and estimating unknown values are important practices in many professions. Marketers, for example, track market growth and sales trends. Retail salespeople compare this year's sales with last year's sales. Private investors try to predict stock fluctuations, and production engineers attempt to calculate yields for new, untested production runs. Virtually every profession can profit from the ability to predict the unknown.

The 1-2-3 templates and equations in this chapter determine the relationships between different series of data. You can use those relationships to show past trends, estimate unknown data, and make near-term predictions.

You can relate different sets of data with 1-2-3 using two methods: time series analysis and regression analysis. *Time series analysis*, which uses moving averages, can help businesses determine the cyclical fluctuations in the economy and in company sales and growth. *Regression analysis*, which finds the relationship between two or more related series of data, assumes a relationship of a definite form, such as a linear or exponential relationship.

Time series analysis is an important tool for understanding the cyclical nature of business or investments. With the Times Series Analysis template, you can determine the cyclical nature of sales and production rates and the rise and fall of stock prices. The smoothing techniques "even out" the variations caused by short-term effects and reveal underlying patterns.

Regression analysis tries to find a mathematical relationship, which may or may not be time related, between sets of data. With this method, you can find relationships between information such as quantities of raw materials and final output or quality rates and return rates. Each of the regression analysis templates assumes a different type of relationship between data sets. You should use the template that produces the best correlation between your two sets of data.

Appendix A contains a reference list of private and government bureaus that gather and analyze industrial, demographic, and financial data. This data can be useful to you for making your own forecasts.

Entering Lists of Cells

When you create the templates in this chapter, follow these steps to enter the lists of cells:

1. Change column widths to the widths shown in the listing, such as [W5], then enter and justify the labels and section lines for the entire spreadsheet. The labels and lines will act as a skeleton from which you can locate other parts of the template. Study the figure of each template to get an idea of how labels are arranged. Lines between sections are easiest to enter using the repeat command, for example, \=.

2. Enter and format numbers from the template cell listing. The listing's numbers, referred to as values, are either data from the sample problem or constants used in a formula. Entering the numbers will help you see the addresses to be used by range names.

3. Create the range names used in the formulas. The range names must be created before entering formulas that use those names. The range names used in each template are listed in the "Creating the Template" section that relates to each template. The skeleton of labels and numbers you have entered will guide you in creating range names. Create range names with the **/Range Name Create** command. In Release 2, you can review range names and their addresses by issuing the **/Range Name Table**

command. In Release 1A, issue the /rnc command and select a range name with the cursor and Enter keys; this procedure displays the address assigned to the selected name.

In the trend analysis templates, each column of calculations is given a range name. This makes a range of calculations easier to identify in formulas and in the @SUM function. For each of these columns, the heading (which is the same as the range name) describes the calculations in the column. For example, one column heading in the Power Curve Fit template is LN(X)SQR. This heading indicates that the calculation in the column is @LN(X)^2, the square of the log of X, where X is the number from the X data column in the same row as the calculation.

4. After creating the range names, enter the formulas. Major formulas are given in the "Trends Formulas" section that relates to each template as well as in the listing. Chapters 1 and 2 describe how to enter and correct formulas efficiently. After entering a long or complex formula, you should save the template to disk.

All the templates in this chapter contain columns of repeating formulas. Entering these columns of formulas is easy when you use absolute addressing and the /Copy command. Absolute addressing is indicated in the listings by a $ sign before a range name or in an address. Create the top formula in a column of repeating formulas and copy it down into other locations. With this technique, you quickly can enter formulas (such as in the LN(X)SQR column described in step 3) in columns of calculations.

5. When everything is entered, *don't* run your template. You always should save your template before testing. Although the calculations in this chapter are straightforward, some templates may erase data and formulas or create errors when tested. Having an original in these cases can save you unnecessary work.

6. If you have entered the data values shown in the cell listing, the template will execute the sample problem. If the answers are different from the answers shown in the

figure of the template, check the data, then check the range names, and finally print and check the formulas. Chapters 1 and 2 offer tips on how to check formulas.

Time Series Analysis

Whether your business is retail sales, real estate, or stock brokerage, a major element in your success is how well you can predict the future. Using the historical data in your 1-2-3 database, you can reveal cyclical patterns by smoothing away erratic changes and adjusting for outside influences. In many cases, you will be able to make near-term predictions from the patterns you find.

Some businesses are tied closely to seasonal cycles. Although sometimes these cycles are obvious, other times they can be concealed by influential factors such as inflation, employment rates, and regional growth.

Revealing a Changing Population's Effect on Business Cycles

Suppose that you are facing a sales cycle problem. Your region has undergone a recent population explosion that has obscured any cyclical pattern in your business. You need to know whether your sales are increasing from factors other than the area's growth. Luckily, the local economic development board has just released a table showing the growth rate of different market segments in the area. Table 4.1 shows the sales per month over the last three years for your business and the population growth rate of your target market as an index number.

Without the 1-2-3 time series analysis, the sales appear erratic, and pinpointing a consistent cycle is difficult. Using exponential smoothing of the sales rates, the 1-2-3 graph (see fig. 4.1) reveals an obvious sales cycle that appears to have an upward trend. After adjusting sales for population growth, you can see that sales actually are on a steady downward trend. The cycle's downward trend in relation to the increasing population indicates that your business is losing its share of the market.

Table 4.1
Sales and Market Growth Rate

Month	Sales	Index
1	50.0	1.0
2	46.0	1.0
3	47.7	1.005
4	44.0	1.02
5	45.9	1.02
6	45.6	1.025
7	45.0	1.03
8	47.1	1.04
9	50.0	1.07
10	49.5	1.10
11	53.0	1.10
12	57.6	1.11
13	50.9	1.13
14	52.0	1.12
15	47.0	1.125
16	47.8	1.134
17	47.2	1.12
18	46.3	1.13
19	47.0	1.133
20	48.2	1.14
21	54.0	1.15
22	52.0	1.17
23	57.0	1.17
24	59.6	1.186
25	49.0	1.17
26	50.0	1.19
27	49.0	1.2
28	50.2	1.25
29	49.3	1.265
30	48.1	1.27
31	50.4	1.256
32	51.0	1.268
33	54.5	1.286
34	53.0	1.3
35	59.4	1.32
36	64.0	1.35

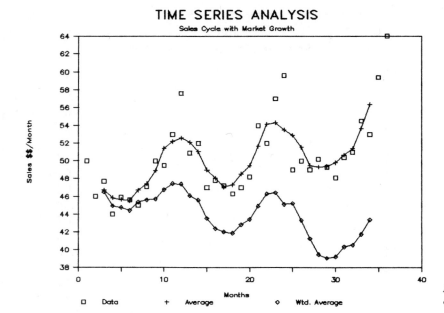

Fig. 4.1. Finding a business sales cycle with time series analysis.

Creating the Template

The 1-2-3 Time Series Analysis template in figure 4.2 analyzes data in two ways: by periodic moving average and by exponential smoothing. The results of each method are displayed with and without weighted adjustments.

Periodic moving averages find an average data value over time. Using the current period as the center of the five time periods, this template averages over five time periods.

The other method, *exponential smoothing*, smooths out extreme fluctuations in data by subtracting a fixed percentage from the current average and adding a fixed percentage from the current period. This process allows the current data to influence the average by a controlled amount. By changing the fixed percentage, you can increase the current period's influence. When the fixed percentage is high, the current period has a greater influence.

Periodic moving averages are calculated by averaging the data (Y) over multiple periods, with the current period (t) as the center point. The periodic moving average formula over five periods is

$$Y_{AVE(t)}=(Y_{t-2}+Y_{t-1}+Y_t+Y_{t+1}+Y_{t+2})/5$$

PERIOD	DATA	FIVE-PERIOD AVERAGE	EXPONENTIAL SMOOTHING, ESF= 0.1	0.5	WEIGHT INDEX	ADJUSTED AVERAGES PERIOD AVERAGE	EXPONENTIAL 0.1	0.5
1	50.0	NA	50.0	50.0	1.0000	NA	50.0	50.0
2	46.0	NA	49.6	48.0	1.0000	NA	49.6	48.0
3	47.7	46.7	49.4	47.9	1.0050	46.5	49.2	47.6
4	44.0	45.8	48.9	45.9	1.0200	44.9	47.9	45.0
5	45.9	45.6	48.6	45.9	1.0200	44.7	47.6	45.0
6	45.6	45.5	48.3	45.8	1.0250	44.4	47.1	44.6
7	45.0	46.7	47.9	45.4	1.0300	45.4	46.6	44.1
8	47.1	47.4	47.9	46.2	1.0400	45.6	46.0	44.5
9	50.0	48.9	48.1	48.1	1.0700	45.7	44.9	45.0
10	49.5	51.4	48.2	48.8	1.1000	46.8	43.8	44.4
11	53.0	52.2	48.7	50.9	1.1000	47.5	44.3	46.3
12	57.6	52.6	49.6	54.3	1.1100	47.4	44.7	48.9
13	50.9	52.1	49.7	52.6	1.1300	46.1	44.0	46.5
14	52.0	51.1	49.9	52.3	1.1200	45.6	44.6	46.7
15	47.0	49.0	49.7	49.6	1.1250	43.5	44.1	44.1
16	47.8	48.1	49.5	48.7	1.1340	42.4	43.6	43.0
17	47.2	47.1	49.2	48.0	1.1200	42.0	44.0	42.8
18	46.3	47.3	48.9	47.1	1.1300	41.9	43.3	41.7
19	47.0	48.5	48.8	47.1	1.1330	42.8	43.0	41.5
20	48.2	49.5	48.7	47.6	1.1400	43.4	42.7	41.8
21	54.0	51.6	49.2	50.8	1.1500	44.9	42.8	44.2
22	52.0	54.2	49.5	51.4	1.1700	46.3	42.3	43.9
23	57.0	54.3	50.3	54.2	1.1700	46.4	43.0	46.3
24	59.6	53.5	51.2	56.9	1.1860	45.1	43.2	48.0
25	49.0	52.9	51.0	53.0	1.1700	45.2	43.6	45.3
26	50.0	51.6	50.9	51.5	1.1900	43.3	42.7	43.3
27	49.0	49.5	50.7	50.2	1.2000	41.3	42.2	41.9
28	50.2	49.3	50.6	50.2	1.2500	39.5	40.5	40.2
29	49.3	49.4	50.5	49.8	1.2650	39.1	39.9	39.3
30	48.1	49.8	50.3	48.9	1.2700	39.2	39.6	38.5
31	50.4	50.7	50.3	49.7	1.2560	40.3	40.0	39.5
32	51.0	51.4	50.3	50.3	1.2680	40.5	39.7	39.7
33	54.5	53.7	50.8	52.4	1.2860	41.7	39.5	40.8
34	53.0	56.4	51.0	52.7	1.3000	43.4	39.2	40.5
35	59.4	NA	51.8	56.1	1.3200	NA	39.3	42.5
36	64.0	NA	53.0	60.0	1.3500	NA	39.3	44.5
	NA					NA		
	NA					NA		

Make an @NA entry below the data column for the same number of rows as one-half the averaging period. This prevents blank cells from being averaged in.

Fig. 4.2. Time Series Analysis template.

This formula isn't used until row 10 because the formula needs two trailing rows of data, rows 8 and 9, before it can operate correctly. The moving average is entered in cell C10 as the following.

@IF(@CELL(B12,"type")="b",@NA,@SUM(B8..B12)/5)

This formula calculates the average of the five data cells centered on B10. The @IF function determines whether the cell at t+2 is blank, which indicates the end of data. If the cell is blank, the average would be incorrect; in these cases, NA is displayed.

Exponential smoothing, the second method, takes the current smoothed value, S_{t-1}; reduces it by a percentage, ESF; and adds to the current smoothed value the same percentage taken from the current data. Because no smoothed value exists to start with, the exponential smoothing formula uses the first piece of data as an estimate. The smoothing becomes more accurate as additional data is included. Large values of ESF make the curve more responsive to short-term change. The exponential smoothing formula is

$$S_t=(1-ESF)*S_{t-1}+ESF*Y_t$$

The first exponentially smoothed values, in D8 and E8, use data directly from B8. The smoothing formula begins in row 9. ESF1 and ESF2 are range names for the exponential smoothing factors in D6 and E6, respectively. The smoothing formulas follow.

Term	Address	Formula
Smoothed Value	D9	@IF(@CELL(B9,"type")="b",@NA, (1–$ESF1)*D8+$ESF1*B9)
Smoothed Value	E9	@IF(@CELL(B9,"type")="b",@NA, (1–$ESF2)*E8+$ESF2*B9)

The dollar signs in front of ESF1 and ESF2 enable you to copy these formulas over the full range of data. The relative cell addresses (those without dollar signs) adjust to accept the correct data. The @IF statement checks for a blank data cell, which indicates the end of the data.

While external factors—such as population growth, inflation, and unemployment—can affect economic cycles, often you can use weighted indices to adjust for these effects. National and state governments and private research companies calculate these indices and make them available to the public. (See Appendix A for the names of some reports containing this information.)

Weighted indices compensate for changes over time by adjusting all the data. After the adjustments, data can be compared relative to a specific time frame. In the example, your business began its time series (sales) analysis in the month that the economic development board used as the base month. The base month was given an adjustment index of 1.0. You make adjustments with a weighted index by dividing the index for a period into the data for that period.

List of cells 4.1 contains everything you need to create the Time Series Analysis template. Enter your data in column B under the heading DATA. The first column, which indicates the time period, is used only to make data entry easier, not to make calculations.

The FIVE-PERIOD AVERAGE column displays the average value of the five periods centered around the period displayed in each row of column A. The two columns under EXPONENTIAL SMOOTHING contain data calculated with smoothing factors of 0.1 and 0.5. You can enter new smoothing factors by typing them in cells D6 and E6.

Tricks, Traps, and Assumptions

Periodic moving averages should be averaged over an odd number of periods. This produces an even number of periods before and after each selected date. If you average over an even number of periods, the average value produced corresponds to a date in between two periods.

Exponential smoothing tends to lag behind the actual cycle. The smaller the exponential smoothing factor (ESF), the larger the lag and the smoother the curve. Large exponential smoothing factors cause the smoothed data to shift with large changes in periodic data.

You can expand the number of periods in the template beyond 36 by copying the last row of formulas down. If you are using fewer than 36 periods, either enter blanks in the unused data cells or use /Range Erase to clear the cells. The @IF functions display NA where appropriate.

Cyclical patterns and the effects of different exponential smoothing are easiest to identify in a graph. To see the data as points and the averaged or smoothed values as a curve, use an X-Y graph with the time periods as the X data range, the original data as the A data range, and the averaged or smoothed values as the B data range. All ranges must have the same number of cells. Before selecting View, use the Format command to set the A data range to Symbols and the B data range to Lines. This procedure creates a graph in which the smoothed or average data appears as connected lines and the original data as symbols. Figure 4.1 shows the original data for your business as symbols and the weighted and exponentially smoothed data as a curve.

List of Cells 4.1

```
A1:  PR [W6] '
A2:  PR [W6] 'TIME SERIES ANALYSIS
A3:  PR [W6] \=
B3:  PR [W7] \=
C3:  PR \=
D3:  PR \=
E3:  PR \=
F3:  PR [W4] \=
G3:  PR \=
H3:  PR \=
I3:  PR \=
J3:  PR \=
C4:  PR "FIVE-
D4:  PR "       EXPONENTIAL
H4:  PR "      ADJUSTED AVERAGES
C5:  PR "PERIOD
D5:  PR "    SMOOTHING, ESF=
G5:  PR "WEIGHT
H5:  PR "PERIOD
I5:  PR "       EXPONENTIAL
A6:  PR [W6] 'PERIOD
B6:  PR [W7] "DATA
C6:  PR "AVERAGE
D6:  U 0.1
E6:  U 0.5
G6:  PR "INDEX
H6:  PR "AVERAGE
I6:  (F1) PR +ESF1
J6:  (F1) PR +ESF2
A7:  PR [W6] \-
B7:  PR [W7] \-
C7:  PR \-
D7:  PR \-
E7:  PR \-
F7:  PR [W4] \-
G7:  PR \-
H7:  PR \-
I7:  PR \-
J7:  PR \-
A8:  PR [W6] 1
B8:  (F1) U [W7] 50
C8:  (F1) PR @NA
D8:  (F1) PR +B8
E8:  (F1) PR +B8
G8:  (F4) U 1
H8:  (F1) PR +C8/G8
I8:  (F1) PR +D8/G8
J8:  (F1) PR +E8/G8
A9:  PR [W6] 2
B9:  (F1) U [W7] 46
C9:  (F1) PR @NA
D9:  (F1) PR @IF(@CELL("type",B9..B9)="v",$ESF1*B9+(1-$ESF1)*D8,@NA)
E9:  (F1) PR @IF(@CELL("type",B9..B9)="v",$ESF2*B9+(1-$ESF2)*E8,@NA)
G9:  (F4) U 1
H9:  (F1) PR +C9/G9
I9:  (F1) PR +D9/G9
J9:  (F1) PR +E9/G9
A10: PR [W6] 3
B10: (F1) U [W7] 47.7
C10: (F1) PR @IF(@CELL("type",B12..B12)<>"v",@NA,@SUM(B8..B12)/5)
D10: (F1) PR @IF(@CELL("type",B10..B10)="v",$ESF1*B10+(1-$ESF1)*D9,@NA)
E10: (F1) PR @IF(@CELL("type",B10..B10)="v",$ESF2*B10+(1-$ESF2)*E9,@NA)
G10: (F4) U 1.005
```

```
H10: (F1) PR +C10/G10
I10: (F1) PR +D10/G10
J10: (F1) PR +E10/G10
A11: PR [W6] 4
B11: (F1) U [W7] 44
C11: (F1) PR @IF(@CELL("type",B13..B13)<>"v",@NA,@SUM(B9..B13)/5)
D11: (F1) PR @IF(@CELL("type",B11..B11)="v",$ESF1*B11+(1-$ESF1)*D10,@NA)
E11: (F1) PR @IF(@CELL("type",B11..B11)="v",$ESF2*B11+(1-$ESF2)*E10,@NA)
G11: (F4) U 1.02
H11: (F1) PR +C11/G11
I11: (F1) PR +D11/G11
J11: (F1) PR +E11/G11
A12: PR [W6] 5
B12: (F1) U [W7] 45.9
C12: (F1) PR @IF(@CELL("type",B14..B14)<>"v",@NA,@SUM(B10..B14)/5)
D12: (F1) PR @IF(@CELL("type",B12..B12)="v",$ESF1*B12+(1-$ESF1)*D11,@NA)
E12: (F1) PR @IF(@CELL("type",B12..B12)="v",$ESF2*B12+(1-$ESF2)*E11,@NA)
G12: (F4) U 1.02
H12: (F1) PR +C12/G12
I12: (F1) PR +D12/G12
J12: (F1) PR +E12/G12
A13: PR [W6] 6
B13: (F1) U [W7] 45.6
C13: (F1) PR @IF(@CELL("type",B15..B15)<>"v",@NA,@SUM(B11..B15)/5)
D13: (F1) PR @IF(@CELL("type",B13..B13)="v",$ESF1*B13+(1-$ESF1)*D12,@NA)
E13: (F1) PR @IF(@CELL("type",B13..B13)="v",$ESF2*B13+(1-$ESF2)*E12,@NA)
G13: (F4) U 1.025
H13: (F1) PR +C13/G13
I13: (F1) PR +D13/G13
J13: (F1) PR +E13/G13
A14: PR [W6] 7
B14: (F1) U [W7] 45
C14: (F1) PR @IF(@CELL("type",B16..B16)<>"v",@NA,@SUM(B12..B16)/5)
D14: (F1) PR @IF(@CELL("type",B14..B14)="v",$ESF1*B14+(1-$ESF1)*D13,@NA)
E14: (F1) PR @IF(@CELL("type",B14..B14)="v",$ESF2*B14+(1-$ESF2)*E13,@NA)
G14: (F4) U 1.03
H14: (F1) PR +C14/G14
I14: (F1) PR +D14/G14
J14: (F1) PR +E14/G14
A15: PR [W6] 8
B15: (F1) U [W7] 47.1
C15: (F1) PR @IF(@CELL("type",B17..B17)<>"v",@NA,@SUM(B13..B17)/5)
D15: (F1) PR @IF(@CELL("type",B15..B15)="v",$ESF1*B15+(1-$ESF1)*D14,@NA)
E15: (F1) PR @IF(@CELL("type",B15..B15)="v",$ESF2*B15+(1-$ESF2)*E14,@NA)
G15: (F4) U 1.04
H15: (F1) PR +C15/G15
I15: (F1) PR +D15/G15
J15: (F1) PR +E15/G15
A16: PR [W6] 9
B16: (F1) U [W7] 50
C16: (F1) PR @IF(@CELL("type",B18..B18)<>"v",@NA,@SUM(B14..B18)/5)
D16: (F1) PR @IF(@CELL("type",B16..B16)="v",$ESF1*B16+(1-$ESF1)*D15,@NA)
E16: (F1) PR @IF(@CELL("type",B16..B16)="v",$ESF2*B16+(1-$ESF2)*E15,@NA)
G16: (F4) U 1.07
H16: (F1) PR +C16/G16
I16: (F1) PR +D16/G16
J16: (F1) PR +E16/G16
A17: PR [W6] 10
B17: (F1) U [W7] 49.5
C17: (F1) PR @IF(@CELL("type",B19..B19)<>"v",@NA,@SUM(B15..B19)/5)
D17: (F1) PR @IF(@CELL("type",B17..B17)="v",$ESF1*B17+(1-$ESF1)*D16,@NA)
E17: (F1) PR @IF(@CELL("type",B17..B17)="v",$ESF2*B17+(1-$ESF2)*E16,@NA)
G17: (F4) U 1.1
H17: (F1) PR +C17/G17
I17: (F1) PR +D17/G17
J17: (F1) PR +E17/G17
```

```
A18: PR [W6] 11
B18: (F1) U [W7] 53
C18: (F1) PR @IF(@CELL("type",B20..B20)<>"v",@NA,@SUM(B16..B20)/5)
D18: (F1) PR @IF(@CELL("type",B18..B18)="v",$ESF1*B18+(1-$ESF1)*D17,@NA)
E18: (F1) PR @IF(@CELL("type",B18..B18)="v",$ESF2*B18+(1-$ESF2)*E17,@NA)
G18: (F4) U 1.1
H18: (F1) PR +C18/G18
I18: (F1) PR +D18/G18
J18: (F1) PR +E18/G18
A19: PR [W6] 12
B19: (F1) U [W7] 57.6
C19: (F1) PR @IF(@CELL("type",B21..B21)<>"v",@NA,@SUM(B17..B21)/5)
D19: (F1) PR @IF(@CELL("type",B19..B19)="v",$ESF1*B19+(1-$ESF1)*D18,@NA)
E19: (F1) PR @IF(@CELL("type",B19..B19)="v",$ESF2*B19+(1-$ESF2)*E18,@NA)
G19: (F4) U 1.11
H19: (F1) PR +C19/G19
I19: (F1) PR +D19/G19
J19: (F1) PR +E19/G19
A20: PR [W6] 13
B20: (F1) U [W7] 50.9
C20: (F1) PR @IF(@CELL("type",B22..B22)<>"v",@NA,@SUM(B18..B22)/5)
D20: (F1) PR @IF(@CELL("type",B20..B20)="v",$ESF1*B20+(1-$ESF1)*D19,@NA)
E20: (F1) PR @IF(@CELL("type",B20..B20)="v",$ESF2*B20+(1-$ESF2)*E19,@NA)
G20: (F4) U 1.13
H20: (F1) PR +C20/G20
I20: (F1) PR +D20/G20
J20: (F1) PR +E20/G20
A21: PR [W6] 14
B21: (F1) U [W7] 52
C21: (F1) PR @IF(@CELL("type",B23..B23)<>"v",@NA,@SUM(B19..B23)/5)
D21: (F1) PR @IF(@CELL("type",B21..B21)="v",$ESF1*B21+(1-$ESF1)*D20,@NA)
E21: (F1) PR @IF(@CELL("type",B21..B21)="v",$ESF2*B21+(1-$ESF2)*E20,@NA)
G21: (F4) U 1.12
H21: (F1) PR +C21/G21
I21: (F1) PR +D21/G21
J21: (F1) PR +E21/G21
A22: PR [W6] 15
B22: (F1) U [W7] 47
C22: (F1) PR @IF(@CELL("type",B24..B24)<>"v",@NA,@SUM(B20..B24)/5)
D22: (F1) PR @IF(@CELL("type",B22..B22)="v",$ESF1*B22+(1-$ESF1)*D21,@NA)
E22: (F1) PR @IF(@CELL("type",B22..B22)="v",$ESF2*B22+(1-$ESF2)*E21,@NA)
G22: (F4) U 1.125
H22: (F1) PR +C22/G22
I22: (F1) PR +D22/G22
J22: (F1) PR +E22/G22
A23: PR [W6] 16
B23: (F1) U [W7] 47.8
C23: (F1) PR @IF(@CELL("type",B25..B25)<>"v",@NA,@SUM(B21..B25)/5)
D23: (F1) PR @IF(@CELL("type",B23..B23)="v",$ESF1*B23+(1-$ESF1)*D22,@NA)
E23: (F1) PR @IF(@CELL("type",B23..B23)="v",$ESF2*B23+(1-$ESF2)*E22,@NA)
G23: (F4) U 1.134
H23: (F1) PR +C23/G23
I23: (F1) PR +D23/G23
J23: (F1) PR +E23/G23
A24: PR [W6] 17
B24: (F1) U [W7] 47.2
C24: (F1) PR @IF(@CELL("type",B26..B26)<>"v",@NA,@SUM(B22..B26)/5)
D24: (F1) PR @IF(@CELL("type",B24..B24)="v",$ESF1*B24+(1-$ESF1)*D23,@NA)
E24: (F1) PR @IF(@CELL("type",B24..B24)="v",$ESF2*B24+(1-$ESF2)*E23,@NA)
G24: (F4) U 1.12
H24: (F1) PR +C24/G24
I24: (F1) PR +D24/G24
J24: (F1) PR +E24/G24
A25: PR [W6] 18
B25: (F1) U [W7] 46.3
C25: (F1) PR @IF(@CELL("type",B27..B27)<>"v",@NA,@SUM(B23..B27)/5)
```

```
D25: (F1) PR @IF(@CELL("type",B25..B25)="v",$ESF1*B25+(1-$ESF1)*D24,@NA)
E25: (F1) PR @IF(@CELL("type",B25..B25)="v",$ESF2*B25+(1-$ESF2)*E24,@NA)
G25: (F4) U 1.13
H25: (F1) PR +C25/G25
I25: (F1) PR +D25/G25
J25: (F1) PR +E25/G25
A26: PR [W6] 19
B26: (F1) U [W7] 47
C26: (F1) PR @IF(@CELL("type",B28..B28)<>"v",@NA,@SUM(B24..B28)/5)
D26: (F1) PR @IF(@CELL("type",B26..B26)="v",$ESF1*B26+(1-$ESF1)*D25,@NA)
E26: (F1) PR @IF(@CELL("type",B26..B26)="v",$ESF2*B26+(1-$ESF2)*E25,@NA)
G26: (F4) U 1.133
H26: (F1) PR +C26/G26
I26: (F1) PR +D26/G26
J26: (F1) PR +E26/G26
A27: PR [W6] 20
B27: (F1) U [W7] 48.2
C27: (F1) PR @IF(@CELL("type",B29..B29)<>"v",@NA,@SUM(B25..B29)/5)
D27: (F1) PR @IF(@CELL("type",B27..B27)="v",$ESF1*B27+(1-$ESF1)*D26,@NA)
E27: (F1) PR @IF(@CELL("type",B27..B27)="v",$ESF2*B27+(1-$ESF2)*E26,@NA)
G27: (F4) U 1.14
H27: (F1) PR +C27/G27
I27: (F1) PR +D27/G27
J27: (F1) PR +E27/G27
A28: PR [W6] 21
B28: (F1) U [W7] 54
C28: (F1) PR @IF(@CELL("type",B30..B30)<>"v",@NA,@SUM(B26..B30)/5)
D28: (F1) PR @IF(@CELL("type",B28..B28)="v",$ESF1*B28+(1-$ESF1)*D27,@NA)
E28: (F1) PR @IF(@CELL("type",B28..B28)="v",$ESF2*B28+(1-$ESF2)*E27,@NA)
G28: (F4) U 1.15
H28: (F1) PR +C28/G28
I28: (F1) PR +D28/G28
J28: (F1) PR +E28/G28
A29: PR [W6] 22
B29: (F1) U [W7] 52
C29: (F1) PR @IF(@CELL("type",B31..B31)<>"v",@NA,@SUM(B27..B31)/5)
D29: (F1) PR @IF(@CELL("type",B29..B29)="v",$ESF1*B29+(1-$ESF1)*D28,@NA)
E29: (F1) PR @IF(@CELL("type",B29..B29)="v",$ESF2*B29+(1-$ESF2)*E28,@NA)
G29: (F4) U 1.17
H29: (F1) PR +C29/G29
I29: (F1) PR +D29/G29
J29: (F1) PR +E29/G29
A30: PR [W6] 23
B30: (F1) U [W7] 57
C30: (F1) PR @IF(@CELL("type",B32..B32)<>"v",@NA,@SUM(B28..B32)/5)
D30: (F1) PR @IF(@CELL("type",B30..B30)="v",$ESF1*B30+(1-$ESF1)*D29,@NA)
E30: (F1) PR @IF(@CELL("type",B30..B30)="v",$ESF2*B30+(1-$ESF2)*E29,@NA)
G30: (F4) U 1.17
H30: (F1) PR +C30/G30
I30: (F1) PR +D30/G30
J30: (F1) PR +E30/G30
A31: PR [W6] 24
B31: (F1) U [W7] 59.6
C31: (F1) PR @IF(@CELL("type",B33..B33)<>"v",@NA,@SUM(B29..B33)/5)
D31: (F1) PR @IF(@CELL("type",B31..B31)="v",$ESF1*B31+(1-$ESF1)*D30,@NA)
E31: (F1) PR @IF(@CELL("type",B31..B31)="v",$ESF2*B31+(1-$ESF2)*E30,@NA)
G31: (F4) U 1.186
H31: (F1) PR +C31/G31
I31: (F1) PR +D31/G31
J31: (F1) PR +E31/G31
A32: PR [W6] 25
B32: (F1) U [W7] 49
C32: (F1) PR @IF(@CELL("type",B34..B34)<>"v",@NA,@SUM(B30..B34)/5)
D32: (F1) PR @IF(@CELL("type",B32..B32)="v",$ESF1*B32+(1-$ESF1)*D31,@NA)
E32: (F1) PR @IF(@CELL("type",B32..B32)="v",$ESF2*B32+(1-$ESF2)*E31,@NA)
G32: (F4) U 1.17
```

```
H32: (F1) PR +C32/G32
I32: (F1) PR +D32/G32
J32: (F1) PR +E32/G32
A33: PR [W6] 26
B33: (F1) U [W7] 50
C33: (F1) PR @IF(@CELL("type",B35..B35)<>"v",@NA,@SUM(B31..B35)/5)
D33: (F1) PR @IF(@CELL("type",B33..B33)="v",$ESF1*B33+(1-$ESF1)*D32,@NA)
E33: (F1) PR @IF(@CELL("type",B33..B33)="v",$ESF2*B33+(1-$ESF2)*E32,@NA)
G33: (F4) U 1.19
H33: (F1) PR +C33/G33
I33: (F1) PR +D33/G33
J33: (F1) PR +E33/G33
A34: PR [W6] 27
B34: (F1) U [W7] 49
C34: (F1) PR @IF(@CELL("type",B36..B36)<>"v",@NA,@SUM(B32..B36)/5)
D34: (F1) PR @IF(@CELL("type",B34..B34)="v",$ESF1*B34+(1-$ESF1)*D33,@NA)
E34: (F1) PR @IF(@CELL("type",B34..B34)="v",$ESF2*B34+(1-$ESF2)*E33,@NA)
G34: (F4) U 1.2
H34: (F1) PR +C34/G34
I34: (F1) PR +D34/G34
J34: (F1) PR +E34/G34
A35: PR [W6] 28
B35: (F1) U [W7] 50.2
C35: (F1) PR @IF(@CELL("type",B37..B37)<>"v",@NA,@SUM(B33..B37)/5)
D35: (F1) PR @IF(@CELL("type",B35..B35)="v",$ESF1*B35+(1-$ESF1)*D34,@NA)
E35: (F1) PR @IF(@CELL("type",B35..B35)="v",$ESF2*B35+(1-$ESF2)*E34,@NA)
G35: (F4) U 1.25
H35: (F1) PR +C35/G35
I35: (F1) PR +D35/G35
J35: (F1) PR +E35/G35
A36: PR [W6] 29
B36: (F1) U [W7] 49.3
C36: (F1) PR @IF(@CELL("type",B38..B38)<>"v",@NA,@SUM(B34..B38)/5)
D36: (F1) PR @IF(@CELL("type",B36..B36)="v",$ESF1*B36+(1-$ESF1)*D35,@NA)
E36: (F1) PR @IF(@CELL("type",B36..B36)="v",$ESF2*B36+(1-$ESF2)*E35,@NA)
G36: (F4) U 1.265
H36: (F1) PR +C36/G36
I36: (F1) PR +D36/G36
J36: (F1) PR +E36/G36
A37: PR [W6] 30
B37: (F1) U [W7] 48.1
C37: (F1) PR @IF(@CELL("type",B39..B39)<>"v",@NA,@SUM(B35..B39)/5)
D37: (F1) PR @IF(@CELL("type",B37..B37)="v",$ESF1*B37+(1-$ESF1)*D36,@NA)
E37: (F1) PR @IF(@CELL("type",B37..B37)="v",$ESF2*B37+(1-$ESF2)*E36,@NA)
G37: (F4) U 1.27
H37: (F1) PR +C37/G37
I37: (F1) PR +D37/G37
J37: (F1) PR +E37/G37
A38: PR [W6] 31
B38: (F1) U [W7] 50.4
C38: (F1) PR @IF(@CELL("type",B40..B40)<>"v",@NA,@SUM(B36..B40)/5)
D38: (F1) PR @IF(@CELL("type",B38..B38)="v",$ESF1*B38+(1-$ESF1)*D37,@NA)
E38: (F1) PR @IF(@CELL("type",B38..B38)="v",$ESF2*B38+(1-$ESF2)*E37,@NA)
G38: (F4) U 1.256
H38: (F1) PR +C38/G38
I38: (F1) PR +D38/G38
J38: (F1) PR +E38/G38
A39: PR [W6] 32
B39: (F1) U [W7] 51
C39: (F1) PR @IF(@CELL("type",B41..B41)<>"v",@NA,@SUM(B37..B41)/5)
D39: (F1) PR @IF(@CELL("type",B39..B39)="v",$ESF1*B39+(1-$ESF1)*D38,@NA)
E39: (F1) PR @IF(@CELL("type",B39..B39)="v",$ESF2*B39+(1-$ESF2)*E38,@NA)
G39: (F4) U 1.268
H39: (F1) PR +C39/G39
I39: (F1) PR +D39/G39
J39: (F1) PR +E39/G39
```

```
A40: PR [W6] 33
B40: (F1) U [W7] 54.5
C40: (F1) PR @IF(@CELL("type",B42..B42)<>"v",@NA,@SUM(B38..B42)/5)
D40: (F1) PR @IF(@CELL("type",B40..B40)="v",$ESF1*B40+(1-$ESF1)*D39,@NA)
E40: (F1) PR @IF(@CELL("type",B40..B40)="v",$ESF2*B40+(1-$ESF2)*E39,@NA)
G40: (F4) U 1.286
H40: (F1) PR +C40/G40
I40: (F1) PR +D40/G40
J40: (F1) PR +E40/G40
A41: PR [W6] 34
B41: (F1) U [W7] 53
C41: (F1) PR @IF(@CELL("type",B43..B43)<>"v",@NA,@SUM(B39..B43)/5)
D41: (F1) PR @IF(@CELL("type",B41..B41)="v",$ESF1*B41+(1-$ESF1)*D40,@NA)
E41: (F1) PR @IF(@CELL("type",B41..B41)="v",$ESF2*B41+(1-$ESF2)*E40,@NA)
G41: (F4) U 1.3
H41: (F1) PR +C41/G41
I41: (F1) PR +D41/G41
J41: (F1) PR +E41/G41
A42: PR [W6] 35
B42: (F1) U [W7] 59.4
C42: (F1) PR @IF(@CELL("type",B44..B44)<>"v",@NA,@SUM(B40..B44)/5)
D42: (F1) PR @IF(@CELL("type",B42..B42)="v",$ESF1*B42+(1-$ESF1)*D41,@NA)
E42: (F1) PR @IF(@CELL("type",B42..B42)="v",$ESF2*B42+(1-$ESF2)*E41,@NA)
G42: (F4) U 1.32
H42: (F1) PR +C42/G42
I42: (F1) PR +D42/G42
J42: (F1) PR +E42/G42
A43: PR [W6] 36
B43: (F1) U [W7] 64
C43: (F1) PR @IF(@CELL("type",B45..B45)<>"v",@NA,@SUM(B41..B45)/5)
D43: (F1) PR @IF(@CELL("type",B43..B43)="v",$ESF1*B43+(1-$ESF1)*D42,@NA)
E43: (F1) PR @IF(@CELL("type",B43..B43)="v",$ESF2*B43+(1-$ESF2)*E42,@NA)
G43: (F4) U 1.35
H43: (F1) PR +C43/G43
I43: (F1) PR +D43/G43
J43: (F1) PR +E43/G43
```

Multiple Linear Regression Curve Fit

In your experience, you may have tried to draw a straight line through a "cloud" of data plotted on an X-Y grid. The line, you hoped, would give you the general trend from the data and enable you to predict a Y value when you knew the X value. Although drawing a line to predict trends is easy, you can never be sure how well the line fits the data. When Y depends on multiple sets of X, the problem becomes far too complex for a hand-drawn line.

Linear regression analysis and multiple regression analysis are the most well-known methods of finding trends, predicting the near future, and calculating dependent or unknown values. *Linear regression analysis* uses a set of X and Y data to calculate a line with the least amount of error. *Multiple regression analysis* uses multiple sets of data to find a multidimensional plane with the least amount of error in predicting Y.

The following two examples illustrate how linear regression and multiple regression work. In the first example, a nearly direct relationship appears to exist between direct-mail advertising and orders for gift packs. Linear regression is needed in this first case. The second example predicts the hatch rate for a fish hatchery from three sets of input: food, oxygen level, and temperature. Multiple regression is used in this second case.

Predicting Direct-Mail Orders with a Straight-Line Projection

Suppose that you have a thriving 10-year-old, mail-order business that sells organic fruit and nuts grown on your farm. Some segments of your business have a production limit, and you must be careful that you don't receive too many orders. Because fresh fruit and rapid turnaround are your hallmark, you must predict the number of orders you will get so that enough workers and inventory will be available. Your fruit baskets are so well known and sought after that you control orders by the number of direct-mail pieces you send. Using the non-Christmas-season mailing history in table 4.2, can you determine how much mail you should send in order to sell 12,000 baskets of Macintosh apples?

Table 4.2
Mailing History

Macintosh basket mailing pieces	Macintosh basket orders in two weeks
60000	4750
70000	7200
85000	6800
100000	9698
120000	9980
85000	7589
130000	12890
120000	8345
100000	8678
120000	11006

Figure 4.3 shows the straight line plotted through the mailing response data. In figure 4.4 you can see from the projected values that you should mail 140,000 advertising pieces in order to receive approximately 12,000 orders for baskets of Macintosh apples. The correlation coefficient, R Squared=.789 (in the statistics section of fig. 4.4), indicates that the line fits the data well.

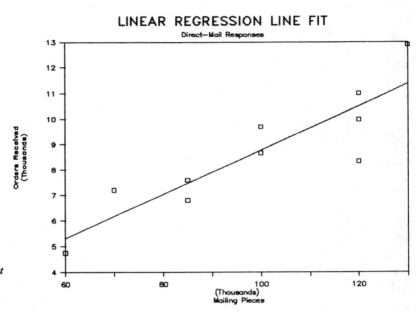

Fig. 4.3. Direct-mail responses that fit a straight line graph well.

Problems are not often as simple and straightforward as this example. More often, a result depends on more than one input. For instance, suppose that you have a fish hatchery, and you have been tracking the days needed for fingerlings to go from hatch to release. You have recorded a number of variables that you think may affect that time. Table 4.3 shows the data collected so far. Using multiple regression analysis, can you determine what equation fits the data and which is the least important factor? Before showing this information to your boss, what should you be aware of?

The equation predicting the days until release is

$$T=-1.37798*Food+1.708532*Oxygen+2.676077*Temp.-171.176$$

with an R Squared value of .5053, a low level of fit.

In addition to the test revealing a low correlation coefficient, R Squared, the equation shows the reverse of the expected growth for-

	A	B	C	D	E	F	G	H	I
1									
2	LINEAR AND MULTIPLE REGRESSION ANALYSIS								
3	===								
4	The linear equation for multiple independent variables is								
5	Y = A*X1 + B*X2 + C*X3 + D*X4 + E*X5 + ... + Constant								
6	This is a straight line when all coefficients other than A are zero.								
7									
8	Enter known X and Y values in the DATA ENTRY section.								
9	Erase cells that do not contain new data.								
10	Increase or decrease rows at a middle row.								
11	Enter X values to project new Ys in the PROJECTED VALUES section.								
12	Hold down Alt and press L.								
13									
14	===								
15	PROJECTED VALUES								
16									
17				Enter X values used in Y projection.					
18	Y Project		X1	X2	X3	X4	X5		
19									
20	5301		60000						
21	6171		70000						
22	7041		80000						
23	7911		90000						
24	8781		100000						
25	9650		110000						
26	10520		120000						
27	11390		130000						
28	12260		140000						
29	13130		150000						
30									
31									
32	DATA ENTRY								
33									
34				KNOWN					
35	ESTIMATED								
36									
37	Y		X1	X2	X3	X4	X5		
38	5301.056		4750	60000					
39	6170.939		7200	70000					
40	7475.763		6800	85000					
41	8780.588		9698	100000					
42	10520.35		9980	120000					

```
43  7475.763    7589    85000
44  11390.23   12890   130000
45  10520.35    8345   120000
46  8780.588    8678   100000
47  10520.35   11006   120000
48  =======================================
49  =======================================
50  STATISTICS AND COEFFICIENTS
51
52  Data entered automatically by 1-2-3.
53               Regression Output:
54      Constant                 81.75892
55      Std Err of Y Est         1128.802
56      R Squared                0.789088
57      No. of Observations            10
58      Degrees of Freedom              8
59      Coefficient Labels     A    B    C    D    E
60      X Coefficient(s)  0.086988
61      Std Err of Coef.  0.015900
62  =======================================
63
64  MACRO
65
66  =======================================
67  LINEAR REGRESSION MACRO
68
69  \1   /ruA60.H61~           Unprotect area to be blanked
70       {BLANK D60.H61}~      Erase old coefficient area
71       /rpA60.H61~           Protect X coeff. area
72       {GOTO}G1~{GOTO}A31~   Display data area
73       {GOTO}XRANGE~         Cursor at top left of X data
74       /drr                  Reset data regression
75       x{?}~                 Define new X-range
76       q                     Exit regression
77       {GOTO}YRANGE~         Cursor at top of Y data
78       /dry.{END}{DOWN}~     Define Y-range
79       oOUTPUT~g             Define output, then go
80       {GOTO}G1~{GOTO}A14~   Show projected data.
81
82
83
84
85
```

Fig. 4.4. Linear and Multiple Regression Analysis template.

Table 4.3
Fingerling Release Time

Y	X1	X2	X3
Days until release	Food	Oxygen	Temperature
100	4	23	90
104	5	24	90.2
108	6	25	20.4
110	4	25	90.6
109	3	24	90.8
108	2	23	91
107	3	22	91.2
106	4	21	91.4
105	5	22	91.6
104	6	24	91.8

mula. According to the equation, increasing the food shortens the time until release, which sounds reasonable. But increasing the oxygen content of the water also should help the fish grow. The equation shows that increasing the oxygen level slows fish growth. Before presenting your information to the boss, collecting more information in a more controlled environment would be wise.

Trends Formulas

The linear formula that relates independent X variables to a Y being solved for is

Y= CONSTANT + A*X1 + B*X2 + C*X3 + . . .

for as many variables, such as food and oxygen, as are necessary. The template in figure 4.4 solves multiple regressions that have from 1 to 16 independent variables, X, which Y depends on. This template uses the /Data Regression commands to solve for the constant; for each variable's coefficient, A, B, C, and so forth; and for the R Squared number.

Although the template uses the /Data Regression commands in Release 2 of 1-2-3, you can develop a Release 1A template for two independent variables by using the formulas shown in Appendix E.

Creating the Template

The Linear and Multiple Regression Analysis template is particularly easy to create because it uses the /**Data Regression** command in Release 2 to do the work. The short macro in the template clears old data, sets data ranges, and executes the /dr command. You either can use the macro or enter the /dr command manually.

The template is divided into five sections. The top two sections provide instructions and show projected values of Y for different values of independent X variables. The third section, under KNOWN, accepts the known Y and X data. You can enter as many as five sets of independent X data. Below the DATA ENTRY section, 1-2-3 displays the coefficients and constant for the linear equation. Also included is information about the accuracy of the line. The \l macro is in the last section.

The template uses the original column width settings and general numeric formatting, so you do not need to do any special formatting. The /dr command produces most of the information in the STATISTICS AND COEFFICIENTS section. All you need to enter are the label in cells A52 and the coefficient labels in cells B59 through H59.

Range names are used to make the X coefficients in the formulas and in the macro easier to understand. The range names are

Address	*Range Name*
B53	OUTPUT
B68	\L
C38	YRANGE
D38	XRANGE
D60	A
E54	CONSTANT
E60	B
F60	C
G60	D
H60	E

An efficient way of creating range names for the X coefficients, A through E, is to use /**Range Name Label Down** and to highlight the labels A through E in cells D59..H59. This procedure names the cells below the labels with the label names.

List of cells 4.2 shows the labels, values, and formulas that create this template. After entering the Linear and Multiple Regression Analysis template, save the template to disk. Then use the fish hatchery and direct mail examples to test whether the template works correctly. Enter the X and Y data sets in the columns from D38 through H47. Press Alt-l. You must enter X data in adjacent rows, beginning with the row under X1 at D38. Do not leave any blanks.

When the macro requests the X-range for X data, outline the X area from D38 through H47, which contains the pertinent data. Press Enter. The resulting A, B, C, D, and CONSTANT values should be the same as those in the sample problems.

Problems you solve may have more or less data than is used in the template. If you have less data than the rows in DATA ENTRY, enter the data anyway. If you have more data, use the /Worksheet Insert Row command to add more rows. In either case, make sure that the data contains no blanks, but does have a blank at the bottom of the column. When the macro requests the X-range, select only the range containing your X data.

The PROJECTED VALUES section holds as many as 10 sets of X values used to estimate an unknown Y. Unused cells in the Y Project column appear as NA. To add rows in the PROJECTED VALUES section, use /Worksheet Insert Row. After inserting additional rows, copy the formula in A20..A29 into the extra rows.

Tricks, Traps, and Assumptions

Straight-line growth or decline rarely continues unchecked. Therefore, using linear regression analysis to calculate unknown values that lie either within the range of sample data or near the edge of data is best. The unbridled projections made during the home computer boom are excellent examples of projections that extended too far beyond the sample data. Some of the most vocal analysts made growth estimates years into the future, which were based on straight-line projections calculated during a peak growth year. The projections did not foresee market saturation or the inevitable competition caused by high growth and profits. Even as the home computer industry nosed into decline, analysts continued to forecast sky-rocketing sales.

Before using one of the other trend analysis templates in this chapter, use the linear regression template as an initial estimate for problems with a single independent variable. Linear and multiple regression are often acceptable for short ranges and for predictions that fall within the range of existing data.

R Squared in the STATISTICS AND COEFFICIENTS section of the Release 2 template shows how well the calculated curve and projected values of Y fit the actual data. The closer R Squared is to 1, the better the correlation between the projection and the actual data. An R Squared of .7 or better shows acceptable reliability. Although disagreement exists about the acceptable range of R Squared for different types of problems, everyone agrees that lower values of R Squared indicate that the projection does not fit the data well.

At least three pairs of X and Y data must exist for the template to work with one independent X. In addition, the same number of X and Y data must exist. The data can be in decimals and can be entered in any order.

Do not leave blank cells within any X or Y data ranges. Do, however, leave a blank cell at the bottom of the Y data range; otherwise, the \l macro will not work.

Do not use a set of X independent variables that is a constant multiple of another set of X variables. The multiple regression will not work, and the error message Cannot Invert Matrix! will appear.

List of Cells 4.2

```
A2:  'LINEAR AND MULTIPLE REGRESSION ANALYSIS
A3:  \=
B3:  \=
C3:  \=
D3:  \=
E3:  \=
F3:  \=
G3:  \=
H3:  \=
A4:  'The linear equation for multiple independent variables is
B5:  'Y = A*X1 + B*X2 + C*X3 + D*X4 + E*X5 + ... + Constant
A6:  'This is a straight line when all coefficients other than A are zero.
A8:  'Enter known X and Y values in the DATA ENTRY section.
B9:  'Erase cells that do not contain new data.
B10: 'Increase or decrease rows at a middle row.
A11: 'Enter X values to project new Ys in the PROJECTED VALUES section.
A12: U 'Hold down Alt and press L.
A14: \=
B14: \=
C14: \=
D14: \=
E14: \=
F14: \=
G14: \=
H14: \=
A15: 'PROJECTED VALUES
A16: \-
B16: \-
C16: \-
D16: \-
E16: \-
F16: \-
G16: \-
```

```
H16: \-
D17: 'Enter X values used in Y projection.
A18: 'Y Project
D18: "X1
E18: "X2
F18: "X3
G18: "X4
H18: "X5
A19: \-
D19: \-
E19: \-
F19: \-
G19: \-
H19: \-
A20: (F0) @IF(@COUNT(D20..H20)=0,@NA,$A*D20+$B*E20+$C*F20+$D*G20+$E*H20+$CONSTANT)
D20: U 60000
A21: (F0) @IF(@COUNT(D21..H21)=0,@NA,$A*D21+$B*E21+$C*F21+$D*G21+$E*H21+$CONSTANT)
D21: U 70000
A22: (F0) @IF(@COUNT(D22..H22)=0,@NA,$A*D22+$B*E22+$C*F22+$D*G22+$E*H22+$CONSTANT)
D22: U 80000
A23: (F0) @IF(@COUNT(D23..H23)=0,@NA,$A*D23+$B*E23+$C*F23+$D*G23+$E*H23+$CONSTANT)
D23: U 90000
A24: (F0) @IF(@COUNT(D24..H24)=0,@NA,$A*D24+$B*E24+$C*F24+$D*G24+$E*H24+$CONSTANT)
D24: U 100000
A25: (F0) @IF(@COUNT(D25..H25)=0,@NA,$A*D25+$B*E25+$C*F25+$D*G25+$E*H25+$CONSTANT)
D25: U 110000
A26: (F0) @IF(@COUNT(D26..H26)=0,@NA,$A*D26+$B*E26+$C*F26+$D*G26+$E*H26+$CONSTANT)
D26: U 120000
A27: (F0) @IF(@COUNT(D27..H27)=0,@NA,$A*D27+$B*E27+$C*F27+$D*G27+$E*H27+$CONSTANT)
D27: U 130000
A28: (F0) @IF(@COUNT(D28..H28)=0,@NA,$A*D28+$B*E28+$C*F28+$D*G28+$E*H28+$CONSTANT)
D28: U 140000
A29: (F0) @IF(@COUNT(D29..H29)=0,@NA,$A*D29+$B*E29+$C*F29+$D*G29+$E*H29+$CONSTANT)
D29: U 150000
A31: \=
B31: \=
C31: \=
D31: \=
E31: \=
F31: \=
G31: \=
H31: \=
A32: 'DATA ENTRY
A33: \-
B33: \-
C33: \-
D33: \-
E33: \-
F33: \-
G33: \-
H33: \-
A35: 'ESTIMATED
E35: 'KNOWN
A36: \-
C36: \-
D36: \-
E36: \-
F36: \-
G36: \-
H36: \-
A37: 'Y
C37: "Y
D37: "X1
E37: "X2
F37: "X3
G37: "X4
H37: "X5
A38: @IF(@COUNT(C38..H38)=0,@NA,$A*XRANGE+$B*E38+$C*F38+$D*G38+$E*H38+$CONSTANT)
```

```
C38: U 4750
D38: U 60000
A39: @IF(@COUNT(C39..H39)=0,@NA,$A*D39+$B*E39+$C*F39+$D*G39+$E*H39+$CONSTANT)
C39: U 7200
D39: U 70000
A40: @IF(@COUNT(C40..H40)=0,@NA,$A*D40+$B*E40+$C*F40+$D*G40+$E*H40+$CONSTANT)
C40: U 6800
D40: U 85000
A41: @IF(@COUNT(C41..H41)=0,@NA,$A*D41+$B*E41+$C*F41+$D*G41+$E*H41+$CONSTANT)
C41: U 9698
D41: U 100000
A42: @IF(@COUNT(C42..H42)=0,@NA,$A*D42+$B*E42+$C*F42+$D*G42+$E*H42+$CONSTANT)
C42: U 9980
D42: U 120000
A43: @IF(@COUNT(C43..H43)=0,@NA,$A*D43+$B*E43+$C*F43+$D*G43+$E*H43+$CONSTANT)
C43: U 7589
D43: U 85000
A44: @IF(@COUNT(C44..H44)=0,@NA,$A*D44+$B*E44+$C*F44+$D*G44+$E*H44+$CONSTANT)
C44: U 12890
D44: U 130000
A45: @IF(@COUNT(C45..H45)=0,@NA,$A*D45+$B*E45+$C*F45+$D*G45+$E*H45+$CONSTANT)
C45: U 8345
D45: U 120000
A46: @IF(@COUNT(C46..H46)=0,@NA,$A*D46+$B*E46+$C*F46+$D*G46+$E*H46+$CONSTANT)
C46: U 8678
D46: U 100000
A47: @IF(@COUNT(C47..H47)=0,@NA,$A*D47+$B*E47+$C*F47+$D*G47+$E*H47+$CONSTANT)
C47: U 11006
D47: U 120000
A49: \=
B49: \=
C49: \=
D49: \=
E49: \=
F49: \=
G49: \=
H49: \=
A50: 'STATISTICS AND COEFFICIENTS
A51: \-
B51: \-
C51: \-
D51: \-
E51: \-
F51: \-
G51: \-
H51: \-
A52: 'Data entered automatically by 1-2-3.
C53: 'Regression Output:
B54: 'Constant
E54: 81.758928571
B55: 'Std Err of Y Est
E55: 1128.8027789
B56: 'R Squared
E56: 0.7890887221
B57: 'No. of Observations
E57: 10
B58: 'Degrees of Freedom
E58: 8
B59: 'Coefficient Labels
D59: "A
E59: "B
F59: "C
G59: "D
H59: "E
B60: 'X Coefficient(s)
D60: 0.0869882937
```

```
B61:  'Std Err of Coef.
D61:  0.0159002079
A63:  \=
B63:  \=
C63:  \=
D63:  \=
E63:  \=
F63:  \=
G63:  \=
H63:  \=
A64:  'MACRO
A65:  \-
B65:  \-
C65:  \-
D65:  \-
E65:  \-
F65:  \-
G65:  \-
H65:  \-
B67:  'LINEAR REGRESSION MACRO
A68:  '\l
B68:  '/ruA60.H61~
E68:  'Unprotect area to be blanked
B69:  ' {BLANK D60.H61}~
E69:  'Erase old coefficient area
B70:  '/rpA60.H61~
E70:  'Protect X coeff. area
B71:  ' {GOTO}G1~{GOTO}A31~
E71:  'Display data area
B72:  ' {GOTO}XRANGE~
E72:  'Cursor at top left of X data
B73:  '/drr
E73:  'Reset data regression
B74:  'x{?}~
E74:  'Define new X-range
B75:  'q
E75:  'Exit regression
B76:  ' {GOTO}YRANGE~
E76:  'Cursor at top of Y data
B77:  '/dry.{END}{DOWN}~
E77:  'Define Y-range
B78:  'oOUTPUT~g
E78:  'Define output, then go
B79:  ' {GOTO}G1~{GOTO}A14~
E79:  'Show projected data
```

The Power Curve Fit

Engineering and technical problems often involve fitting a curve to a set of data in which one piece of data is the square, cube, or fourth power of another. Starting at zero, the slope for this type of curve becomes steeper and steeper with each small horizontal increase.

Many of the basic laws of science and geometry have equations with a term raised to a power. When you think a problem is influenced by a basic law of physics or geometry, try fitting the data with a power curve. Suppose, for example, that you are trying to find an equation relating the number of tuna in a school to the school's length. You hope to use the information to design nets that catch tuna, but do not kill porpoises.

Finding the Equation of a School of Tuna

You have used sonar readings, aerial photography, and fishery studies to gather the information in table 4.4. The table relates the estimated number of tuna in a school to one-half the apparent length of the school on the surface of the water. Using the partial list of data in the table, can you determine the probable equation for estimating the school's size? Does your equation seem reasonable?

Table 4.4
Relationship between Estimated Number of Tuna
and Half Surface Length of School

Half surface length of school (100 ft.)	Estimated number of tuna
1	200
2	580
3	18900
4	26500
5	16500
6	65700
7	56000
8	98000

Figure 4.5 shows the shape of the curve plotted from the Power Curve Fit template's equation. Figure 4.6 shows the A and B coefficients and the equation for the curve, shown at the top of the template. The curve has the equation

Tuna=193.66*HalfLength^3.09

R Squared, the measure of how well the curve fits the data, is .9063, a high value, which shows a very good fit. That an equation like this would produce a curve this well defined is unlikely. However, closer analysis shows that the equation for the tuna school is similar to the equation for the volume of a sphere. Because fish schools take on a changing oblate or spherical shape, the equation seems to have the right form.

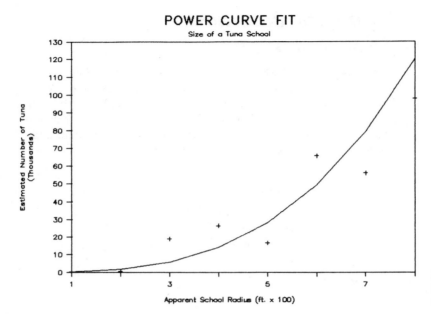

Fig. 4.5. The power curve fit used to predict the size of a tuna school.

Trends Formulas

The formula of a power curve is

$$Y = A * X^B$$

where A and B are coefficients (constant numbers). Using regression analysis, you can use the following formulas to find these two coefficients. In these formulas, sets of X and Y data are paired by the same subscript. For example, $\ln X_i * \ln Y_i$ should use the X and Y values that were entered as a pair. N is the total number of data pairs.

$$A = \exp\left[\frac{\text{Sum}(\ln Y_i)}{N} - \frac{B * \text{Sum}(\ln X_i)}{N} \right]$$

$$B = \frac{\text{Sum}(\ln X_i * \ln Y_i) - \frac{\text{Sum}(\ln X_i)\text{Sum}(\ln Y_i)}{N}}{\text{Sum}((\ln X_i)^2) - \frac{(\text{Sum}(\ln X_i))^2}{N}}$$

```
          A         B         C         D         E         F         G         H
 1
 2 POWER CURVE FIT
 3 ========================================================================
 4
 5 The power curve has the form Y=A*X^B
 6 For the current data the coefficients, A and B are
 7                A 193.6646
 8                B   3.0924
 9
10 Correlation coefficients close to 1 indicate a good curve fit.
11 The correlation coefficient, R Squared, for this data is
12          R Squared  0.9063
13
14 ========================================================================
15 PROJECTED VALUES
16 ------------------------------------------------------------------------
17 Enter positive values under X to calculate projected Y values.
18          X              Proj. Y
19          1                  194
20          2                 1652
21          3                 5788
22          4                14089
23          5                28091
24          6                49366
25          7                79516
26          8               120168
27
28 ========================================================================
29 DATA ENTRY
30 ------------------------------------------------------------------------
31 X and Y data values must be greater than zero.
32
33          N         8
34
35 X and Y Data Entry                    Calculation Terms
36 ----------------             ---------------------------------------------
37       X         Y           LN(X)  LN(X)SQR    LN(Y)  LN(Y)SQR LN(X)LN(Y)
38       1        200           0.00    0.00       5.30    28.07    0.00
39       2        580           0.69    0.48       6.36    40.49    4.41
40       3      18900           1.10    1.21       9.85    96.96   10.82
41       4      26500           1.39    1.92      10.18   103.73   14.12
42       5      16500           1.61    2.59       9.71    94.31   15.63
43       6      65700           1.79    3.21      11.09   123.05   19.88
44       7      56000           1.95    3.79      10.93   119.53   21.27
45       8      98000           2.08    4.32      11.49   132.08   23.90
46
```

Fig. 4.6. The Power Curve Fit template.

R Squared tells you how well the curve fits the data. The closer R Squared is to one, the better the fit. The equation for R Squared is

$$\text{R Squared} = \frac{\left[\text{SUM}((\ln X_i)(\ln Y_i)) - \dfrac{\text{SUM}(\ln X_i)\text{SUM}(\ln Y_i)}{N} \right]^2}{\left[\text{SUM}((\ln X_i)^2) - \dfrac{(\text{SUM}(\ln X_i))^2}{N} \right] \left[\text{SUM}((\ln Y_i)^2) - \dfrac{(\text{SUM}(\ln Y_i))^2}{N} \right]}$$

Creating the Template

Although the equations are complex, building the template isn't difficult. In the DATA ENTRY section of the template (see fig. 4.6), the first two columns hold X and Y data values. The other columns are the terms in the preceding formulas before they are summed. Giving each of the columns a range name makes the formulas easy to enter. The range names used in the Power Curve Fit template follow.

Address	Range Name
A38..A45	X
B33	N
C7	A
C8	B
D38..D45	LN(X)
E38..E45	LN(X)SQR
F38..F45	LN(Y)
G38..G45	LN(Y)SQR
H38..H45	LN(X)LN(Y)

In figure 4.6, you can see that these range names—X, LN(X), LN(X)SQR, LN(Y), LN(Y)SQR, and LN(X)LN(Y)—are the same names as the column labels in the DATA ENTRY section. Naming an entire column this way makes an @SUM function such as @SUM(LN(Y)SQR) easy to understand.

After you have named each column of calculations, you can enter the formulas, using the range names. The formulas for the coefficients, R Squared, and the projected value of Y follow.

Term	Address	Formula
A	C7	@EXP(((@SUM(LN(Y))–B*@SUM(LN(X)))/N)
B	C8	(@SUM(LN(X)LN(Y))–@SUM(LN(X))* @SUM(LN(Y))/N)/ (@SUM(LN(X)SQR)–@SUM(LN(X))^2/N)
R Squared	C12	+B^2*(@SUM(LN(X)SQR)– @SUM(LN(X))^2/N)/ (@SUM(LN(Y)SQR)–@SUM(LN(Y))^2/N)
N	B33	@COUNT(X)
Proj. Y	C19	+$A*A19^$B

Create the template by setting column G's width to 10 and entering list of cells 4.3. After you have entered the labels, values, and formulas, unprotect the data entry areas. Then protect the spreadsheet by giving the /Worksheet Global Protect Enable command. Save your template to disk, then test whether it works correctly.

Use the tuna data to test the template. You can graph the curve and the experimental data by using an X-Y graph. Use the X data under PROJECTED VALUES as the X graph range. Use the Proj. Y values as the A graph range. Make the actual Y values the B graph range. Both the actual Y and projected Y values can be graphed on the same graph when both sets of X values are the same. To make your graph appear like the one in figure 4.5, use the /Graph Option Format command to format the A range as a line (the power curve) and the B range as symbols (the test data).

You can add more room for data or projected values by inserting rows in the middle of columns and then copying all the equations from the row above into the new space. Some equations in the Data Entry rows go out to column H. When you copy equations into the inserted rows, be sure to include the equations as far out as column H.

Tricks, Traps, and Assumptions

This template works correctly only for X and Y values greater than zero. The X values under PROJECTED VALUES also must be greater than zero. Never leave blanks in the columns of X and Y data.

If your data indicates a rapid growth, you also should try the exponential growth curve fit.

List of Cells 4.3

```
A2: PR 'POWER CURVE FIT
A3: PR \=
B3: PR \=
C3: PR [W9] \=
D3: PR [W9] \=
E3: PR [W9] \=
F3: PR [W9] \=
G3: PR [W10] \=
H3: PR \=
A5: PR 'The power curve has the form Y=A*X^B
A6: PR 'For the current data the coefficients, A and B are
B7: PR "A
C7: (F4) PR [W9] @EXP((@SUM(LN(Y))-B*@SUM(LN(X)))/N)
B8: PR "B
C8: (F4) PR [W9] (@SUM(LN(X)LN(Y))-@SUM(LN(X))*@SUM(LN(Y))/N)/(@SUM(LN(X)SQR)-@SUM(LN(X))^2/N)
A10: PR 'Correlation coefficients close to 1 indicate a good curve fit.
A11: PR 'The correlation coefficient, R Squared, for this data is
B12: PR 'R Squared
```

```
C12: (F4) PR [W9] +B^2*(@SUM(LN(X)SQR)-@SUM(LN(X))^2/N)/(@SUM(LN(Y)SQR)-@SUM(LN(Y))^2/N)
A14: PR \=
B14: PR \=
C14: PR [W9] \=
D14: PR [W9] \=
E14: PR [W9] \=
F14: PR [W9] \=
G14: PR [W10] \=
H14: PR \=
A15: PR 'PROJECTED VALUES
A16: PR \-
B16: PR \-
C16: PR [W9] \-
D16: PR [W9] \-
E16: PR [W9] \-
F16: PR [W9] \-
G16: PR [W10] \-
H16: PR \-
A17: PR 'Enter positive values under X to calculate projected Y values.
A18: PR "X
C18: PR [W9] "Proj. Y
A19: (F0) U 1
C19: (F0) PR [W9] +$A*A19^$B
A20: (F0) U 2
C20: (F0) PR [W9] +$A*A20^$B
A21: (F0) U 3
C21: (F0) PR [W9] +$A*A21^$B
A22: (F0) U 4
C22: (F0) PR [W9] +$A*A22^$B
A23: (F0) U 5
C23: (F0) PR [W9] +$A*A23^$B
A24: (F0) U 6
C24: (F0) PR [W9] +$A*A24^$B
A25: (F0) U 7
C25: (F0) PR [W9] +$A*A25^$B
A26: (F0) U 8
C26: (F0) PR [W9] +$A*A26^$B
A28: PR \=
B28: PR \=
C28: PR [W9] \=
D28: PR [W9] \=
E28: PR [W9] \=
F28: PR [W9] \=
G28: PR [W10] \=
H28: PR \=
A29: PR 'DATA ENTRY
A30: PR \-
B30: PR \-
C30: PR [W9] \-
D30: PR [W9] \-
E30: PR [W9] \-
F30: PR [W9] \-
G30: PR [W10] \-
H30: PR \-
A31: PR 'X and Y data values must be greater than zero.
A33: PR "N
B33: PR @COUNT(X)
A35: PR 'X and Y Data Entry
E35: PR [W9] 'Calculation Terms
A36: PR \-
B36: PR \-
D36: PR [W9] \-
E36: PR [W9] \-
F36: PR [W9] \-
G36: PR [W10] \-
H36: PR \-
A37: PR "X
```

```
B37: PR "Y
D37: (F6) PR [W9] "LN(X)
E37: PR [W9] "LN(X)SQR
F37: PR [W9] "LN(Y)
G37: PR [W10] "LN(Y)SQR
H37: PR "LN(X)LN(Y)
A38: U 1
B38: U 200
D38: (F2) PR [W9] @LN(A38)
E38: (F2) PR [W9] +D38^2
F38: (F2) PR [W9] @LN(B38)
G38: (F2) PR [W10] +F38^2
H38: (F2) PR +D38*F38
A39: U 2
B39: U 580
D39: (F2) PR [W9] @LN(A39)
E39: (F2) PR [W9] +D39^2
F39: (F2) PR [W9] @LN(B39)
G39: (F2) PR [W10] +F39^2
H39: (F2) PR +D39*F39
A40: U 3
B40: U 18900
D40: (F2) PR [W9] @LN(A40)
E40: (F2) PR [W9] +D40^2
F40: (F2) PR [W9] @LN(B40)
G40: (F2) PR [W10] +F40^2
H40: (F2) PR +D40*F40
A41: U 4
B41: U 26500
D41: (F2) PR [W9] @LN(A41)
E41: (F2) PR [W9] +D41^2
F41: (F2) PR [W9] @LN(B41)
G41: (F2) PR [W10] +F41^2
H41: (F2) PR +D41*F41
A42: U 5
B42: U 16500
D42: (F2) PR [W9] @LN(A42)
E42: (F2) PR [W9] +D42^2
F42: (F2) PR [W9] @LN(B42)
G42: (F2) PR [W10] +F42^2
H42: (F2) PR +D42*F42
A43: U 6
B43: U 65700
D43: (F2) PR [W9] @LN(A43)
E43: (F2) PR [W9] +D43^2
F43: (F2) PR [W9] @LN(B43)
G43: (F2) PR [W10] +F43^2
H43: (F2) PR +D43*F43
A44: U 7
B44: U 56000
D44: (F2) PR [W9] @LN(A44)
E44: (F2) PR [W9] +D44^2
F44: (F2) PR [W9] @LN(B44)
G44: (F2) PR [W10] +F44^2
H44: (F2) PR +D44*F44
A45: U 8
B45: U 98000
D45: (F2) PR [W9] @LN(A45)
E45: (F2) PR [W9] +D45^2
F45: (F2) PR [W9] @LN(B45)
G45: (F2) PR [W10] +F45^2
H45: (F2) PR +D45*F45
```

Exponential Growth Curve

Rapid growth rates, whether in nature or in business, usually can be described with an exponential curve. This type of growth happens in animal populations with plentiful food and little competition or predation. Such growth also occurs in the initial stages of some rapidly expanding businesses.

The Exponential Curve Fit template is an excellent tool for examining rapid or initial growth rates. You can use it to examine growth rates as diverse as sales volume and tissue cultures. But be careful; forecasting with an exponential curve can be dangerous unless you are aware of similar growth histories and of all the outside elements that affect the growth rate.

Fitting a Curve to Rapid Growth

Suppose that you own a small publishing house and have found a new channel of distribution that consumers find convenient and efficient. Sales through this channel are exploding. During this early growth phase, the sales curve appears to build at an increasingly faster rate. Using the sales data in table 4.5, can you determine what the sales curve is and what sales are probable for the 23rd week? What must you be aware of when forecasting with the exponential curve fit?

Table 4.5
Book Sales

Week	Sales (in hundreds)
4	52
6	76
8	245
10	548
12	487
14	1234
16	998
18	1123
20	2145

The template reveals that the book sales fit a curve with the equation

$$\text{Sales} = 31.59 * e^{(.22 * \text{Week})}$$

Figure 4.7 illustrates this curve and shows how rapidly sales expand with exponential growth. The equation for the curve was produced from data in the top part of the template (see fig. 4.8).

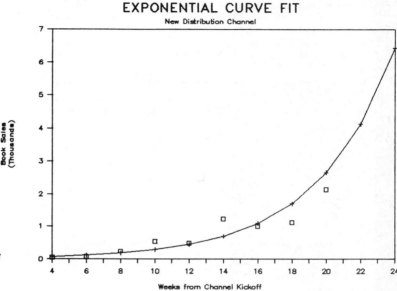

EXPONENTIAL CURVE FIT

New Distribution Channel

Fig. 4.7. Rapid growth of book sales that seems to fit an exponential curve.

The coefficient of correlation, R Squared, is equal to .89, an acceptable curve. Substituting 23 for the Week variable, X (under PROJECTED VALUES), produces a Proj. Y of 5152 (hundred units) in the 23rd week.

Your publishing company must be careful of extending sales curves, especially exponential growth curves, too far. Exponential growth does not go unlimited in either nature or business. In this case, sales quickly will exceed the support structure, and enough time will have passed for the competition to begin moving into the new distribution channel. Companies that use a middle level of distribution also must be cautious when forecasting sales based on shipments during the time in which the distribution "pipeline" fills.

Figure 4.8 shows the solution to the curve for the sales data. The PRO-JECTED VALUES portion of the template shows projections of new data points in future weeks. The X values are weeks, and the Y values are sales volumes in hundreds of units. The DATA ENTRY AND CALCULATION

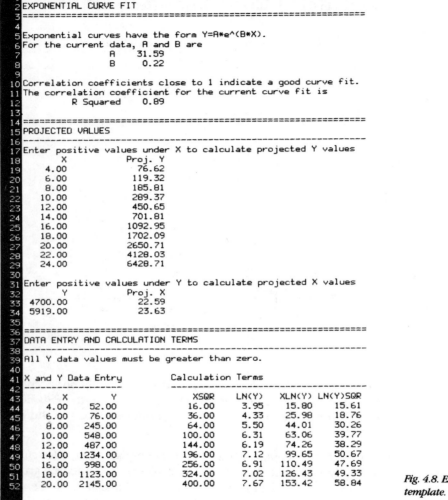

```
          A       B        C        D        E        F        G        H
1
2 EXPONENTIAL CURVE FIT
3 ================================================================
4
5 Exponential curves have the form Y=A*e^(B*X).
6 For the current data, A and B are
7                 A      31.59
8                 B       0.22
9
10 Correlation coefficients close to 1 indicate a good curve fit.
11 The correlation coefficient for the current curve fit is
12           R Squared     0.89
13
14 ================================================================
15 PROJECTED VALUES
16 ----------------------------------------------------------------
17 Enter positive values under X to calculate projected Y values
18        X               Proj. Y
19      4.00                76.62
20      6.00               119.32
21      8.00               185.81
22     10.00               289.37
23     12.00               450.65
24     14.00               701.81
25     16.00              1092.95
26     18.00              1702.09
27     20.00              2650.71
28     22.00              4128.03
29     24.00              6428.71
30
31 Enter positive values under Y to calculate projected X values
32        Y               Proj. X
33   4700.00                22.59
34   5919.00                23.63
35
36 ================================================================
37 DATA ENTRY AND CALCULATION TERMS
38 ----------------------------------------------------------------
39 All Y data values must be greater than zero.
40
41 X and Y Data Entry           Calculation Terms
42 ------------------           ------------------------------------
43     X         Y                XSQR     LN(Y)   XLN(Y)  LN(Y)SQR
44   4.00      52.00             16.00      3.95    15.80     15.61
45   6.00      76.00             36.00      4.33    25.98     18.76
46   8.00     245.00             64.00      5.50    44.01     30.26
47  10.00     548.00            100.00      6.31    63.06     39.77
48  12.00     487.00            144.00      6.19    74.26     38.29
49  14.00    1234.00            196.00      7.12    99.65     50.67
50  16.00     998.00            256.00      6.91   110.49     47.69
51  18.00    1123.00            324.00      7.02   126.43     49.33
52  20.00    2145.00            400.00      7.67   153.42     58.84
```

Fig. 4.8. Exponential Curve Fit template.

TERMS section shows the pairs of X and Y data as the first two columns on the left. The other four columns contain data used in calculating the curve.

Trends Formulas

The equation for the exponential curve is calculated by using the least squares fit method to find an equation in the following form.

$Y = A * e^{BX}$

The A and B coefficients are calculated from the following formulas.

$$A = \exp\left[\frac{\text{Sum}(\ln Y_i)}{N} - B * \frac{\text{Sum}(X_i)}{N}\right]$$

$$B = \frac{\text{Sum}(X_i * \ln Y_i) - \dfrac{\text{Sum}(X_i)\ \text{Sum}(\ln Y_i)}{N}}{\text{Sum}(X_i^2) - \dfrac{(\text{Sum}(X_i))^2}{N}}$$

X_i and Y_i are matched pairs of data, and all Ys are positive. X and Y can be decimals and can be entered as pairs in any order. N is the number of total pairs.

The coefficient of correlation, R Squared, measures how closely the curve fits the data. If R Squared is zero, no exponential curve correlation exists between the data and the curve. A better correlation may exist with another type of curve described in this chapter. For example, the power curve fit and exponential curve fit produce curves that appear similar, but one may fit the data better and produce an R Squared that is closer to 1. A curve that exactly fits the data has an R Squared close to 1. Calculate the value of R Squared with the following.

$$\text{R Squared} = \frac{\left[\text{Sum}(X_i * \ln Y_i) - \dfrac{\text{Sum}(X_i)\text{Sum}(\ln Y_i)}{N}\right]^2}{\left[\text{Sum}(X_i^2) - \dfrac{(\text{Sum}(X_i))^2}{N}\right]\left[\text{Sum}((\ln Y_i)^2) - \dfrac{(\text{Sum}(\ln Y_i))^2}{N}\right]}$$

The projected values on the curve for a given X are

Proj. $Y = A * e^{BX}$

The predicted values on the curve for a given Y are

Proj. $X = (1/B) \ln(Y/A)$

Creating the Template

The easiest way to enter these formulas is to create columns of X and Y calculations like those shown in the template under the Calculation Terms columns (see fig. 4.8). You can label these columns with descriptive range names and use the range names in the formulas. The template uses the following range names.

Address	Range Name
A44..A52	X
C7	A
C8	B
D44..D52	XSQR
E44..E52	LN(Y)
F44..F52	XLN(Y)
G44..G52	LN(Y)SQR

The column headings in the calculation portion of figure 4.8 are the same as the range names of the columns underneath. Using these descriptive range names makes the @SUM functions easy to enter and to understand. The formulas for A, B, and R Squared, respectively, follow.

Term	Address	Formula
A	C7	@EXP(@SUM(LN(Y))/@COUNT(X) −B*@SUM(X)/@COUNT(X))
B	C8	(@SUM(XLN(Y))−@SUM(X)*@SUM(LN(Y))/ @COUNT(X))/(@SUM(XSQR) −(@SUM(X)^2)/@COUNT(X))
R Squared	C12	+B^2*(@SUM(XSQR)−@SUM(X)^2/ @COUNT(X))/(@SUM(LN(Y)SQR) −@SUM(LN(Y))^2/@COUNT(X))

In these formulas, @COUNT(X) has replaced N from the equations.

Before you create the formulas, create the preceding range names. Enter the formulas as shown in list of cells 4.4.

Enter the X and Y data in the columns labeled X and Y Data Entry. Do not leave blank cells in the data; otherwise, @COUNT will not be able to count accurately.

All Y data must be positive. X and Y values may be decimals and can be entered in any order, but must be kept together in pairs. At least two pairs of X and Y must exist in order for the template to work.

You can add additional data entry area or projected data area by inserting rows in the middle of the existing columns. Do not insert or delete rows at the top or bottom of the columns; this destroys the range names. After you have inserted rows, copy all the formulas from a complete row into the inserted area.

Tricks, Traps, and Assumptions

Be careful not to project growth curves too far. In both nature and business, available resources, competitors, and predators limit growth rates that continue for too long or increase too rapidly.

In a simplified view of how industries grow, the initial growth for a new industry is often exponential. As the industry matures, growth changes from exponential to straight line. When the number of new purchasers declines, the curve "tops out" with logarithmic growth, which then flattens out to a shallow linear growth rate reflecting the number of replacement purchases. Unless the industry is infused with innovation, alternative products or functional replacements may cause the industry eventually to decline.

The X-Y graph is an excellent way of plotting the curve you calculate. Expand the X and Proj. Y area so that you can plot approximately 10 sets of X and Proj. Y values. Use the /Data Fill command to enter a continuous, evenly spaced sequence of numbers under X. Use these numbers as the X data range for the graph. The Proj. Y values should be used as the A data range. The graph format of the A data range should be a line in order to make the curve visible.

List of Cells 4.4

```
A2:  'EXPONENTIAL CURVE FIT
A3:  \=
B3:  \=
C3:  \=
D3:  \=
E3:  \=
F3:  \=
G3:  \=
A5:  'Exponential curves have the form Y=A*e^(B*X).
A6:  'For the current data, A and B are
B7:  "A
C7:  @EXP((@SUM(LN(Y))/@COUNT(X)-B*@SUM(X)/@COUNT(X))
B8:  "B
C8:  (@SUM(XLN(Y))-@SUM(X)*@SUM(LN(Y))/@COUNT(X))/(@SUM(XSQR)-(@SUM(X)^2)/@COUNT(X))
A10: 'Correlation coefficients close to 1 indicate a good curve fit.
A11: 'The correlation coefficient for the current curve fit is
B12: 'R Squared
C12: +B^2*(@SUM(XSQR)-@SUM(X)^2/@COUNT(X))/(@SUM(LN(Y)SQR)-@SUM(LN(Y))^2/@COUNT(X))
```

```
A14: \=
B14: \=
C14: \=
D14: \=
E14: \=
F14: \=
G14: \=
A15: 'PROJECTED VALUES
A16: \-
B16: \-
C16: \-
D16: \-
E16: \-
F16: \-
G16: \-
A17: 'Enter positive values under X to calculate projected Y values
A18: "X
C18: "Proj. Y
A19: U 4
C19: +$A*@EXP($B*A19)
A20: U 6
C20: +$A*@EXP($B*A20)
A21: U 8
C21: +$A*@EXP($B*A21)
A22: U 10
C22: +$A*@EXP($B*A22)
A23: U 12
C23: +$A*@EXP($B*A23)
A24: U 14
C24: +$A*@EXP($B*A24)
A25: U 16
C25: +$A*@EXP($B*A25)
A26: U 18
C26: +$A*@EXP($B*A26)
A27: U 20
C27: +$A*@EXP($B*A27)
A28: U 22
C28: +$A*@EXP($B*A28)
A29: U 24
C29: +$A*@EXP($B*A29)
A31: 'Enter positive values under Y to calculate projected X values
A32: "Y
C32: "Proj. X
A33: U 4700
C33: @LN(A33/$A)/$B
A34: U 5919
C34: @LN(A34/$A)/$B
A36: \=
B36: \=
C36: \=
D36: \=
E36: \=
F36: \=
G36: \=
A37: 'DATA ENTRY AND CALCULATION TERMS
A38: \-
B38: \-
C38: \-
D38: \-
E38: \-
F38: \-
G38: \-
A39: 'All Y data values must be greater than zero.
A41: 'X and Y Data Entry
D41: 'Calculation Terms
A42: \-
B42: \-
```

```
D42:  \-
E42:  \-
F42:  \-
G42:  \-
A43:  "X
B43:  "Y
D43:  "XSQR
E43:  "LN(Y)
F43:  "XLN(Y)
G43:  "LN(Y)SQR
A44:  U 4
B44:  U 52
D44:  +A44^2
E44:  @LN(B44)
F44:  +A44*E44
G44:  +E44^2
A45:  U 6
B45:  U 76
D45:  +A45^2
E45:  @LN(B45)
F45:  +A45*E45
G45:  +E45^2
A46:  U 8
B46:  U 245
D46:  +A46^2
E46:  @LN(B46)
F46:  +A46*E46
G46:  +E46^2
A47:  U 10
B47:  U 548
D47:  +A47^2
E47:  @LN(B47)
F47:  +A47*E47
G47:  +E47^2
A48:  U 12
B48:  U 487
D48:  +A48^2
E48:  @LN(B48)
F48:  +A48*E48
G48:  +E48^2
A49:  U 14
B49:  U 1234
D49:  +A49^2
E49:  @LN(B49)
F49:  +A49*E49
G49:  +E49^2
A50:  U 16
B50:  U 998
D50:  +A50^2
E50:  @LN(B50)
F50:  +A50*E50
G50:  +E50^2
A51:  U 18
B51:  U 1123
D51:  +A51^2
E51:  @LN(B51)
F51:  +A51*E51
G51:  +E51^2
A52:  U 20
B52:  U 2145
D52:  +A52^2
E52:  @LN(B52)
F52:  +A52*E52
G52:  +E52^2
```

Logarithmic Curve Fit

Industries and animal populations often grow rapidly at first, then decrease with time. Limited resources, competition, or predation cause the slowdown. Populations (whether industry or animal) that are approaching the saturation point grow along a logarithmic curve. The logarithmic curve illustrates a rapid growth, followed by a gradual decrease in growth rate. After growth and resources balance out, growth may continue at the same rate at which resources increase. When industries grow, they eventually reach the saturation point; from that point on, replacements or population growth account for most new sales. Growth rates for industries that have reached this level are nearly straight lines.

Plotting the Growth of a Maturing Industry

Suppose that you are making projections for a venture capital proposal, and you must estimate the industry size and future growth rate for a revolutionary new water-sport product: the wave skimmer. After researching the growth of such sports as snow skiing, board sailing, and catamaran sailing, you have made estimates of the industry's size as it begins to mature. You expect maturity to occur rapidly, between the 4th and 13th years. Using the partial data list in table 4.6, can you determine the shape and formula of the logarithmic curve with the best fit? What types of external factors could affect the growth of the entire industry drastically?

Figure 4.9 shows the X and Y data entered in columns A and B in the template's DATA ENTRY section. The top section of the template displays the constant A and coefficient B used in the formula, which is

Units=–6651+4647*ln(Year)

The equation generates a logarithmic curve (see fig. 4.10), which you create by entering years 4 through 13 under X in the PROJECTED VALUES section. An X-Y graph plots the values of X against Proj. Y. Using the line format connects all the X-Y points.

The correlation coefficient, R Squared, for the curve is .88, which shows that the curve fits the data well.

You need to include in your report that the curve represents the total "pie" available to all competitors. Unless you can find a way to protect your market, your share will be reduced by the competition.

Table 4.6
Total Industry Growth Estimates

Year	Installed units (in hundreds)
4	123
5	390
6	1135
7	1879
8	3850
9	4678
10	3687
11	5120
12	4126
13	4985

The entire industry's growth can be limited unnaturally by forces such as government laws banning the use of your wave skimmer or bad publicity concerning accidents during use of the product. The industry's growth also could take a large positive jump to a higher growth curve if a more exciting, safer wave skimmer were developed.

Trends Formulas

The logarithmic curve has an equation in the form

$$Y = A + B*\ln(X)$$

Use the following formulas to calculate the A and B coefficients.

$$A = \frac{\text{Sum}(Y_i) - B*\text{Sum}(\ln X_i)}{N}$$

$$B = \frac{\text{Sum}(Y_i*\ln X_i) - \dfrac{\text{Sum}(\ln X_i)*\text{Sum}(Y_i)}{N}}{\text{Sum}((\ln X_i)^2) - \dfrac{(\text{Sum}(\ln X_i))^2}{N}}$$

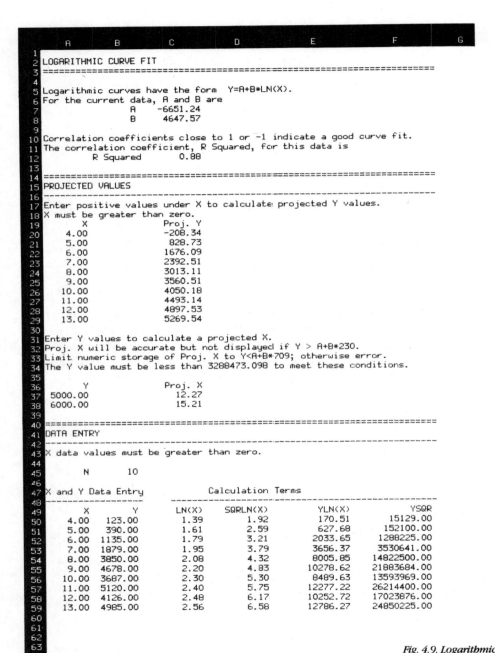

```
        A        B          C          D           E                F              G
1
2  LOGARITHMIC CURVE FIT
3  ================================================================================
4
5  Logarithmic curves have the form   Y=A+B*LN(X).
6  For the current data, A and B are
7                   A     -6651.24
8                   B      4647.57
9
10 Correlation coefficients close to 1 or -1 indicate a good curve fit.
11 The correlation coefficient, R Squared, for this data is
12          R Squared       0.88
13
14 ================================================================================
15 PROJECTED VALUES
16 --------------------------------------------------------------------------------
17 Enter positive values under X to calculate projected Y values.
18 X must be greater than zero.
19          X               Proj. Y
20        4.00             -208.34
21        5.00              828.73
22        6.00             1676.09
23        7.00             2392.51
24        8.00             3013.11
25        9.00             3560.51
26       10.00             4050.18
27       11.00             4493.14
28       12.00             4897.53
29       13.00             5269.54
30
31 Enter Y values to calculate a projected X.
32 Proj. X will be accurate but not displayed if Y > A+B*230.
33 Limit numeric storage of Proj. X to Y<A+B*709; otherwise error.
34 The Y value must be less than 3288473.098 to meet these conditions.
35
36          Y               Proj. X
37     5000.00               12.27
38     6000.00               15.21
39
40 ================================================================================
41 DATA ENTRY
42 --------------------------------------------------------------------------------
43 X data values must be greater than zero.
44
45          N        10
46
47 X and Y Data Entry              Calculation Terms
48 --------------------        ----------------------------------------------------
49          X        Y       LN(X)    SQRLN(X)      YLN(X)           YSQR
50        4.00    123.00      1.39      1.92        170.51         15129.00
51        5.00    390.00      1.61      2.59        627.68        152100.00
52        6.00   1135.00      1.79      3.21       2033.65       1288225.00
53        7.00   1879.00      1.95      3.79       3656.37       3530641.00
54        8.00   3850.00      2.08      4.32       8005.85      14822500.00
55        9.00   4678.00      2.20      4.83      10278.62      21883684.00
56       10.00   3687.00      2.30      5.30       8489.63      13593969.00
57       11.00   5120.00      2.40      5.75      12277.22      26214400.00
58       12.00   4126.00      2.48      6.17      10252.72      17023876.00
59       13.00   4985.00      2.56      6.58      12786.27      24850225.00
60
61
62
63
64
```

Fig. 4.9. Logarithmic Curve Fit template.

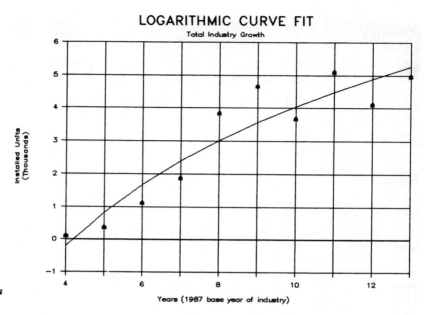

Fig. 4.10. Logarithmic growth in a maturing industry.

In these equations, X_i and Y_i are pairs of data. At least two pairs of data must exist, and they must be positive. X and Y data pairs can be decimals and can be entered as pairs in any order. N is the number of data pairs.

The correlation coefficient, R Squared, measures how closely the curve fits the data. The closer R Squared is to 1, the better the curve fits. If R Squared is zero, no correlation exists between the data and the curve. You can calculate R Squared from the following formulas.

$$\text{R Squared} = \frac{\left[\text{Sum}(Y_i * \ln X_i) - \frac{\text{Sum}(\ln X_i)\text{Sum}(Y_i)}{N} \right]^2}{\left[\text{Sum}((\ln X_i)^2) - \frac{(\text{Sum}(\ln X_i))^2}{N} \right] \left[\text{Sum}((Y_i)^2) - \frac{(\text{Sum}(Y_i))^2}{N} \right]}$$

After you know the values for the constant A and coefficient B, you can project an unknown X or Y value by using the following formulas.

Proj. $Y = A + B * \ln(X)$

Proj. $X = \exp \left[\dfrac{Y-A}{B} \right]$

Creating the Template

As you have seen before, these complex formulas are easiest to enter if you use range names instead of cell addresses. To make entering the formulas easier, use the following range names.

Address	Range Name
A50..A59	X
B45	N
B50..B59	Y
C50..C59	LN(X)
C7	A
C8	B
D50..D59	SQRLN(X)
E50..E59	YLN(X)
F50..F59	YSQR

Compare these range names to those in figure 4.9, and you can see that the range names X, Y, LN(X), SQRLN(X), YLN(X), and YSQR give the names of columns in the DATA ENTRY section of the template. Naming an entire column this way makes an @SUM function such as @SUM(LN(X)) easy to type and understand.

The 1-2-3 formulas that use these range names in the template follow.

Term	Address	Formula
A	C7	(@SUM(Y)−B*@SUM(LN(X)))/N
B	C8	(@SUM(YLN(X))−@SUM(LN(X))*@SUM(Y)/N)/ (@SUM(SQRLN(X))−@SUM(LN(X))^2/N)
R Squared	C12	+B^2*((@SUM(SQRLN(X))−@SUM(LN(X))^2/N))/ (@SUM(YSQR)−@SUM(Y)^2/N)
Proj. Y	C20	+$A+$B*@LN(A20)
Proj. X	C37	@EXP((A37−$A)/$B)

You can copy the formulas in cells C20 and C37 down the column to fill the cells from C20 through C29 and C37 and C38. List of cells 4.5 is for the entire Logarithmic Curve Fit template.

To use the template, enter X and Y data in columns A and B in the DATA ENTRY section. If you need additional rows, insert them in the middle of the DATA ENTRY section and copy the equations for an entire row down into the new area. Remember: Inserting or deleting in the first or last rows in these ranges destroys the accuracy of the range names.

You can create graphs of the curve like the one in figure 4.10 by inserting rows in the X and Proj. Y rows in the section labeled PROJECTED VALUES. Use the /Data Fill command to fill the X data range with continuous, evenly spaced numbers. Use a line or an X-Y graph and plot both the X data in the X graph range and the Proj. Y data in the A graph range. You can add the original Y data as the B graph range if the original X values are exactly the same and are in the same order as the X data under PROJECTED VALUES.

Tricks, Traps, and Assumptions

Do not mistake industry life curves for the curves of product life cycles. In general, industries mature at a logarithmic rate. Products may grow and decline within this same time frame. Industries seem predictable after the fact, but many variables in the areas of timing, competition, advertising, and consumer attitude affect products. Therefore, predicting an individual product's sales rate from industry curves is hazardous.

At least two pairs of X_i, Y_i data must exist. Pairs are matched during calculation according to their i subscripts. All Y data must be positive. X and Y values may be decimals.

List of Cells 4.5

```
A2:  PR 'LOGARITHMIC CURVE FIT
A3:  PR \=
B3:  PR \=
C3:  PR [W12] \=
D3:  PR [W12] \=
E3:  PR [W15] \=
F3:  PR [W15] \=
A5:  PR 'Logarithmic curves have the form   Y=A+B*LN(X).
A6:  PR 'For the current data, A and B are
B7:  PR "A
C7:  (F2) PR [W12] (@SUM(Y)-B*@SUM(LN(X)))/N
B8:  PR "B
C8:  (F2) PR [W12] (@SUM(YLN(X))-@SUM(LN(X))*@SUM(Y)/N)/(@SUM(SQRLN(X))-@SUM(LN(X))^2/N)
A10: PR 'Correlation coefficients close to 1 or -1 indicate a good curve fit.
A11: PR 'The correlation coefficient, R Squared, for this data is
B12: PR "R Squared
C12: (F2) PR [W12] +B^2*((@SUM(SQRLN(X))-@SUM(LN(X))^2/N))/(@SUM(YSQR)-@SUM(Y)^2/N)
A14: PR \=
B14: PR \=
C14: PR [W12] \=
D14: PR [W12] \=
E14: PR [W15] \=
F14: PR [W15] \=
A15: PR 'PROJECTED VALUES
A16: PR \-
B16: PR \-
```

```
C16: PR [W12] \-
D16: PR [W12] \-
E16: PR [W15] \-
F16: PR [W15] \-
A17: PR 'Enter positive values under X to calculate projected Y values.
A18: PR 'X must be greater than zero.
A19: PR "X
C19: PR [W12] "Proj. Y
A20: (F2) U 4
C20: (F2) PR [W12] +$A+$B*@LN(A20)
A21: (F2) U 5
C21: (F2) PR [W12] +$A+$B*@LN(A21)
A22: (F2) U 6
C22: (F2) PR [W12] +$A+$B*@LN(A22)
A23: (F2) U 7
C23: (F2) PR [W12] +$A+$B*@LN(A23)
A24: (F2) U 8
C24: (F2) PR [W12] +$A+$B*@LN(A24)
A25: (F2) U 9
C25: (F2) PR [W12] +$A+$B*@LN(A25)
A26: (F2) U 10
C26: (F2) PR [W12] +$A+$B*@LN(A26)
A27: (F2) U 11
C27: (F2) PR [W12] +$A+$B*@LN(A27)
A28: (F2) U 12
C28: (F2) PR [W12] +$A+$B*@LN(A28)
A29: (F2) U 13
C29: (F2) PR [W12] +$A+$B*@LN(A29)
A31: PR 'Enter Y values to calculate a projected X.
A32: PR 'Proj. X will be accurate but not displayed if Y > A+B*230.
A33: PR 'Limit numeric storage of Proj. X to Y<A+B*709; otherwise error.
A34: PR 'The Y value must be less than
D34: PR [W12] 709*B+A
E34: PR [W15] 'to meet these conditions.
A36: PR "Y
C36: PR [W12] "Proj. X
A37: (F2) U 5000
C37: (F2) PR [W12] @EXP((A37-$A)/$B)
A38: (F2) U 6000
C38: (F2) PR [W12] @EXP((A38-$A)/$B)
A40: PR \=
B40: PR \=
C40: PR [W12] \=
D40: PR [W12] \=
E40: PR [W15] \=
F40: PR [W15] \=
A41: PR 'DATA ENTRY
A42: PR \-
B42: PR \-
C42: PR [W12] \-
D42: PR [W12] \-
E42: PR [W15] \-
F42: PR [W15] \-
A43: PR 'X data values must be greater than zero.
A45: PR "N
B45: PR @COUNT(X)
A47: PR 'X and Y Data Entry
D47: PR [W12] 'Calculation Terms
A48: PR \-
B48: PR \-
C48: PR [W12] "      -------
D48: PR [W12] \-
E48: PR [W15] \-
F48: PR [W15] \-
A49: PR "X
B49: PR "Y
```

```
C49: (F6) PR [W12] "LN(X)
D49: PR [W12] "SQRLN(X)
E49: PR [W15] "YLN(X)
F49: PR [W15] "YSQR
A50: (F2) U 4
B50: (F2) U 123
C50: (F2) PR [W12] @LN(A50)
D50: (F2) PR [W12] +C50^2
E50: (F2) PR [W15] +B50*C50
F50: (F2) PR [W15] +B50^2
A51: (F2) U 5
B51: (F2) U 390
C51: (F2) PR [W12] @LN(A51)
D51: (F2) PR [W12] +C51^2
E51: (F2) PR [W15] +B51*C51
F51: (F2) PR [W15] +B51^2
A52: (F2) U 6
B52: (F2) U 1135
C52: (F2) PR [W12] @LN(A52)
D52: (F2) PR [W12] +C52^2
E52: (F2) PR [W15] +B52*C52
F52: (F2) PR [W15] +B52^2
A53: (F2) U 7
B53: (F2) U 1879
C53: (F2) PR [W12] @LN(A53)
D53: (F2) PR [W12] +C53^2
E53: (F2) PR [W15] +B53*C53
F53: (F2) PR [W15] +B53^2
A54: (F2) U 8
B54: (F2) U 3850
C54: (F2) PR [W12] @LN(A54)
D54: (F2) PR [W12] +C54^2
E54: (F2) PR [W15] +B54*C54
F54: (F2) PR [W15] +B54^2
A55: (F2) U 9
B55: (F2) U 4678
C55: (F2) PR [W12] @LN(A55)
D55: (F2) PR [W12] +C55^2
E55: (F2) PR [W15] +B55*C55
F55: (F2) PR [W15] +B55^2
A56: (F2) U 10
B56: (F2) U 3687
C56: (F2) PR [W12] @LN(A56)
D56: (F2) PR [W12] +C56^2
E56: (F2) PR [W15] +B56*C56
F56: (F2) PR [W15] +B56^2
A57: (F2) U 11
B57: (F2) U 5120
C57: (F2) PR [W12] @LN(A57)
D57: (F2) PR [W12] +C57^2
E57: (F2) PR [W15] +B57*C57
F57: (F2) PR [W15] +B57^2
A58: (F2) U 12
B58: (F2) U 4126
C58: (F2) PR [W12] @LN(A58)
D58: (F2) PR [W12] +C58^2
E58: (F2) PR [W15] +B58*C58
F58: (F2) PR [W15] +B58^2
A59: (F2) U 13
B59: (F2) U 4985
C59: (F2) PR [W12] @LN(A59)
D59: (F2) PR [W12] +C59^2
E59: (F2) PR [W15] +B59*C59
F59: (F2) PR [W15] +B59^2
```

Quadratic Regression Curve Fit

When you are not sure which curve to fit to your data, try quadratic regression. The quadratic regression curve fits many different curve shapes, whether they are straight lines, curves that arc up, or curves that arc down.

Quadratic regression also may be the best curve to use if you need to find a maximum or minimum. On a graph like the one in figure 4.11, the maximum output is the curve's highest point. If the curve were shaped like a U, the curve's lowest point would be the minimum output of Y.

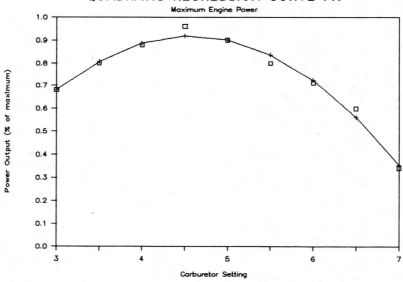

Fig. 4.11. Finding maximum engine output with quadratic regression.

Finding Maximum Output

Suppose that you are testing your proprietary carburetor design with a new fuel additive. You have gathered the information in table 4.7, which relates engine power to carburetor settings. You can use the 1-2-3 Quadratic Regression template to determine the carburetor setting for the highest power output.

Table 4.7
Relationship between Carburetor Setting
and Engine Power

Carburetor setting	Power rating
3.0	.68
3.5	.80
4.0	.88
4.5	.96
5.0	.90
5.5	.80
6.0	.71
6.5	.60
7.0	.34

Figure 4.11 shows how the carburetor settings on either side of 4.5 give less than maximum power. The equation that produces this graph is

Power=−1.0994+.8825*Setting−.0965*Setting^2

The values for the equation are shown in the top section of the template (see fig. 4.12). The template shows the equation and the value for each constant and coefficient.

Trends Formulas

The quadratic equation combines the equation of a straight line with a power curve. The result can be curves that are straight lines, a curve with X to the power of 2, or a parabola (a curve that changes direction), as in the example. The equation that produces these results is

Y=A+B*X+C*X^2

The equations used to calculate the constant A and the coefficients B and C are long and complex. They are shown here for reference. The formulas to enter in 1-2-3 have been divided into segments and use range names; therefore, they are easier to enter. In the following equations, N is the number of X and Y data pairs. The subscript i indicates that X and Y data from a pair is matched during some calculations, for example, X_i*Y_i. The full equations follow.

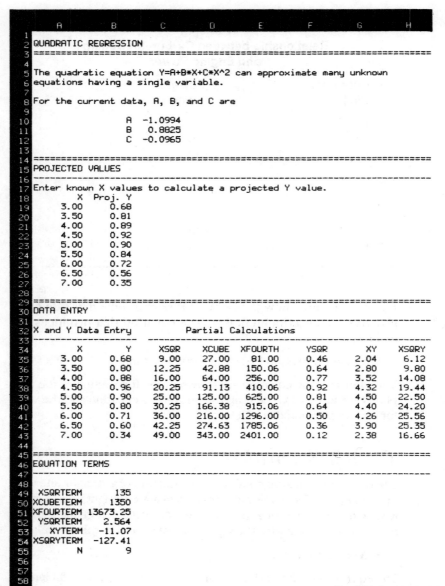

```
       A        B        C        D        E        F        G        H
 1
 2 QUADRATIC REGRESSION
 3 ==================================================================
 4
 5 The quadratic equation Y=A+B*X+C*X^2 can approximate many unknown
 6 equations having a single variable.
 7
 8 For the current data, A, B, and C are
 9
10               A  -1.0994
11               B   0.8825
12               C  -0.0965
13
14 ==================================================================
15 PROJECTED VALUES
16 ------------------------------------------------------------------
17 Enter known X values to calculate a projected Y value.
18        X    Proj. Y
19      3.00     0.68
20      3.50     0.81
21      4.00     0.89
22      4.50     0.92
23      5.00     0.90
24      5.50     0.84
25      6.00     0.72
26      6.50     0.56
27      7.00     0.35
28
29 ==================================================================
30 DATA ENTRY
31 ------------------------------------------------------------------
32 X and Y Data Entry          Partial Calculations
33 ------------------------------------------------------------------
34      X       Y      XSQR    XCUBE   XFOURTH   YSQR     XY    XSQRY
35    3.00    0.68     9.00    27.00     81.00   0.46    2.04    6.12
36    3.50    0.80    12.25    42.88    150.06   0.64    2.80    9.80
37    4.00    0.88    16.00    64.00    256.00   0.77    3.52   14.08
38    4.50    0.96    20.25    91.13    410.06   0.92    4.32   19.44
39    5.00    0.90    25.00   125.00    625.00   0.81    4.50   22.50
40    5.50    0.80    30.25   166.38    915.06   0.64    4.40   24.20
41    6.00    0.71    36.00   216.00   1296.00   0.50    4.26   25.56
42    6.50    0.60    42.25   274.63   1785.06   0.36    3.90   25.35
43    7.00    0.34    49.00   343.00   2401.00   0.12    2.38   16.66
44
45 ==================================================================
46 EQUATION TERMS
47 ------------------------------------------------------------------
48
49  XSQRTERM       135
50 XCUBETERM      1350
51 XFOURTERM  13673.25
52  YSQRTERM     2.564
53    XYTERM    -11.07
54 XSQRYTERM   -127.41
55         N         9
56
57
58
59
60
```

Fig. 4.12. Quadratic Regression template.

$$A = \frac{SUM(Y_i) - B*SUM(X_i) - C*SUM(X_i^2)}{N}$$

$$B = \frac{[N*SUM(X_i*Y_i) - SUM(X_i)*SUM(Y_i)] - C*[N*SUM(X_i^3) - SUM(X_i)*SUM(X_i^2)]}{N*SUM(X_i^2) - (SUM(X_i))^2}$$

$$C = \frac{T_1 - T_2}{[N*SUM(X_i^2) - (SUM(X_i))^2][N*SUM(X_i^4) - (SUM(X_i^2))^2] - [N*SUM(X_i^3) - SUM(X_i)*SUM(X_i^2)]^2}$$

$$T_1 = [N*SUM(X_i^2) - (SUM(X_i))^2][N*SUM(X_i^2*Y_i) - SUM(X_i^2)*SUM(Y_i)]$$

$$T_2 = [N*SUM(X_i^3) - SUM(X_i)*SUM(X_i^2)][N*SUM(X_i*Y_i) - SUM(X_i)*SUM(Y_i)]$$

Creating the Template

The formulas are easier to enter in your spreadsheet than they might appear. The first step is to precalculate terms that will be summed. For example, the calculation $SUM(X_i*Y_i)$ is performed by creating a column containing the values of X_i*Y_i. This column, labeled XY under Partial Calculations, then can be summed with the @SUM function. The precalculated numbers are located under the Partial Calculations heading in the DATA ENTRY section of the template.

Give each of the columns of precalculated numbers a descriptive range name that you can use in the formulas. The following range names are used in the template.

Address	*Range Name*
A35..A43	X
B35..B43	Y
B49	XSQRTERM
B50	XCUBETERM
B51	XFOURTERM
B52	YSQRTERM
B53	XYTERM
B54	XSQRYTERM
B55	N
C10	A
C11	B
C12	C
C35..C43	XSQR
D35..D43	XCUBE
E35..E43	XFOURTH
F35..F43	YSQR
G35..G43	XY
H35..H43	XSQRY

Dividing large formulas into segments and entering each segment in its own cell makes formula entry much easier. Giving each of these segments a descriptive name, such as XSQRTERM, makes formula entry easier still.

A number of simple calculations are performed in the `Partial Calculations` columns of the `DATA ENTRY` section. The formulas for these precalculations are in list of cells 4.6. You can create the formulas for the first row, A35..H35, and then copy them into rows 36 through 43. Using range names, the long formulas that calculate the constant A and the coefficients B and C become much shorter. The formulas for the Quadratic Regression template follow.

Term	Address	Formula
A	C10	(@SUM(Y)–C*@SUM(XSQR)–B*@SUM(X))/N
B	C11	(XYTERM–C*XCUBETERM)/XSQRTERM
C	C12	(XSQRTERM*XSQRYTERM– XCUBETERM*XYTERM)/ (XSQRTERM*XFOURTERM–XCUBETERM^2)
Proj. Y	B19	+$A+$B*A19+$C*A19^2
XSQRTERM	B49	+N*@SUM(XSQR)–@SUM(X)^2
XCUBETERM	B50	+N*@SUM(XCUBE)–@SUM(X)*@SUM(XSQR)
XFOURTERM	B51	+N*@SUM(XFOURTH)–@SUM(XSQR)^2
YSQRTERM	B52	+N*@SUM(YSQR)–@SUM(Y)^2
XYTERM	B53	+N*@SUM(XY)–@SUM(X)*@SUM(Y)
XSQRYTERM	B54	+N*@SUM(XSQRY)–@SUM(XSQR)*@SUM(Y)
N	B55	@COUNT(X)

Create the template by changing column A's width to 10 and entering list of cells 4.6. Be sure that you create the range names before you enter the formulas that use the names.

After you enter the labels, values, and formulas, save your template to disk. The cell listing 4.6 contains the data from the sample problem. Check to make sure that the problem is solved accurately.

Enter your data under the X and Y `Data Entry` label in the `DATA ENTRY` section. You can enter pairs of X and Y data in any order. If the X values are not in consecutive order and at even increments, the graph will not be accurate.

If you need additional data entry rows, insert them in the middle of the DATA ENTRY area by issuing the command /Worksheet Insert Row. Do not insert or delete a row at the beginning or end of a named range. After inserting rows, copy the formulas from row A35..H35 into the new blank rows. You can expand the PROJECTED VALUES area in the same way.

Tricks, Traps, and Assumptions

Some problems don't have a maximum or minimum, and their curve may continue to increase or decrease. In such cases, try using one of the other curve fits to see whether you can obtain a better R Squared value.

List of Cells 4.6

```
A2: PR [W10] 'QUADRATIC REGRESSION
A3: PR [W10] \=
B3: PR \=
C3: PR \=
D3: PR \=
E3: PR \=
F3: PR \=
G3: PR \=
H3: PR \=
A5: PR [W10] 'The quadratic equation Y=A+B*X+C*X^2 can approximate many unknown
A6: PR [W10] 'equations having a single variable.
A8: PR [W10] 'For the current data, A, B, and C are
B10: PR "A
C10: (F4) PR (@SUM(Y)-C*@SUM(XSQR)-B*@SUM(X))/N
B11: PR "B
C11: (F4) PR (XYTERM-C*XCUBETERM)/XSQRTERM
B12: PR "C
C12: (F4) PR (XSQRTERM*XSQRYTERM-XCUBETERM*XYTERM)/(XSQRTERM*XFOURTERM-XCUBETERM^2)
A14: PR [W10] \=
B14: PR \=
C14: PR \=
D14: PR \=
E14: PR \=
F14: PR \=
G14: PR \=
H14: PR \=
A15: PR [W10] 'PROJECTED VALUES
A16: PR [W10] \-
B16: PR \-
C16: PR \-
D16: PR \-
E16: PR \-
F16: PR \-
G16: PR \-
H16: PR \-
A17: PR [W10] 'Enter known X values to calculate a projected Y value.
A18: PR [W10] "X
B18: PR "Proj. Y
```

```
A19: (F2) U [W10] 3
B19: (F2) PR +$A+$B*A19+$C*A19^2
A20: (F2) U [W10] 3.5
B20: (F2) PR +$A+$B*A20+$C*A20^2
A21: (F2) U [W10] 4
B21: (F2) PR +$A+$B*A21+$C*A21^2
A22: (F2) U [W10] 4.5
B22: (F2) PR +$A+$B*A22+$C*A22^2
A23: (F2) U [W10] 5
B23: (F2) PR +$A+$B*A23+$C*A23^2
A24: (F2) U [W10] 5.5
B24: (F2) PR +$A+$B*A24+$C*A24^2
A25: (F2) U [W10] 6
B25: (F2) PR +$A+$B*A25+$C*A25^2
A26: (F2) U [W10] 6.5
B26: (F2) PR +$A+$B*A26+$C*A26^2
A27: (F2) U [W10] 7
B27: (F2) PR +$A+$B*A27+$C*A27^2
A29: PR [W10] \=
B29: PR \=
C29: PR \=
D29: PR \=
E29: PR \=
F29: PR \=
G29: PR \=
H29: PR \=
A30: PR [W10] 'DATA ENTRY
A31: PR [W10] \-
B31: PR \-
C31: PR \-
D31: PR \-
E31: PR \-
F31: PR \-
G31: PR \-
H31: PR \-
A32: PR [W10] 'X and Y Data Entry
D32: PR 'Partial Calculations
A33: PR [W10] \-
B33: PR \-
C33: PR '  -------
D33: PR \-
E33: PR \-
F33: PR \-
G33: PR \-
H33: PR \-
A34: PR [W10] "X
B34: PR "Y
C34: (F2) PR "XSQR
D34: PR "XCUBE
E34: PR "XFOURTH
F34: (F2) PR "YSQR
G34: (F2) PR "XY
H34: (F2) PR "XSQRY
A35: (F2) U [W10] 3
B35: (F2) U 0.68
C35: (F2) PR +A35^2
D35: (F2) PR +A35^3
E35: (F2) PR +A35^4
F35: (F2) PR +B35^2
G35: (F2) PR +A35*B35
H35: (F2) PR +C35*B35
A36: (F2) U [W10] 3.5
B36: (F2) U 0.8
C36: (F2) PR +A36^2
D36: (F2) PR +A36^3
E36: (F2) PR +A36^4
```

```
F36: (F2) PR +B36^2
G36: (F2) PR +A36*B36
H36: (F2) PR +C36*B36
A37: (F2) U [W10] 4
B37: (F2) U 0.88
C37: (F2) PR +A37^2
D37: (F2) PR +A37^3
E37: (F2) PR +A37^4
F37: (F2) PR +B37^2
G37: (F2) PR +A37*B37
H37: (F2) PR +C37*B37
A38: (F2) U [W10] 4.5
B38: (F2) U 0.96
C38: (F2) PR +A38^2
D38: (F2) PR +A38^3
E38: (F2) PR +A38^4
F38: (F2) PR +B38^2
G38: (F2) PR +A38*B38
H38: (F2) PR +C38*B38
A39: (F2) U [W10] 5
B39: (F2) U 0.9
C39: (F2) PR +A39^2
D39: (F2) PR +A39^3
E39: (F2) PR +A39^4
F39: (F2) PR +B39^2
G39: (F2) PR +A39*B39
H39: (F2) PR +C39*B39
A40: (F2) U [W10] 5.5
B40: (F2) U 0.8
C40: (F2) PR +A40^2
D40: (F2) PR +A40^3
E40: (F2) PR +A40^4
F40: (F2) PR +B40^2
G40: (F2) PR +A40*B40
H40: (F2) PR +C40*B40
```

5

Statistics and
Database Analysis

Your 1-2-3 database contains a wealth of information that may not be evident on the surface. This chapter explains how to access that information and use it in a number of ways. The basic statistics section shows you how to increase the accuracy of 1-2-3's @STD and @VAR functions. Using statistics, you can analyze your database, determine quality control levels, predict the probability of meeting sales quotas, and find the percentages of customer approval from a survey. 1-2-3 also can help you control quality, design product warranties, and check customer opinions.

The text histogram and cross-tabulation templates help you find hidden information in your 1-2-3 database. Because 1-2-3 databases show only a few records or rows of information at a time, analyzing the relationships between all the pieces is difficult. But with these two templates, you will be able to see all the hidden relationships and reveal a bigger "picture."

The text histogram template produces a table that shows the number of times that selected words appear in a database field. The template's program works like the /Data Distribution command, but with text instead of numbers. You create a list of words, and the template searches any database field to find the number of times each word on the list occurs in the database.

If you use surveys or compare information in different database fields, the cross-tabulation template can save you a lot of time. A valuable tool for checking customer surveys or sales records, the template builds a graph that shows you as many as 30 different cross-views of data. In addition, by using different formula and text criteria, you can compare information from different fields. For example, the graph can show you how a store's customer profile varies on each day of the week. You can use that kind of information to help you target your advertising.

Basic Statistics

Most people don't have the time or resources to gather every possible measurement or test result. A more efficient method is to take small random samples and use 1-2-3's @STD and @VAR functions to calculate the standard deviation and variance. However, when samples are small, these 1-2-3 functions tend to underestimate standard deviation and variance. This section shows you how to correct for the low estimate.

Before you use 1-2-3's @STD and @VAR functions, you should determine whether the measurements you are testing fit the normal probability distribution. If they do not, @STD and @VAR may not be appropriate, and tests such as the quality control test in the next section will not be accurate.

1-2-3's @STD and @VAR functions use the n or biased method of calculation, which works best with a large number of sample measurements. Most statisticians use an unbiased or n−1 method of calculating standard deviation and variance. This latter method is more accurate for a small number of sample measurements. Using the Biased to Unbiased Statistics template, you easily can convert between biased and unbiased statistics.

Using standard deviation and variance, you can compare the ways in which measurements from different samples are distributed around the mean (average). Standard deviation is also useful for approximating the percentage of measurements that occurs within a predefined range. Knowing this percentage can help you determine whether measurements fit a class of problems with a normal probability distribution. If the measurements do fit, their probability and statistics are easy to work with, and you can use the Probability in a Normal Distribution template in the next section to solve many types of probability problems.

Standard deviation and variance are most accurate with events or measurements that have a normal probability distribution. Normal probability distribution appears frequently in nature; events are more likely to occur near the mean and just as likely to occur below the mean as above it. Figure 5.1 shows the normal probability curve, also known as the bell-shaped curve. Many naturally occurring events happen with a frequency that is plotted like the bell-shaped curve. The curve plots a measurement on the horizontal axis and the frequency with which the measurement occurs on the vertical axis. In figure 5.1, the mean is shown as Z=0 on the horizontal scale.

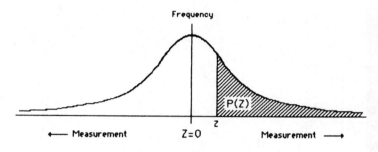

Fig. 5.1. The normal probability curve.

Probability of Z or Greater Measurement Occurring

Improving 1-2-3's @STD and @VAR Functions

For events or measurements with a normal probability distribution, you can use standard deviation (the @STD function) to find the percentage of measurements that fall within a specific range of the mean—within one, two, or three standard deviations. (Use the Probability in a Normal Distribution template if you need to calculate the percentage or probability of a measurement that falls in any range of measurements.)

Plotting how frequently measurements happen and comparing the curve with the normal curve is another way to determine whether measurements fit the normal distribution. For example, suppose that a high-school track coach takes 200 random samples of times for students running a mile-and-a-half. The coach enters the samples into the DATABASE section of the Biased to Unbiased Statistics template, shown in figure 5.2. (To save you typing time, the example in fig. 5.2 shows only 32 samples. However, you should take more than 32 samples.)

BIASED TO UNBIASED STATISTICS

Statistic	Biased (1-2-3)	Unbiased
Number	32	32
Mean (average)	12.52343	12.52343
Standard deviation	2.525711	2.566124
Variance	6.379216	6.584997

Normal Dist. Ranges (upper range limit)	N	Biased Distribution Ranges	N	Unbiased Distribution Ranges	N
Mean - 3 Std	0.05	4.95	0	4.83	0
Mean - 2 Std	0.75	7.47	0	7.39	0
Mean - 1 Std	4.32	10.00	5	9.96	5
Mean	10.88	12.52	12	12.52	12
Mean + 1 Std	10.88	15.05	10	15.09	10
Mean + 2 Std	4.32	17.57	5	17.66	5
Mean + 3 Std	0.75	20.10	0	20.22	0
Greater	0.05		0		0

DISTRIBUTION MACRO

\d	{GOTO}I5~{GOTO}A5~	Set display area
	/ddDATABASE~BRANGE~	Create biased distribution table
	/ddDATABASE~UBRANGE~	Create unbiased distribution table
	/grgtb	Reset graph and set bar graph
	xNORMN~	Set X-axis
	aBIASEDN~	Left bar is 1-2-3 biased dist.
	bNORMN~	Center bar is normal distribution
	cUNBIASEDN~	Right bar is unbiased dist.
	vq	View graph

39	================================
40	DATABASE
41	--------------------------------
42	RUNTIMES
43	12.3
44	10.7
45	14.7
46	9.9
47	10.2
48	9.6
49	14.5
50	12.0
51	10.0
52	12.6
53	9.0
54	14.5
55	17.0
56	17.3
57	10.0
58	9.3
59	11.0
60	15.3
61	8.3
62	11.0
63	14.5
64	13.3
65	11.0
66	10.0
67	14.5
68	14.3
69	14.5
70	12.0
71	14.5
72	17.0
73	15.2
74	10.8
75	
76	
77	
78	

Fig. 5.2. Biased to Unbiased Statistics template.

The upper portion of the template shows the number of times entered, the mean (average) time, the biased and unbiased standard deviation, and the biased and unbiased variance. The frequency that times will occur in a normal probability distribution appears under the N in the Normal Dist. Ranges section. In this example, 4.32 students should have run with times between 2 standard deviations below the mean time and 1 standard deviation below the mean (between 7.47 and 10 minutes).

When you press Alt-d, the template calculates how the students' times were distributed and generates a plot of the actual distribution versus the normal distribution. The graph, shown in figure 5.3, shows three bars for each standard deviation. The center bar shows the number of race times in a time range if the probability distribution were normal (a bell-shaped curve). The left bar shows the number of times using a biased distribution, and the right bar shows the number of times using an unbiased distribution. The closer the unbiased bars are to the center bar, the closer the runners' times are to having a normal distribution. The small number of times in this sample are unusually close to a good distribution.

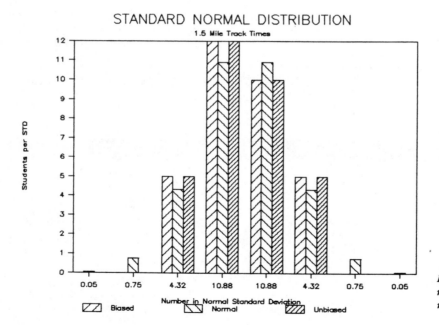

Fig. 5.3. The distribution of running times compared to a normal distribution.

Because only 32 measurements are used in the example, a big difference does not exist between biased and unbiased standard deviation and variance. If all 200 race times were entered, the difference between them would be larger, and the biased (1-2-3) method would have underestimated even more.

If measurements you make are not distributed in a bell-shaped curve, the measurements probably do not have a normal probability distribution. In this case, you should not use the quality control and probability testing methods explained in the section "Probability in a Normal Distribution."

Basic Statistics Formulas

The formula that 1-2-3 uses to calculate @VAR, the biased variance, is

$$@VAR=SUM(X_i-Average)^2/N$$

The biased @STD function that 1-2-3 uses is

$$@STD=\sqrt{SUM(X_i-Average)^2/N}$$

N is the number of samples. The subscript $_i$ indicates that each measurement, X, must have the average subtracted before squaring. When all measurements and averages are subtracted, they are summed. The unbiased standard deviation uses the same formulas, but N–1 replaces N.

To convert the @VAR function to the unbiased variance, use the formula

$$@VAR(range)*N/(N-1)$$

To convert the @STD function to the unbiased standard deviation, use the formula

$$@STD(range)*@SQRT(N/(N-1))$$

@COUNT(range) or @DCOUNT(range) can be used in place of N because these functions count the number of measurements in the range. Cells G9 and G10 in the template contain the unbiased formulas.

Measurements in a normal probability distribution are evenly distributed on either side of the mean. They produce the following percentage of measurements within different ranges of the mean.

Range of Measurement	Percentage of Population in the Range
Mean +/− 1 * Std Dev	68%
Mean +/− 2 * Std Dev	95%
Mean +/− 3 * Std Dev	99.7%

Creating the Template

The unbiased formulas and biased and unbiased ranges can be entered into the template as easily recognized formulas. But first, you must create the following range names.

Address	Range Name
A43..A74	DATABASE
B17..B24	NORMN
B29	\D
D7	N
D8	MEAN
D9	STD
D17..D23	BRANGE
E17..E24	BIASEDN
G8	UMEAN
G9	USTD
G17..G23	UBRANGE
H17..H24	UNBIASEDN

Using range names in formulas is easier than entering cell addresses, and you are less likely to make typographical errors. The following formulas use these range names.

Term	Address	Formula
Unbiased STD	G9	@STD(DATABASE)*@SQRT(@COUNT(DATABASE) /(@COUNT(DATABASE)−1))
Unbiased VAR	G10	@VAR(DATABASE)*@COUNT(DATABASE) /(@COUNT(DATABASE)−1)

The formulas in D17..D23 and G17..G23 create two columns of measurement ranges that correspond to the measurements at the biased and unbiased standard deviations. These columns have the range names BRANGE and UBRANGE, which the **/Data Distribution** command uses over the DATABASE range to create a table that shows how many measurements fall within the divisions of BRANGE and UBRANGE. For example, the \d macro in figure 5.2 uses the /**Data Distribution** command in its second and third rows. The column of numbers named DATABASE is first compared with the divisions in BRANGE, the biased range, and then with the divisions in UBRANGE, the unbiased range. To the right of BRANGE and UBRANGE, the /dd command displays the number of values in DATABASE found in each division.

Before you enter the spreadsheet and data, change column A's width to 13 and column C's width to 5. Create the preceding range names, then enter list of cells 5.1.

Tricks, Traps, and Assumptions

The percentage of measurements that falls within one, two, and three standard deviations of the mean can help verify that the measurements fit the normally distributed or bell-shaped curve. If you need to find. how measurements are distributed in ranges other than one, two, or three standard deviations from the mean, use the Probability in a Normal Distribution template in the next section.

You can merge your database directly into the basic statistics template by using the /**File Combine Copy** command. After merging your database, give the range name DATABASE to the database field (the column of data) being checked.

List of Cells 5.1

```
A2: [W13] 'BIASED TO UNBIASED STATISTICS
A3: [W13] \=
B3: \=
C3: [W5] \=
D3: \=
E3: \=
F3: \=
G3: \=
H3: \=
A5: [W13] 'Statistic
D5: 'Biased (1-2-3)
G5: 'Unbiased
A6: [W13] \-
D6: \-
E6: \-
G6: \-
A7: [W13] 'Number
D7: @COUNT(DATABASE)
G7: @COUNT(DATABASE)
```

```
A8:  [W13] 'Mean (average)
D8:  @AVG(DATABASE)
G8:  @AVG(DATABASE)
A9:  [W13] 'Standard deviation
D9:  @STD(DATABASE)
G9:  @STD(DATABASE)*@SQRT(@COUNT(DATABASE)/(@COUNT(DATABASE)-1))
A10: [W13] 'Variance
D10: @VAR(DATABASE)
G10: @VAR(DATABASE)*@COUNT(DATABASE)/(@COUNT(DATABASE)-1)
A14: [W13] 'Normal Dist. Ranges
D14: 'Biased Distribution
G14: 'Unbiased Distribution
A15: [W13] '(upper range limit) N
D15: "Ranges
E15: "N
G15: "Ranges
H15: "N
A16: [W13] \-
B16: \-
D16: \-
E16: \-
G16: \-
H16: \-
A17: [W13] 'Mean - 3 Std
B17: (F2) 0.0015*N
D17: (F2) +MEAN-3*STD
E17: (F0) 0
G17: (F2) +UMEAN-3*USTD
H17: (F0) 0
A18: [W13] 'Mean - 2 Std
B18: (F2) 0.0235*N
D18: (F2) +MEAN-2*STD
E18: (F0) 0
G18: (F2) +UMEAN-2*USTD
H18: (F0) 0
A19: [W13] 'Mean - 1 Std
B19: (F2) 0.135*N
D19: (F2) +MEAN-1*STD
E19: (F0) 5
G19: (F2) +UMEAN-1*USTD
H19: (F0) 5
A20: [W13] 'Mean
B20: (F2) 0.34*N
D20: (F2) +MEAN
E20: (F0) 12
G20: (F2) +UMEAN
H20: (F0) 12
A21: [W13] 'Mean + 1 Std
B21: (F2) 0.34*N
D21: (F2) +MEAN+1*STD
E21: (F0) 10
G21: (F2) +UMEAN+1*USTD
H21: (F0) 10
A22: [W13] 'Mean + 2 Std
B22: (F2) 0.135*N
D22: (F2) +MEAN+2*STD
E22: (F0) 5
G22: (F2) +UMEAN+2*USTD
H22: (F0) 5
A23: [W13] 'Mean + 3 Std
B23: (F2) 0.0235*N
D23: (F2) +MEAN+3*STD
E23: (F0) 0
G23: (F2) +UMEAN+3*USTD
H23: (F0) 0
A24: [W13] 'Greater
B24: (F2) 0.0015*N
```

```
E24: (F0) 0
H24: (F0) 0
A26: [W13] \=
B26: \=
C26: [W5] \=
D26: \=
E26: \=
F26: \=
G26: \=
H26: \=
A27: [W13] 'DISTRIBUTION MACRO
A28: [W13] \-
B28: \-
C28: [W5] \-
D28: \-
E28: \-
F28: \-
G28: \-
H28: \-
A29: [W13] '\d
B29: '{GOTO}I5~{GOTO}A5~
E29: 'Set display area
B30: '/ddDATABASE~BRANGE~
E30: 'Create biased distribution table
B31: '/ddDATABASE~UBRANGE~
E31: 'Create unbiased distribution table
B32: '/grgtb
E32: 'Reset graph and set bar graph
B33: 'xNORMN~
E33: 'Set X-axis
B34: 'aBIASEDN~
E34: 'Left bar is 1-2-3 biased dist.
B35: 'bNORMN~
E35: 'Center bar is normal distribution
B36: 'cUNBIASEDN~
E36: 'Right bar is unbiased dist.
B37: 'vq
E37: 'View graph
A39: [W13] \=
B39: \=
C39: [W5] \=
D39: \=
E39: \=
F39: \=
G39: \=
H39: \=
A40: [W13] 'DATABASE
A41: [W13] \-
B41: \-
C41: [W5] \-
D41: \-
E41: \-
F41: \-
G41: \-
H41: \-
A42: [W13] 'RUNTIMES
A43: (F1) [W13] 12.3
A44: (F1) [W13] 10.7
A45: (F1) [W13] 14.7
A46: (F1) [W13] 9.9
A47: (F1) [W13] 10.2
A48: (F1) [W13] 9.6
A49: (F1) [W13] 14.5
A50: (F1) [W13] 12
A51: (F1) [W13] 10
A52: (F1) [W13] 12.55
```

```
A53: (F1) [W13] 9
A54: (F1) [W13] 14.5
A55: (F1) [W13] 17
A56: (F1) [W13] 17.3
A57: (F1) [W13] 10
A58: (F1) [W13] 9.3
A59: (F1) [W13] 11
A60: (F1) [W13] 15.3
A61: (F1) [W13] 8.3
A62: (F1) [W13] 11
A63: (F1) [W13] 14.5
A64: (F1) [W13] 13.3
A65: (F1) [W13] 11
A66: (F1) [W13] 10
A67: (F1) [W13] 14.5
A68: (F1) [W13] 14.3
A69: (F1) [W13] 14.5
A70: (F1) [W13] 12
A71: (F1) [W13] 14.5
A72: (F1) [W13] 17
A73: (F1) [W13] 15.2
A74: (F1) [W13] 10.8
```

Probability in a Normal Distribution

By checking the probability distributions of product, service, or customer opinion data, you can pinpoint areas that need improvement. Probabilities show you how long to make product warranties, what levels of quality control to demand, and whether customer opinion surveys reveal the truth.

Many naturally occurring events happen with a frequency that plots similar to the bell-shaped curve in figure 5.1. The bell-shaped curve, more accurately described as the normal probability distribution, plots a measurement on the horizontal axis and the frequency with which the measurement occurs on the vertical axis.

Analysis of continuous measurements and pass/fail type measurements can help you decide whether an event is highly probable. Using the Probability in a Normal Distribution template, you easily can test such factors as the quality of a milling machine's output or the pass/fail rate for purchased components.

Setting Quality Control Levels

Manufacturers often have to meet design specifications within quality control limits. In such situations, knowing the quality that a machine or assembly line produces is valuable. For example, suppose that a design sheet specifies that a milling machine will drill holes whose centers are at 98.61 +/− .12mm. Random samples from the machine show that it has produced holes with a mean (average) center of 98.6mm and a standard deviation of .07mm. Using these statistics, can you determine what percentage of holes from the machine will be outside the specifications?

Figure 5.4 is a graphic representation of the solution. The curve shows how frequently the machine drills a hole at a specific location or greater. The percentage of holes out of tolerance is calculated by finding the percentage of holes greater than the smallest limit, then determining the percentage greater than the largest limit. The difference, shown with single cross-shading in the figure, is the percentage within tolerance.

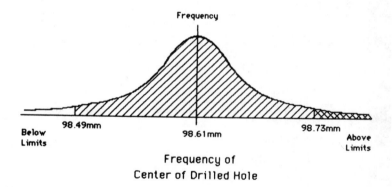

Fig. 5.4. Holes drilled within tolerance shown in single-shaded area.

In the template, the lower limit of 98.49mm is entered as YDATA along with the mean and standard deviation. The Probability in a Normal Distribution template in figure 5.5 shows that 95.1532 percent of the holes have centers located above the lower limit of 98.49mm (98.61−.12). The probability of a hole being above the upper limit, 98.73mm (98.61+.12), is 3.1645 percent. The difference between the two, 91.9887 percent, is the percentage of centers within limits. (This leaves 8.0113 percent (100% minus 91.9887 percent) of holes with centers that are out of limits.

In the milling machine example, measurements are taken over a continuous range and the results are expressed in a bell-shaped curve. But some tests produce the binomial, or pass/fail, kind of results. In pass/fail tests, the probability curve becomes a bar graph. In many pass/fail cases, however, the bell-shaped curve can be used to approximate binomial probability.

```
         A          B          C          D          E          F          G
 1
 2  PROBABILITY IN A NORMAL DISTRIBUTION
 3  ==================================================================
 4
 5  Enter successful measurements.
 6     YDATA          98.49
 7
 8  Enter the mean.
 9     MEAN           98.6
10
11  Enter the standard deviation.
12     DEV            0.07
13
14  ==================================================================
15  PROBABILITY
16  ------------------------------------------------------------------
17  Probability of Y or more successful tests
18  P(Y) is accurate to  +/- 7.5 X 10^-8
19
20     P(Y)       0.951532       Y  In limits
21
22  ==================================================================
23  CALCULATIONS
24  ------------------------------------------------------------------
25  Z, the normalized value of YDATA, is used for calculation.
26  The absolute value of Z must be less than 21.097.
27  In a normalized distribution, mean is 0, and std. deviation is 1.
28
29  Z         -1.571428571
30  F(Z)       0.116061807
31
32  T          1.5723485526
33
34  Use /Range Name Label Right to name the following constants.
35  P             0.2316419
36  B1            0.31938153
37  B2           -0.356563782
38  B3            1.781477937
39  B4           -1.821255978
40  B5            1.330274429
41
42
43  MEAN and DEVIATION for binomial tests (TRUE/FALSE or PASS/FAIL)
44  ==================================================================
45  MEAN = total population * probability of success (or failure)
46        Ex. 2000 * .02 = 40
47
48  DEV = SQRT(total pop. * prob. * (1-prob.)
49        Ex. 2000 * .02 * .98 = 39.2
50
51
52
```

Fig. 5.5. Probability in a Normal Distribution template.

For binomial tests, you must make one adjustment to your data. Because the binomial curve is not smooth, but is made up of many flat-topped bars, the width of each bar must be taken into account. To accomplish this task, subtract one-half, half the width of a bar, from the number of successful trials.

Consider this example of a binomial problem. Components purchased from a supplier are failing the acceptance inspection at a high rate. The components are supposed to have a failure rate of less than .5 percent. A random sample of 1,000 components turned up 9 failures. The supplier claims that the failure rate is temporarily high because of "bad luck" and that the statistics will even out over time. What is the probability that, overall, the components really are within tolerance?

The average and standard deviations for component failures are 5 and 2.23, respectively. (The method for calculating these deviations is described later in the chapter.) Because this is a pass/fail-type test, .5 must be subtracted from the 9 failures, so 8.5 is entered as YDATA. If, overall, the components are within tolerance, the probability of 8.5 (9–.5) or more failing acceptance is 6.4 percent. Because this probability is small, you can assume that the supplier is not meeting your acceptance criteria.

Probability Formulas

The upper section of the screen in figure 5.5 displays the first part of the milling machine problem. With the mean and standard deviation entered, the 1-2-3 template calculates the probability that a hole at location YDATA or greater will be drilled. This probability is the area under the bell-shaped curve to the right of YDATA in figure 5.4.

Before the area under the curve is calculated, the data must be adjusted so that it fits a standard curve with a mean centered on zero and a standard deviation of one. Using this standard curve makes other formulas simpler and calculations easier. The equation that "normalizes" YDATA to fit the standard curve is

   Z=(YDATA–MEAN)/DEV

YDATA, MEAN, and DEV are values from the problem. The frequency for Z, which is F(Z), and the probability of Z or greater, which is P(Z), are the same as the frequency and probability of YDATA.

After YDATA is converted to Z, any point on the curve can be found with

$$F(Z)= \frac{e^{-z^2/2}}{2\pi}$$

The probability of Z or greater occurring is equal to the area under the normalized curve and to the right of Z—that is, the shaded area under the curve. Calculating this probability exactly requires complex math that is unavailable in 1-2-3. But 1-2-3 can make a very accurate approximation with

$$P(Y)=F(Z) * (B1*T + B2*T^2 + B3*T^3 + B4*T^4 + B5*T^5)$$

where

$$T=1/(1+P*Z)$$

The constants are

P	=	.2316419
B1	=	.31938153
B2	=	-.356563782
B3	=	1.781477937
B4	=	-1.821255978
B5	=	1.330274429

For problems with continuous measurement, such as the milling machine, you can use 1-2-3's @AVG and @STD functions to calculate the mean and standard deviation. For small samples, you should convert @AVG and @STD from the biased to the unbiased method, as described in the previous section.

If you are solving problems with pass/fail or yes/no responses, you must calculate the mean and standard deviation with

MEAN = N * probability of success

DEVIATION = (N * probability * (1-probability))

N is the number of successful trials, and probability is the percentage of successes (or failures). In the component failure problem, N is 1,000, and the probability of success is .05. In the component problem, a success is finding a failed component.

Creating and Testing the Template

You can enter the formulas for Z, F(Z), and P(Z) into 1-2-3 just as they are shown, but you must first create the following range names. In this template, each range named cell is to the right of a label with the same name, so you can enter the labels, then use /**Range N**ame **L**abel **R**ight to create the range names. The resulting named cells are

Address	Range Name
B6	YDATA
B9	MEAN
B12	DEV
B29	Z
B30	F(Z)
B32	T
B35	P
B36	B1
B37	B2
B38	B3
B39	B4
B40	B5

After you create these names, use them when you enter the formulas. This procedure makes the formulas more understandable and less prone to error. The formulas follow.

Term	Address	Formula
P(Y)	B20	+F(Z)*(B1*T+B2*T^2+B3*T^3+ B4*T^4+B5*T^5)
Z	B29	(YDATA–MEAN)/DEV
F(Z)	B30	(@EXP(–Z^2/2))/(@SQRT(2*@PI))
T	B30	1/(1+P*Z)

You can leave the default column widths at 9 and enter the entire spreadsheet from list of cells 5.2.

After entering the labels, values, and formulas, unprotect the cells preceded by U. Use the /Worksheet Global Protection Enable command to protect the spreadsheet. Save your template to disk, then use the sample problems to test whether the formulas work correctly.

Tricks, Traps, and Assumptions

If you are not sure whether the data you are working with fits a normal distribution pattern, read the section on basic statistics. You can use the template in that section to check your data's distribution.

The method used to approximate the probability of YDATA or greater happening is very accurate if the events being measured have a normal distribution. P(Z), the same as P(YDATA), is accurate to +/– 7.5×10^{-8}.

Using this approximation limits Z, the normalized YDATA, to values between +/− 21.097. You rarely would need to know the frequencies of measurements this far from the mean. The template automatically monitors the limit of Z when you enter YDATA, MEAN, and DEV. If YDATA is out of limits, too far from the mean, a warning indicator appears in cell D20.

Problems that measure yes/no or pass/fail must calculate the mean and standard deviation by using the preceding equations. The mean and standard deviation are then entered into the top of the spreadsheet along with YDATA, the number of successful trials. For these binomial problems, you must subtract .5 before entering YDATA.

Determining the validity and interpretation of statistical information can be difficult. For problems that do not fit a normal distribution or that appear too complex for these templates, consult a professional familiar with statistical analysis.

List of Cells 5.2

```
A2: PR 'PROBABILITY IN A NORMAL DISTRIBUTION
A3: PR \=
B3: PR [W13] \=
C3: PR \=
D3: PR \=
E3: PR \=
F3: PR \=
G3: PR \=
A5: PR 'Enter successful measurements.
A6: PR "YDATA
B6: U [W13] 98.49
A8: PR 'Enter the mean.
A9: PR "MEAN
B9: U [W13] 98.6
A11: PR 'Enter the standard deviation.
A12: PR "DEV
B12: U [W13] 0.07
A14: PR \=
B14: PR [W13] \=
C14: PR \=
D14: PR \=
E14: PR \=
F14: PR \=
G14: PR \=
A15: PR 'PROBABILITY
A16: PR \-
B16: PR [W13] \-
C16: PR \-
D16: PR \-
E16: PR \-
F16: PR \-
G16: PR \-
A17: PR "Probability of Y or more successful tests
```

```
A18: PR 'P(Y) is accurate to  +/- 7.5 X 10^-8
A20: PR "P(Y)
B20: (F6) PR [W13] +F(Z)*(B1*T+B2*T^2+B3*T^3+B4*T^4+B5*T^5)
C20: PR "Y
D20: PR @IF(@ABS(Z)>21.097,"Out of limits","In limits")
A22: PR \=
B22: PR [W13] \=
C22: PR \=
D22: PR \=
E22: PR \=
F22: PR \=
G22: PR \=
A23: PR 'CALCULATIONS
A24: PR \-
B24: PR [W13] \-
C24: PR \-
D24: PR \-
E24: PR \-
F24: PR \-
G24: PR \-
A25: PR 'Z, the normalized value of YDATA, is used for calculation.
A26: PR 'The absolute value of Z must be less than 21.097.
A27: PR 'In a normalized distribution, mean is 0, and std. deviation is 1.
A29: PR 'Z
B29: PR [W13] (YDATA-MEAN)/DEV
A30: PR 'F(Z)
B30: PR [W13] (@EXP(-Z^2/2))/(@SQRT(2*@PI))
A32: PR 'T
B32: PR [W13] 1/(1+P*Z)
A34: PR 'Use /Range Name Label Right to name the following constants.
A35: PR 'P
B35: PR [W13] 0.2316419
A36: PR 'B1
B36: PR [W13] 0.31938153
A37: PR 'B2
B37: PR [W13] -0.356563782
A38: PR 'B3
B38: PR [W13] 1.781477937
A39: PR 'B4
B39: PR [W13] -1.821255978
A40: PR 'B5
B40: PR [W13] 1.330274429
A43: PR 'MEAN and DEVIATION for binomial tests (TRUE/FALSE or PASS/FAIL)
A44: PR \=
B44: PR [W13] \=
C44: PR \=
D44: PR \=
E44: PR \=
F44: PR \=
G44: PR \=
A45: PR 'MEAN = total population * probability of success (or failure)
B46: PR [W13] 'Ex. 2000 * .02 = 40
A48: PR 'DEV = SQRT(total pop. * prob. * (1-prob.)
B49: PR [W13] 'Ex. 2000 * .02 * .98 = 39.2
```

Text Histogram

The **/Data Distribution** command is an excellent way of finding the
frequency and range of numbers in your database, but the command
doesn't work with text. The Histogram for Text and Numeric Data
template solves that problem by creating a data distribution table and

bar graph that can show you how often text, such as names or descriptions, appears in your database. The template can help you find how many similarly named items are in an inventory, how many employees have similar backgrounds, or how frequently names appear in a list.

You can specify which field or column that you want to search in the database and what text to count in that field. You can type the database to be searched or use the /File Combine Copy command to merge a database from another file.

Checking Job Distribution in a Personnel File

Small companies can use data distribution tables and bar graphs to create profiles of employee job skills. By comparing primary job skills and secondary job skills, managers can find areas in which cross-training or additional hiring will be necessary to fulfill future needs.

The database at the bottom of figure 5.6 contains two fields from a small personnel file stored in 1-2-3. Giving this database the range name DATABASE and pressing Alt-t produces the data in the HISTOGRAM section of the template and the bar graph in figure 5.7. The profile of the job skills available in the company is easy to see from the graph.

The Text Distribution Macro

The FIELD NAME section of the template shows the name of the field being searched, which is PRIMEJOB, and a list of the job descriptions being searched for. The text distribution macro uses the field name and list of job descriptions as query criteria for an @DCOUNT function. In turn, each job description is used as a criterion, and the number that @DCOUNT finds appears in the FREQUENCY IN FIELD column. The macro abbreviates the job descriptions to four letters and uses the numbers and abbreviations to generate a bar graph.

The macro \t begins by copying PRIMEJOB into the criteria cell at A32. The cursor starts at the top of the job description list and copies the description into the criteria area at A33. @DCOUNT then uses the information in CRITERIA, cells A32 and A33, to check information in the range DATABASE. @DCOUNT counts all records in the first column that match the criteria. The {EDIT}{CALC} combination changes the @DCOUNT function into a value. When the cursor moves to the next lower cell location, the {IF} macro uses @CELL-POINTER("type")="b" to determine whether the cell at the new cursor location is blank. If the cell is blank, the macro skips to the LABELER macro.

The column counted does not have to be the same as the column containing the criteria. A column other than the first can be used, but the column must not contain blank cells; otherwise, the count may be inaccurate. The first column is specified in the @DCOUNT function by an offset of zero.

The LABELER macro copies the job descriptions into the column under HISTOGRAM LABELS. A combination of @LEFT and @CELLPOINTER shortens each name to a four-letter abbreviation. @CELLPOINTER ("contents") returns the string at the current cursor location, and @LEFT shortens that string to four letters. The {EDIT}{CALC} combination is used again to freeze the @LEFT and @CELLPOINTER formula into a permanent four-character label. The LABELER macro repeats unless {IF} detects that ("type")="b", which means that the cursor is on a blank cell. If the cell is blank, the macro skips to the GRAPHER macro.

The GRAPHER macro uses the frequency numbers and abbreviated labels to create a simple bar graph that shows the number of times each job description appears in the database. After the graph is created, you can use the options available under /Graph to dress up the graph and save it for printing.

```
        A          B            C           D            E        F          G          H
1
2  HISTOGRAM FOR TEXT AND NUMERIC DATA
3  ===================================================================================
4
5  Enter or /File Combine Copy your database into the DATABASE section.
6  Give your database and field names the range name DATABASE.
7  Enter the field name and search text to be counted for the histogram.
8  Press Alt-t for a histogram of text data.
9  ===================================================================================
10 ===================================================================================
11 HISTOGRAM
12
13 ===================================================================================
14 FIELD      SEARCH                   FREQUENCY                 HISTOGRAM
15 NAME       TEXT                     IN FIELD                  LABELS
16 ----------------------------------------------------------------------------
17 PRIMEJOB   Assembler                   5                      Asse
18            Designer                    2                      Desi
19            Sales                       3                      Sale
20            SSupport                    2                      SSup
21            Marketing                   4                      Mark
22            Financial                   1                      Fina
23            Planning                    1                      Plan
24            Shipping                    2                      Ship
25
26
27
28 ===================================================================================
29 MACROS
30
31 Text Search Criteria
32 PRIMEJOB
33 Shipping
34
35           TEXT HISTOGRAM
36 \t        {GOTO}I10~{GOTO}A10~                      Display screen
37           {GOTO}TEXT~                               To top of field names
38           /cA17~CRITERIA~                           Field name into criteria
39 TAGAIN    /c~A33~                                   Current cell into criteria
40           {RIGHT 2}                                 Position in frequency column
41           @DCOUNT(DATABASE,0,CRITERIA)              Count with criteria
42           {EDIT}{CALC}                              Change @DCOUNT to value
43           {DOWN}{LEFT 2}
44           {IF @CELLPOINTER("type")="b"}{LABELER}    If blank go to LABELER
45           {TAGAIN}                                  Repeat for next criteria
46
47           MAKE LABELS FOR HISTOGRAM BARS
48 LABELER   {GOTO}TEXT~                               Start at top of text list
49           /c.{END}{DOWN}~LABELS~                    Copy list into label area
```

```
51  LAGAIN   @LEFT(@CELLPOINTER("contents"),4)   Shorten label to 4 letters
52           {EDIT}{CALC}                         Change display to string
53           {DOWN}                               Next label
54           {IF @CELLPOINTER("type")="b"}{GRAPHER}   If blank go to GRAPHER
55           {LAGAIN}                             Repeat for next label
56
57           CREATE AND DISPLAY GRAPH
58  GRAPHER  {GOTO}FREQ~                          Start at top of freq list
59           /grg                                 Clear previous graphs
60           tb                                   Set bar graph
61           a.{END}{DOWN}~                       Specify A range
62           q                                    Quit
63           {GOTO}LABELS~                        Start at top of labels
64           /goda.{END}{DOWN}~aqq                Specify A labels
65           vq                                   View and pause
66           {QUIT}                               Quit
67
68  ===================================================
69  DATABASE
70  ---------------------------------------------------
71
72           LNAME      PRIMEJOB
73           Smythe     Assembler
74           James      Designer
75           Querno     Sales
76           Dvorak     SSupport
77           Dennis     Marketing
78           Muir       Assembler
79           Bernard    Designer
80           Dickens    Sales
81           Irving     Shipping
82           Bonar      Marketing
83           Milton     Assembler
84           Stein      Sales
85           Christie   Marketing
86           Dali       Assembler
87           Mao        Financial
88           Ramirez    Planning
89           Goethe     Shipping
90           Dennis     Marketing
91           Swanson    Assembler
92           Oates      SSupport
93
94
95
96
97
98
99
```

Fig. 5.6. Histogram for Text and Numeric Data template.

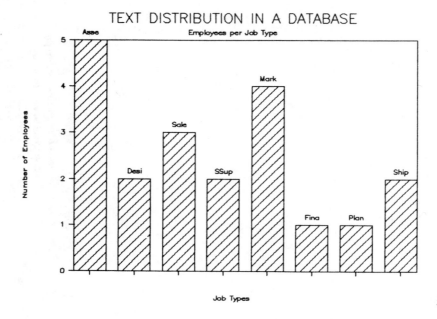

Fig. 5.7. The number and types of jobs in a personnel file.

Creating and Testing the Template

The text distribution template operates from a three-part macro that uses the following range names.

Address	Range Name
A32..A33	CRITERIA
A72..B92	DATABASE
B17	TEXT
B36	\T
B39	TAGAIN
B48	LABELER
B51	LAGAIN
B58	GRAPHER
D17	FREQ
F17	LABELS

You can assign the range names used in the macro (\T, TAGAIN, LA-BELER, LAGAIN, and GRAPHER) by issuing the command /**Range Name Label Right** and highlighting the range that covers those names.

After you enter the labels, values, and macro, using list of cells 5.3, save your template to disk. Then test to see whether the template works correctly.

To examine a large database, you can copy the database into the DA-TABASE section at the bottom of the template. You can do so in either of two ways. Using the first method, you delete nondatabase information from your spreadsheet, move the database to the upper left corner of the spreadsheet, and save the spreadsheet with a new file name. You then can merge this file into the Histogram for Text and Numeric Data template by starting the template and positioning the cursor at the upper left corner of the DATABASE section. Then you issue the /File Combine Copy Entire command and respond with the new file's name. When the database is copied, assign the data the range name DATABASE.

The second method of bringing your database into the template is to give the database in your spreadsheet a range name, such as MYDATA, and to save the spreadsheet again. Then, you start the template, move the cursor into the DATABASE section, and issue the /File Combine Copy Named-Range command. Enter the range name MYDATA and the name of your spreadsheet file containing MYDATA. When your data appears, assign it the range name DATABASE.

Tricks, Traps, and Assumptions

Names used as criteria, those under FIELD NAME and SEARCH TEXT, must be exactly the same as those in the database. To avoid typographical errors, copy rather than type names from the database into the columns under FIELD NAME and SEARCH TEXT.

The @DCOUNT function counts nonblank cells in a column of the database that you specify. This template uses column 0 but could have used another column. Choose a column that will never contain blanks; columns with blanks cause incorrect counts.

List of Cells 5.3

```
A2:  'HISTOGRAM FOR TEXT AND NUMERIC DATA
A3:  \=
B3:  \=
C3:  \=
D3:  \=
E3:  \=
F3:  \=
G3:  \=
H3:  \=
A5:  'Enter or /File Combine Copy your database into the DATABASE section.
A6:  'Give your database and field names the range name DATABASE.
A7:  'Enter the field name and search text to be counted for the histogram.
A8:  U 'Press Alt-t for a histogram of text data.
A10: \=
B10: \=
C10: \=
D10: \=
E10: \=
F10: \=
G10: \=
H10: \=
A11: 'HISTOGRAM
A12: \-
B12: \-
C12: \-
D12: \-
E12: \-
F12: \-
G12: \-
H12: \-
A14: 'FIELD
B14: 'SEARCH
D14: 'FREQUENCY
F14: 'HISTOGRAM
A15: 'NAME
B15: 'TEXT
D15: 'IN FIELD
F15: 'LABELS
A16: \-
B16: \-
D16: \-
F16: \-
A17: 'PRIMEJOB
B17: 'Assembler
D17: 5
F17: 'Asse
B18: 'Designer
D18: 2
F18: 'Desi
B19: 'Sales
D19: 3
F19: 'Sale
B20: 'SSupport
D20: 2
F20: 'SSup
B21: 'Marketing
D21: 4
F21: 'Mark
B22: 'Financial
D22: 1
F22: 'Fina
B23: 'Planning
D23: 1
```

```
F23:  'Plan
B24:  'Shipping
D24:  2
F24:  'Ship
A28:  \=
B28:  \=
C28:  \=
D28:  \=
E28:  \=
F28:  \=
G28:  \=
H28:  \=
A29:  'MACROS
A30:  \-
B30:  \-
C30:  \-
D30:  \-
E30:  \-
F30:  \-
G30:  \-
H30:  \-
A31:  'Text Search Criteria
A32:  'PRIMEJOB
A33:  'Shipping
B35:  'TEXT HISTOGRAM
A36:  '\t
B36:  ' {GOTO}I10~{GOTO}A10~
F36:  'Display screen
B37:  ' {GOTO}TEXT~
F37:  'To top of field names
B38:  '/cA17~CRITERIA~
F38:  'Field name into criteria
A39:  'TAGAIN
B39:  '/c~A33~
F39:  'Current cell into criteria
B40:  ' {RIGHT 2}
F40:  'Position in frequency column
B41:  '@DCOUNT(DATABASE,0,CRITERIA)
F41:  'Count with criteria
B42:  ' {EDIT}{CALC}
F42:  'Change @DCOUNT to value
B43:  ' {DOWN}{LEFT 2}
B44:  ' {IF @CELLPOINTER("type")="b"}{LABELER}
G44:  'If blank go to LABELER
B45:  ' {TAGAIN}
F45:  'Repeat for next criteria
B47:  'MAKE LABELS FOR HISTOGRAM BARS
A48:  'LABELER
B48:  ' {GOTO}TEXT~
F48:  'Start at top of text list
B49:  '/c. {END}{DOWN}~LABELS~
F49:  'Copy list into label area
B50:  ' {GOTO}LABELS~
F50:  'Move to top of label area
A51:  'LAGAIN
B51:  '@LEFT(@CELLPOINTER("contents"),4)
F51:  'Shorten label to 4 letters
B52:  ' {EDIT}{CALC}
F52:  'Change display to string
B53:  ' {DOWN}
F53:  'Next label
B54:  ' {IF @CELLPOINTER("type")="b"}{GRAPHER}
G54:  'If blank go to GRAPHER
B55:  ' {LAGAIN}
F55:  'Repeat for next label
B57:  'CREATE AND DISPLAY GRAPH
```

```
A58:  'GRAPHER
B58:  '{GOTO}FREQ~
F58:  'Start at top of freq list
B59:  '/grg
F59:  'Clear previous graphs
B60:  'tb
F60:  'Set bar graph
B61:  'a.{END}{DOWN}~
F61:  'Specify A range
B62:  'q
F62:  'Quit
B63:  '{GOTO}LABELS~
F63:  'Start at top of labels
B64:  '/goda.{END}{DOWN}~aqq
F64:  'Specify A labels
B65:  'vq
F65:  'View and pause
B66:  '{QUIT}
F66:  'Quit
A68:  \=
B68:  \=
C68:  \=
D68:  \=
E68:  \=
F68:  \=
G68:  \=
H68:  \=
A69:  'DATABASE
A70:  \-
B70:  \-
C70:  \-
D70:  \-
E70:  \-
F70:  \-
G70:  \-
H70:  \-
A72:  'LNAME
B72:  'PRIMEJOB
A73:  'Smythe
B73:  'Assembler
A74:  '.James
B74:  'Designer
A75:  'Querno
B75:  'Sales
A76:  'Dvorak
B76:  'SSupport
A77:  'Dennis
B77:  'Marketing
A78:  'Muir
B78:  'Assembler
A79:  'Bernard
B79:  'Designer
A80:  'Dickens
B80:  'Sales
A81:  'Irving
B81:  'Shipping
A82:  'Bonar
B82:  'Marketing
A83:  'Milton
B83:  'Assembler
A84:  'Stein
B84:  'Sales
A85:  'Christie
B85:  'Marketing
A86:  'Dali
B86:  'Assembler
```

```
A87:  'Mao
B87:  'Financial
A88:  'Ramirez
B88:  'Planning
A89:  'Goethe
B89:  'Shipping
A90:  'Dennis
B90:  'Marketing
A91:  'Swanson
B91:  'Assembler
A92:  'Oates
B92:  'SSupport
```

Cross-Tabulation

Gleaning opinions from customer surveys and analyzing sales data have two things in common. They both require tedious examination of a database, and they both are important to managing and improving your business.

The 1-2-3 Cross-Tabulation template analyzes any type of database information and reveals relationships that sometimes may be difficult to see. Used with a database of survey information, the template can compare responses with an ideal customer profile. For example, you could find out how many families have children in different age brackets and also plan to purchase a new bicycle in the next year. With manual data queries, you can see only one query at a time. With cross-tabulation, you can process many queries at one time and see all the results at once.

You can cross-tabulate any 1-2-3 database with this template. The CROSS-TABULATION section in figure 5.8 shows how a matrix is set up by entering a row of criteria across the top and a column of criteria down column A. You can enter any field name and criteria labels across the top or down the side. Criteria formulas are entered across the top. The number at the intersection of each row and column is the number of records in the database that satisfies both criteria. The cross-tabulation in figure 5.8 has 30 queries (or intersections). You can modify the macro to add more rows or columns and therefore more queries.

	A	B	C	D	E	F	G	H

CROSS-TABULATION

===

Enter or /File Combine Copy your database in the data area.
Enter the field names in row 18 and down column A as shown.
Enter the tabulation (search) criteria below each field name.
Enter formula criteria as a label in row 19.
Put a 1 in row 17 above field names having formula criteria.
Give the database and its field names the range name DATA.
Hold down the Alt key and press T to fill the cross-tabulation.

===

CROSS-TABULATION

Formula Field Criteria	WType Reisl	WType Chard	WType Chabl	WType Cabrnt	1 Units +D78>10	1 Sales$ +E78>400
Seller						
Susan		1	1	0	3	1
Seller						
John	0	2	1	0	1	1
Buyer						
Barney's	0	1	0	1	2	0
Buyer						
ABC Liqr	0	1	1	0	0	0
Buyer						
Sam's	1	0	0	0	1	1

===

MACRO AND CRITERIA

===

DATABASE QUERY CRITERIA

Row Crit	Col Crit
Buyer	Sale$
Buyer	
Sam's	0

```
46
47    \t          TABULATION MACRO AND SUBROUTINES
48                {GOTO}H16~{GOTO}A16~                                              Show cross tab screen
49                {BLANK XTAB}{CALC}                                                Clear cross tab area
50                {PANELOFF}{WINDOWSOFF}                                            Turn off control panel and screen redraw
51                {FOR ROWCNT,0,4,1,ROWCONTROL}                                     Step through rows by incrementing ROWCNT
52                {PANELON}{WINDOWSON}{CALC}{BEEP}                                  Done
53
54    ROWCNT      5
55
56    ROWCONTROL  {CALC}{LET A43,@CHOOSE(ROWCNT,A21,A24,A27,A30,A33)}              Store selected Row Crit in DB query crit
57                {LET A44,@CHOOSE(ROWCNT,A22,A25,A28,A31,A34)}
58                {CALC}
59                {FOR COLCNT,0,5,1,COLCONTROL}                                     Step through columns by incrementing COLCNT
60
61    COLCNT      6
62
63    COLCONTROL  {CALC}{LET B43,@CHOOSE(COLCNT,B18,C18,D18,E18,F18,G18)}          Store selected Col Crit in DB query crit
64                {LET B44,@CHOOSE(COLCNT,B19,C19,D19,E19,F19,G19)}
65                {CALC}
66                {IF @CHOOSE(COLCNT,B17,C17,D17,E17,F17,G17)}{MAKEFORMULA}        If label is formula, then go to MAKEFORMULA
67                {PUT XTAB,COLCNT,ROWCNT*3+1,@DCOUNT(DATA,1,CRITERIA)}            Put count matching criteria into cross tab
68
69    MAKEFORMULA {GOTO}B44~                                                        Go to column criteria cell
70                {EDIT}{HOME}{DEL}~                                                Delete ' from in front of label to make a formula
71                {GOTO}A16~
72                {RETURN}
73    ===============================================================
74
75    YOUR DATABASE
76              Seller    Buyer      WType    Units   Sale$
77              Susan     Barney's   Chard      12     365
78              John      ABC Liqr   Chabl       8     160
79              John      B&B        Chard      15     450
80              Susan     Barney's   Cabrnt     11     340
81              John      ABC Liqr   Chard       8     242
82              Susan     Sam's      Reisl      20     620
83
84
85
86
87
88
89
90
91
92
```

Fig. 5.8. Cross-Tabulation template.

Revealing Sales Information

The CROSS-TABULATION section in figure 5.8 shows a cross-tabulation of queries on wine sales. The upper right corner of the matrix shows that Susan had 1 sale that exceeded $400. The second row shows that John made no Reisling or Cabernet sales but did make 2 Chardonnay and 1 Chablis sale.

The wine sales database is small and doesn't reveal any information that isn't obvious. A larger database, however, might have revealed that some salespeople tend to sell specific products or that some buyers prefer certain wines.

The Cross-Tabulation Macro

The wine sales database, shown in the lower section of figure 5.8, is small enough to let you to see at a glance who has sold different wine types and volumes. But when a database has more than 40 or 50 records (rows), a macro is needed to cross-tabulate information rapidly and accurately.

You could generate the cross-tabulation matrix by manually typing the 30 combinations of field names and criteria into a criteria range, then doing an @COUNT of the database. Performing this task manually, however, obviously would take a long time. If you changed the macro and template to add more rows and columns of queries, your equivalent manual work would expand geometrically.

The \t macro starts 3 macro routines that do an @COUNT on the database, using all 30 criteria combinations. Two {FOR} macros control the row and column field names and criteria that are selected. The {FOR ROWCNT} macro, which is in the \t macro, steps through each row, from 0 to 4. The {LET x,@CHOOSE( )} macros in the first 2 lines of ROWCONTROL use the counter value ROWCNT to select the field name and criteria for the row. The {LET} macro transfers the field and criteria that @CHOOSE selects into the criteria cells A43 and A44.

After a row's field name and criteria are selected, the {FOR COLCNT} macro steps the value of COLCNT from 0 to 5. The first 2 lines in the COLCONTROL routine use this value to select the field name and criteria for each column. Each {LET} macro transfers the column field name and criteria into the query database criteria cells, B43 and B44.

One problem remains. If formulas are entered in row 19, the relative addresses that the formulas contain change when {LET} transfers the formula criteria into the criteria cell at B44. An absolute address cannot be used because criteria formulas must use relative addressing. The solution is to enter formulas in row 19 as labels by preceding each one with an apostrophe. The {IF} macro in the COLCONTROL routine then detects formula-labels and transfers control to the MAKEFORMULA subroutine, which removes the apostrophe once the formula-label is in criteria cell B44. {IF} checks for formulas by checking for the number 1 in row 17.

When a new field name and criteria are in A33..B44, the @DCOUNT function counts how many records satisfy both criteria. The {PUT} macro in the COLCONTROL routine uses ROWCNT and COLCNT to display the @DCOUNT value in the appropriate row and column of the cross-tabulation matrix.

The macro repeats this procedure for each column in a row. Then the macro does the same for the next row and its columns.

Creating and Testing the Template

Macros do all the work in the cross-tabulation matrix. These macros depend on the following range names.

Address	Range Name
A43..B44	CRITERIA
A77..E83	DATA
B21..G34	XTAB
B48	\T
B54	ROWCNT
B56	ROWCONTROL
B61	COLCNT
B63	COLCONTROL
B69	MAKEFORMULA

Enter the labels, values, and macros, using cell listing 5.4. Save the Cross-Tabulation template to disk. Then use the wine sales database to test whether the template works correctly.

Although the wine sales database is small, you can use this quick analysis method even on large databases. Copy your own databases into the template by using /File Combine Copy rather than retyping them. Chapter 2 describes how to copy a database into the template. You must give any database you use the range name DATABASE.

You can change the field names and criteria in the cross-tabulation matrix at any time, then press Alt-t to invoke the tabulation macro. The screen freezes for a minute or more, and a CMD indicator appears at the bottom of the screen. When calculations are completed, the matrix fills up with numbers.

Criteria and field names are entered in A21 to A34 and rows 18 and 19, as shown. You must type all field names and criteria exactly as they appear in the database. You must enter all criteria and field names, including formulas, as labels.

You can enter formulas in row 19 only, and you must enter them as labels. To enter a formula as a label, type an apostrophe before typing the formula. Don't forget to use the relative address of the top cell in the database column you are testing in the formula. Enter a number in row 17 above each formula so that the macro can identify which criteria are formulas.

Tricks, Traps, and Assumptions

You can use the * and ? wild cards in criteria in the same way that you use them in a 1-2-3 data query.

You can prevent criteria mismatches by using the /Copy command to copy field names and labels from the database into rows 18 and 19 and column A. Typed field names and criteria may contain typographical errors that ruin the @COUNT.

You must enter formula criteria as labels and use the relative address of the top cell in the column being examined. An absolute address does not work.

To watch the cross-tabulation matrix being built, remove the {PANELOFF}{WINDOWSOFF} macro commands. Removing these macros, however, slows down execution speed.

Appendix D contains a cross-tabulation matrix for Release 1A of 1-2-3.

List of Cells 5.4

```
A2: [W11] 'CROSS-TABULATION
A3: [W11] \=
B3: \=
C3: \=
D3: \=
E3: \=
F3: \=
G3: \=
A5: [W11] 'Enter or /File Combine Copy your database in the data area.
A6: [W11] 'Enter the field names in row 18 and down column A as shown.
A7: [W11] 'Enter the tabulation (search) criteria below each field name.
A8: [W11] '      Enter formula criteria as a label in row 19.
A9: [W11] '      Put a 1 in row 17 above field names having formula criteria.
A10: [W11] 'Give the database and its field names the range name DATA.
A11: U [W11] 'Hold down the Alt key and press T to fill the cross-tabulation.
A13: [W11] \=
B13: \=
C13: \=
D13: \=
E13: \=
F13: \=
G13: \=
A14: [W11] 'CROSS-TABULATION
A15: [W11] \-
B15: \-
C15: \-
D15: \-
E15: \-
F15: \-
G15: \-
A17: [W11] 'Formula
F17: 1
G17: 1
A18: [W11] 'Field
B18: 'WType
C18: 'WType
D18: 'WType
E18: 'WType
F18: "Units
G18: "Sale$
A19: [W11] 'Criteria
B19: 'Reisl
C19: 'Chard
D19: 'Chabl
E19: 'Cabrnt
F19: "+D78>10
G19: "+E78>400
A20: [W11] \-
B20: \-
C20: \-
D20: \-
E20: \-
F20: \-
G20: \-
A21: [W11] 'Seller
A22: [W11] 'Susan
B22: 1
C22: 1
D22: 0
E22: 1
F22: 3
G22: 1
A23: [W11] \-
```

```
A24: [W11] 'Seller
A25: [W11] 'John
B25: 0
C25: 2
D25: 1
E25: 0
F25: 1
G25: 1
A26: [W11] \-
A27: [W11] 'Buyer
A28: [W11] 'Barney's
B28: 0
C28: 1
D28: 0
E28: 1
F28: 2
G28: 0
A29: [W11] \-
A30: [W11] 'Buyer
A31: [W11] 'ABC Liqr
B31: 0
C31: 1
D31: 1
E31: 0
F31: 0
G31: 0
A32: [W11] \-
A33: [W11] 'Buyer
A34: [W11] 'Sam's
B34: 1
C34: 0
D34: 0
E34: 0
F34: 1
G34: 1
A37: [W11] \=
B37: \=
C37: \=
D37: \=
E37: \=
F37: \=
G37: \=
A38: [W11] 'MACRO AND CRITERIA
A39: [W11] \-
B39: \-
C39: \-
D39: \-
E39: \-
F39: \-
G39: \-
A41: [W11] 'DATABASE QUERY CRITERIA
A42: [W11] 'Row Crit
B42: 'Col Crit
A43: [W11] 'Buyer
B43: 'Sale$
A44: [W11] 'Sam's
B44: +E78>400
B47: 'TABULATION MACRO AND SUBROUTINES
A48: [W11] '\t
B48: '{GOTO}H16~{GOTO}A16~
H48: 'Show cross tab screen
B49: '{BLANK XTAB}{CALC}
H49: 'Clear cross tab area
B50: '{PANELOFF}{WINDOWSOFF}
H50: 'Turn off control panel and screen redraw
B51: '{FOR ROWCNT,0,4,1,ROWCONTROL}
```

```
H51:   'Step through rows by incrementing ROWCNT
B52:   '{PANELON}{WINDOWSON}{CALC}{BEEP}
H52:   'Done
A54:   [W11] 'ROWCNT
B54:   5
A56:   [W11] 'ROWCONTROL
B56:   '{CALC}{LET A43,@CHOOSE(ROWCNT,A21,A24,A27,A30,A33)}
H56:   'Store selected Row Crit in DB query crit
B57:   '{LET A44,@CHOOSE(ROWCNT,A22,A25,A28,A31,A34)}
B58:   '{CALC}
B59:   '{FOR COLCNT,0,5,1,COLCONTROL}
H59:   'Step through columns by incrementing COLCNT
A61:   [W11] 'COLCNT
B61:   6
A63:   [W11] 'COLCONTROL
B63:   '{CALC}{LET B43,@CHOOSE(COLCNT,B18,C18,D18,E18,F18,G18)}
I63:   'Store selected Col Crit in DB query crit
B64:   '{LET B44,@CHOOSE(COLCNT,B19,C19,D19,E19,F19,G19)}
B65:   '{CALC}
B66:   '{IF @CHOOSE(COLCNT,B17,C17,D17,E17,F17,G17)}{MAKEFORMULA}
I66:   'If label is formula, then go to MAKEFORMULA
B67:   '{PUT XTAB,COLCNT,ROWCNT*3+1,@DCOUNT(DATA,1,CRITERIA)}
I67:   'Put count matching criteria into cross tab
A69:   [W11] 'MAKEFORMULA
B69:   '{GOTO}B44~
H69:   'Go to column criteria cell
B70:   '{EDIT}{HOME}{DEL}~
H70:   'Delete ' from in front of label to make a formula
B71:   '{GOTO}A16~
B72:   '{RETURN}
A74:   [W11] \=
B74:   \=
C74:   \=
D74:   \=
E74:   \=
F74:   \=
G74:   \=
A75:   [W11] 'YOUR DATABASE
A76:   [W11] \-
B76:   \-
C76:   \-
D76:   \-
E76:   \-
F76:   \-
G76:   \-
A77:   [W11] 'Seller
B77:   'Buyer
C77:   'WType
D77:   "Units
E77:   "Sale$
A78:   [W11] 'Susan
B78:   'Barney's
C78:   'Chard
D78:   12
E78:   365
A79:   [W11] 'John
B79:   'ABC Liqr
C79:   'Chabl
D79:   8
E79:   160
A80:   [W11] 'John
B80:   'B&B
C80:   'Chard
D80:   15
E80:   450
A81:   [W11] 'Susan
```

```
B81: 'Barney's
C81: 'Cabrnt
D81: 11
E81: 340
A82: [W11] 'John
B82: 'ABC Liqr
C82: 'Chard
D82: 8
E82: 242
A83: [W11] 'Susan
B83: 'Sam's
C83: 'Reisl
D83: 20
E83: 620
```

A

Sources of Demographic, Financial, and Industrial Information

Listed in this appendix are the names of private and government bureaus that gather, analyze, and publish information. In many cases, you can obtain demographic, financial, and industrial information from these sources inexpensively. If you do not need the information on a continuing basis, check with your local library's reference section or interlibrary loan department or with a university library's reference section.

Aside from the listings here, you can contact your state and local economic and taxation agencies for local statistics. Also, some trade groups and trade associations publish research for their members.

Private Sources

The following two books contain common financial ratios for many different types of retail businesses and industries. You can find these two books in the business loan departments of most banks. Or, you can purchase the books directly from the companies at the addresses given.

Robert Morris Associates. *Annual Statement Studies*. Annual. (Robert Morris Associates, 1616 Philadelphia National Bank Building, Philadelphia, PA 19107)

Seventeen commonly used financial ratios for 341 industries. Information, grouped by industry segment and SIC codes, is taken from more than 80,000 financial statements.

Dun and Bradstreet, Inc. *Industry Norms and Key Business Ratios*. Dun's Financial Profile. Annual. (Dun and Bradstreet Credit Services, One Diamond Hill Road, Murray Hill, NJ 07974)

Fourteen key ratios with one- to three-year histories. Information is grouped by industry segment, two- or four-digit SIC code, geographic region, and total assets, and is compiled from approximately one million financial statements.

Government Sources

The United States government is a source of extensive and inexpensive information. The following list includes major government sources of demographic, agricultural, and industrial information. You can use the information to help define trends, target new market areas, and determine competitive standards with which to measure your company and industry.

U.S. Department of Agriculture. *Agricultural Statistics*. Annual.

Material on agricultural production, supplies, consumption, costs, and returns.

U.S. Department of Commerce. Census Bureau. *Annual Survey of Manufacturing*. Annual. (Last published in 1981.)

General statistics on employees, value of shipments, value added, costs, and capital expenditures. Lags by several years; use *County Business Patterns* for more up-to-date information.

U.S. Department of Commerce. Bureau of Economic Analysis. *Business Conditions Digest*. Monthly.

More than 500 economic indicators to help you analyze economic fluctuations. Includes foreign trade.

U.S. Department of Commerce. Census Bureau. *Construction Reports*. Monthly.

A variety of reports for different types of construction. Information on starts, completions, new value, permits, and price indexes.

U.S. Department of Commerce. Census Bureau. *County Business Patterns*. Annual.

Information, according to geographic area and year, on the number of businesses, employees, and payroll for different types of industry.

U.S. Department of Commerce. Census Bureau. *Current Housing Reports*. Annual.

Statistics from the annual housing surveys of areas inside and outside the largest metropolitan areas.

U.S. Department of Commerce. Census Bureau. *Current Business Reports: Monthly Trade, Sales and Inventory*. Monthly.

Statistics for sales and industry of merchant wholesalers for selected types of business in the United States.

U.S. Department of Commerce. Census Bureau. *Current Business Reports: Retail Trade*. Irregular.

Statistics relating to the sales, accounts receivable, and inventories of retail trade in the United States.

U.S. Department of Commerce. Census Bureau. *Current Population Reports*. Irregular.

Estimates and projections of population. Also includes consumer income and buying intentions, family profiles, education, and many other cross sections.

U.S. Department of Commerce. Census Bureau. *Handbook of Cyclical Indicators*, 1984: A supplement to the *Business Conditions Digest*. Annual.

Information on approximately 300 economic time series published in the monthly *Business Conditions Digest*.

U.S. Department of Commerce. Census Bureau. *Statistical Abstract of the United States, National Data Book and Guide to Sources*. Annual.

The largest number of statistics in one book. This should be the starting point for most searches. Includes summaries on social, political, and economic outlooks.

U.S. Department of Commerce. *U.S. Industrial Outlook: Prospects for Over 350 Manufacturing and Service Industries*. Annual.

Reviews of major industries for 1- and 10-year economic forecasts. Includes special analyses on major topics.

U.S. Congress. Council of Economic Advisors. *Economic Indicators*. Monthly.

Information on prices, wages, production, business activity, purchase power, credit, money, and federal finances.

U.S. Department of Labor. Bureau of Labor Statistics. *CPI Detailed Report: Consumer Price Index*. Monthly.

Information on changes in goods and services bought by urban consumers. Index of price changes. Useful for making time series adjustments to other series.

U.S. Department of Labor, Bureau of Labor Statistics, *Wholesale Prices and Price Indexes*. Monthly.

Wholesale price movements by product groups, subgroups, and items.

Two government depository libraries in each congressional district maintain complete collections of these sources. Many other libraries have a partial collection of government documents. You also can purchase copies directly from the U.S. Government Printing Office in Washington, D.C.

Prices for the documents in this list range from $2 for some of the monthly issues to $23 for a copy of the *Statistical Abstract of the United States*. To find out more about these documents and how to order them, contact:

Superintendent of Documents
U.S. Government Printing Office
North Capitol and H Streets, N.W.
Washington, DC 20401

Call (202) 783-3238 for a free guide to government information and a list of government depository libraries. For credit card orders and information on document prices and availability, call (202) 783-3238.

B
Sources of Formulas, Definitions, and Equations

The following sources of financial formulas and definitions greatly expand on the information in the *1-2-3 Business Formula Handbook*.

Abramowitz, Milton, and Irene A. Stegun. *Handbook of Mathematical Functions*, Applied Math Series #55. Washington, D.C.: National Bureau of Standards, U.S. Government Printing Office, 1964.

Beyer, W. H., ed. *Handbook of Tables for Probability and Statistics*. 2nd ed. Cleveland, Ohio: The Chemical Rubber Co., 1968.

Brigham, Eugene F. *Financial Management, Theory and Practice*. 3rd ed. New York: Dryden Press, 1982.

Burington and May. *Handbook of Probability and Statistics with Tables*. 2nd ed. New York: McGraw-Hill, 1970.

Mendenhall, W., and J. E. Reinmuth. *Statistics for Management and Economics*. Belmont, Calif.: Duxbury Press, 1971.

Skrapek, W. A., Bob M. Korkie, and Terrence E. Daniel. *Mathematical Dictionary for Economics and Business Administration*. Boston, Mass.: Allyn and Bacon, Inc., 1976.

Thorndike, David. *Thorndike Encyclopedia of Banking and Financial Tables*. Rev. ed. Boston, Mass.: Warren, Gorham & Lamonth, Inc., 1980.

West, Beverly H., Ellen N. Griesbach, Jerry D. Taylor, and Louis T. Taylor. *The Prentice-Hall Encyclopedia of Mathematics*. Englewood Cliffs, N.J.: Prentice-Hall, 1982.

West, R. C., ed. *Handbook of Tables for Mathematics*. 4th ed. Cleveland, Ohio: The Chemical Rubber Co., 1975.

Weston, J. F., and Eugene F. Brigham. *Managerial Finance*. 5th ed. New York: Dryden Press, 1972.

C

1-2-3 Release 2 and
Release 1A Macro
Conversions

In many cases, the 1-2-3 Release 2 macros in this book can be converted directly to Release 1A macros. The following list will help you make simple conversions. Difficult or long macros used in the templates are converted in Appendix D.

{BEEP}

Release 2 beeps.

Release 1A beeps when {NAME} is used in a macro at an inappropriate location.

{BLANK range}

Release 2 erases the range indicated.

Release 1A uses /Range Erase, /reCELLS.

{BRANCH location}

Release 2 branches macro control to another cell location. This command is not a subroutine call. You must use another {BRANCH} to come back.

In Release 1A, /xg provides the same results.

{FOR counter location,start number,stop number,step number,range}

Release 2 repeats the macro as many times as necessary to count from the start to the stop number, using the step number as the increment.

Release 1A requires a looping macro that counts the number of times the macro repeats. The book *1-2-3 Macro Library* explains how to create looping macros.

{IF condition}

Release 2 continues executing the commands in the cell if the condition in the IF statement is TRUE (not zero).

Release 1A uses the /xi macro.

{LET range,value or string}

Release 2 stores the value or string in the range without moving the cursor from its current location.

Release 1A can use /Copy in a macro or move to a cell, store the value or label, and move back to the original location. For example,

```
/rncHERE~~/rndHERE~/rncHERE~~
{GOTO}location~
value or label~
{GOTO}HERE~
```

{PANELOFF},{PANELON},{WINDOWSOFF},{WINDOWSON}

Release 2 controls whether the control panel and spreadsheet show changes as they occur during macro operation. These commands enhance spreadsheet performance.

Release 1A has no similar feature.

{PUT range,column,row,value or string}

Release 2 uses this macro to put text strings or values into a specific row or column in the matrix of cells defined by range. The cross-tabulation template uses {PUT} to display numbers in the correct row and column.

Release 1A must use a counting loop that moves the cursor from a known location in a range (the upper left corner, for example) to the new location, according to the number of rows and columns specified. Once in the new location, the cursor can enter the number or text.

{RECALCCOL range,condition,iteration}

Release 2 calculates formulas in column order within the indicated range. Recalculation stops when either the condition or the number of iterations is met. The unknown interest templates use {RECALCCOL} to recalculate only the unknown interest portion of the spreadsheet. {RECALCCOL}, as well as {RECALC} (the row-wise calculator), can speed up recalculation in large spreadsheets. The macro always should be followed by {CALC} to update the entire spreadsheet.

Release 1A recalculates the entire spreadsheet. The /Copy command can recalculate part of the spreadsheet by copying a range back onto itself. Always do a {CALC} to include the new calculations in the rest of the spreadsheet.

{RETURN}

Release 2 returns from a subroutine to the calling routine.

Release 1A returns from subroutines with /xr.

{subroutine}

Release 2 names subroutines so that they can be called by name. Use {RETURN} to return from the subroutine.

Release 1A uses the /xc macro to call a subroutine. Use /xr to return.

{QUIT}

Release 2 stops the macro.

Release 1A quits with /xq or a blank cell.

D
1-2-3 Release 1A Macros

If you use Release 1A of 1-2-3, use the following macros instead of the Release 2 macros in this book. Use /**R**ange **N**ame **L**abel **R**ight down the left column of macro labels to name the macro and its subroutines. To learn how you can convert other Release 2 macros in the *1-2-3 Business Formula Handbook*, refer to Appendix C.

Iteration To Calculate Interest of an Annuity

The iteration macro (see list of cells D.1) works with any of the financial templates that use the iteration or circular reference method of calculation. Leave all range names as they are in the Release 2 versions. When the template stops running, it is left in manual re-calculation mode. Execute the macro by holding down the Alt key and pressing C.

List of Cells D.1

```
B45: 'CLEAR AND CALC MACRO
A46: '\c
B46: '{HOME}
E46: 'Position screen
B47: '/reD19~
E47: 'Erase NA if previous errors
B48: '{GOTO}CALCCLR~0~{CALC}
E48: 'Clear old INCR values
B49: '/wgrm
E49: 'Manual recalculation
B50: '/wgri50~
E50: 'Set 50 iterations
B51: '1~{HOME}
E51: 'Allow new values to be used, show screen
B52: '{CALC}
E52: 'Calculate for 50 iterations
B53: '/wgri1~
E53: 'Return to one recalculation
B54: '/wgra
E54: 'Automatic recalculation
B55: '{GOTO}INT~
E55: 'Cursor on interest
B56: '/xi(FIRST INCR/LAST INCR<10)~{GOTO}D19~@NA~{NAME}
F56: 'If solution not accurate, beep and NA
B57: '/ru~/rp~/ru~/rp~
E57: 'Flash answer
```

Financial Management
Rate of Return

The financial management macro for Release 1A (see list of cells D.2)
works nearly the same as the macro for Release 2. Each cell that the
Release 1A macro analyzes is given the range name HERE. This macro
also needs an @NA function in cell D30 at the top of the DISCOUNT
NEG column and in cell F38 at the bottom of the COMPOUND POS
column. The macro uses the @NA in those cells to find the end of the
list of numbers. Leave all range names the same as those in the Release
2 macro. When running this template, do not use global protection.
Execute the macro by holding down the Alt key and pressing S.

List of Cells D.2

```
B44: 'START (Master macro, others are subroutines)
A45: '\s
B45: '{HOME}{GOTO}A21~
F45: 'Position screen
B46: '/wgrm
F46: 'Manual calc
B47: '/dfDISCNT~0~0~~
F47: 'Fill DISCOUNT with 0
B48: '/dfCOMPOUND~0~0~~
F48: 'Fill COMPOUND with 0
B49: '/xc\D~
F49: 'Discount subroutine
B50: '/xc\C~
F50: 'Compound subroutine
B51: '/wgra
F51: 'Automatic calc
B52: '{CALC}{HOME}{NAME}
F52: 'Show results
B54: 'DISCOUNT NEGATIVE CASH FLOWS AND COVER WITH POSITIVE CASH FLOWS
A55: '\d
B55: '/cCASH FLOW~DISCNT~
G55: 'Copy data into DISCOUNT area
B56: '{GOTO}DISCNT~
G56: 'Goto top of DISCOUNT column
B57: '{END}{DOWN}
G57: 'Start at bottom, work up
A58: 'DAGAIN
B58: '/rncHERE~~~/rndHERE~/rncHERE~~~
G58: 'Name current cell
B59: '{UP}{UP}/rncTOP~~~/rndTOP~/rncTOP~~~
G59: 'Name cell two above for NA check
B60: '{GOTO}HERE~
G60: 'Move back to current cell
B61: '/xi(HERE<0)~{EDIT}/(1+SAFERATE)~
G61: 'If cell<0, discount at safe rate
B62: '/xi(HERE<0)~{UP}{EDIT}+{DOWN}~{EDIT}{CALC}~
G62: 'If cell<0, add discount value to cell above
B63: '/xi(HERE<0)~{DOWN}/re~
G63: 'If cell<0, move result up
B64: '/xi(HERE>0)~/cHERE~{RIGHT}{RIGHT}~
G64: 'If cell>0, copy two cells right
B65: '/xi(HERE>0)~/reHERE~
G65: 'If cell>0, erase from DISCOUNT column
B66: '{UP}
G66: 'Move up to next cell
B67: '/xi(@ISNA(TOP))~/xr
G67: 'Return to \S if TOP cell is NA
B68: '/xgDAGAIN~
G68: 'Repeat from DAGAIN
B70: 'COMPOUND POSITIVE CASH FLOWS FORWARD
A71: '\c
B71: '{GOTO}COMPOUND~
G71: 'Start at top of compound area
A72: 'CAGAIN
B72: '/rncHERE~~~/rndHERE~/rncHERE~~~
G72: 'Name current cell
B73: '{DOWN}{DOWN}/rncBTTM~~~/rndBTTM~/rncBTTM~~~
G73: 'Name cell to check for NA (end)
B74: '{GOTO}HERE~
G74: 'Return to current cell
B75: '{EDIT}*(1+REINVESTRATE)~
G75: 'Compound interest on current cell
```

```
B76:  ' {DOWN}{EDIT}+{UP}~{EDIT}{CALC}~
G76:  'Add current cell to one below
B77:  '/reHERE~
G77:  'Erase current cell
B78:  '/xi(@ISNA(BTTM))~/xr
G78:  'Check for NA in BTTM
B79:  '/xgCAGAIN~
G79:  'Repeat from CAGAIN
```

Cross-Tabulation

As in the Release 2 version of the macro, all formula criteria must be entered in row 19 as a label. Precede the formula with an apostrophe (′), a label prefix. Run the Release 1A cross-tabulation macro (see list of cells D.3) by positioning the cursor in row 17 above the column to be tabulated. Hold down the Alt key and press T. The macro checks the cursor's current location, row 17, for a number that signals that a formula criteria is used. If a formula is used, the cell named MARKER is set to 1. The column criteria is then copied into the CRITERIA range. If MARKER has been set to 1, the apostrophe is removed from in front of the formula criteria. From macro cell B53 down, the different row criteria are copied into the CRITERIA range, and an @DCOUNT is used to find out how many records satisfy the criteria. {EDIT}{CALC} changes the @DCOUNT function to a value.

When a column is complete, move the cursor to row 17 above the next column. Press Alt-T again. Do not press Alt-T unless the cursor is positioned correctly.

List of Cells D.3

```
B47:  'TABULATION MACRO AND SUBROUTINES
A48:  '\t
B48:  '/xcFORMCHECK~
G48:  'Check if row 17 indicates a formula.
B49:  '{DOWN}/c{ESC}.{DOWN}~B43~
G49:  'Copy column criteria into criteria range.
B50:  '/xiMARKER=1~/xcMAKEFORM~{DOWN}
G50:  'If MARKER=1, then goto MAKEFORM.
B51:  '{DOWN}{DOWN}{DOWN}{DOWN}/cA21.A22~A43.A44~
G51:  'Copy row criteria into criteria range.
B52:  '@DCOUNT(DATA,0,CRITERIA)~{EDIT}{CALC}
G52:  'Calculate count. Change formula to value.
B53:  '{DOWN}{DOWN}{DOWN}/cA24.A25~A43.A44~
G53:  'Repeat process on next rows.
B54:  '@DCOUNT(DATA,0,CRITERIA)~{EDIT}{CALC}
B55:  '{DOWN}{DOWN}{DOWN}/cA27.A28~A43.A44~
B56:  '@DCOUNT(DATA,0,CRITERIA)~{EDIT}{CALC}
B57:  '{DOWN}{DOWN}{DOWN}/cA30.A31~A43.A44~
B58:  '@DCOUNT(DATA,0,CRITERIA)~{EDIT}{CALC}
B59:  '{DOWN}{DOWN}{DOWN}/cA33.A34~A43.A44~
B60:  '@DCOUNT(DATA,0,CRITERIA)~{EDIT}{CALC}~
B62:  'CHECK FOR FORMULA CRITERIA
A63:  'FORMCHECK
B63:  '/rncHERE~~/rndHERE~/rncHERE~~
G63:  'Name cell in row 17.
B64:  '/xiHERE=0~{GOTO}MARKER~0~{GOTO}HERE~/xr
G64:  'If cell has no number (not a formula), then return.
B65:  '{GOTO}MARKER~1~
G65:  'It is a formula, so set MARKER to 1.
B66:  '{GOTO}HERE~/xr
G66:  'Return to original cell. Return to \t macro.
B68:  'CHANGE FORMULA LABEL TO REAL FORMULA
A69:  'MAKEFORM
B69:  '{GOTO}B44~
G69:  'Goto formula criteria cell.
B70:  '{EDIT}{HOME}{DEL}~
G70:  'Remove apostrophe, changes label into formula.
B71:  '{GOTO}HERE~
G71:  'Go to original cell.
B72:  '/xr
G72:  'Return to \t  macro.
A74:  'MARKER
B74:  0
G74:  'MARKER=1 if criteria is formula.
```

E

1-2-3 Release 1A Formulas for Linear Regression Template

Using 1-2-3 Release 1A and the formulas in this appendix, you can create a linear regression template for one or two independent X variables. When you create your template, use a template such as the Power Curve Fit as a model. That template shows how to create columns of calculated data, such as X1*X2, and then use the @SUM function down the column. Using that technique will make entering the formulas easier.

The formula that relates two independent variables, X1 and X2, to Y is

$$Y=A*X1+B*X2+CONSTANT$$

The X coefficients, A and B, determine how a change in X1 and X2 affects the value of Y. If B is zero, the equation describes a straight line with a slope of A that crosses the Y axis at the value of CONSTANT. When this happens, a slope of +1 is an upward-sloping, 45-degree angle, which indicates a one-to-one relationship between X1 and Y.

The following equations find the X coefficients and CONSTANT for regressions with one or two independent variables. If you need to create a template involving only one set of X data, set the B coefficient and all X2 terms to zero.

$$A = \frac{[N*SUM(X1_i*Y)-SUM(X1_i)*SUM(Y_i)]-B*[N*SUM(X1_i*X2_i)-SUM(X1_i)*SUM(X2_i)]}{N*SUM(X1_i{}^2)-(SUM(X1_i))^2}$$

$$B = \frac{T1-T2}{[N*SUM(X1_i{}^2)-(SUM(X1_i))^2][N*SUM(X2_i{}^2)-(SUM(X2_i))^2]-[N*SUM(X1_i*X2_i)-SUM(X1_i)*SUM(X2_i)]^2}$$

where T1 and T2 are

$$T1=[N*SUM(X1_i{}^2)-(SUM(X1_i))^2][N*SUM(X2_i*Y_i)-SUM(X2_i)*SUM(Y_i)]$$

$$T2=[N*SUM(X1_i*X2_i)-SUM(X1_i)*SUM(X2_i)][N*SUM(X1_i*Y_i)-SUM(X1_i)SUM(Y_i)]$$

$$CONSTANT= \frac{SUM(Y_i)-A*SUM(X1_i)-B*SUM(X2_i)}{N}$$

where Y_i, $X1_i$, and $X2_i$ are the sample data, and i indicates that the data is from the same set. All Ys must be positive, and more than one set of data must exist.

Enter the formulas into your spreadsheet by creating three columns for Y, X1, and X2 data. Adjacent columns in the same rows can hold calculations such as Y^2 and $X*Y$ used in larger formulas. Give each of these data columns a descriptive range name, such as YSQR for Y^2. This procedure makes entering formulas easy. For example, you can enter $SUM(Y_i{}^\wedge 2)$ as @SUM(YSQR). The other trend analysis templates in Chapter 4 use this method of building complex formulas.

The coefficient of correlation, R Squared, measures how well the equation fits the data. For a single X, R Squared is calculated with the following. The R Squared term for multiple X is beyond the scope of this book.

$$R\ Squared = \frac{A * \dfrac{Sum(X1_i)\ Sum(Y_i)}{N} - Sum(X1_i*Y_i)}{Sum(Y_i{}^2) - \dfrac{(Sum\ (Y_i))^2}{N}}$$

If R Squared equals zero, no correlation exists between the data and the line. A line that fits the data exactly has an R Squared of 1.

Index

More Computer Knowledge

LOTUS SOFTWARE TITLES

1-2-3 Business Formula Handbook	19.95
1-2-3 for Business	18.95
1-2-3 Financial Macros	19.95
1-2-3 Macro Library	19.95
1-2-3 Tips, Tricks, and Traps	19.95
Using 1-2-3, 2nd Edition	19.95
Using 1-2-3 Workbook and Disk	29.95
Using Symphony	23.95
Symphony: Advanced Topics	19.95
Symphony Macros and the Command Language	22.95
Symphony Tips, Tricks, and Traps	21.95

IBM TITLES

IBM PC Expansion & Software Guide	29.95
IBM's Personal Computer, 2nd Edition	17.95
Networking IBM PCs: A Practical Guide	18.95
Using PC DOS	21.95
PC DOS Workbook	14.95

APPLICATIONS SOFTWARE TITLES

dBASE III Plus Application	19.95
dBASE III Advanced Programming	22.95
dBASE III Handbook	19.95
Multiplan Models for Business	15.95
R:base 5000 User's Guide	19.95
Using AppleWorks	16.95
Using Dollars and Sense	14.95
Using Enable	17.95
Using Excel	19.95
Excel Macro Library	19.95
Using Javelin	19.95
Using Paradox	19.95
Using Reflex	19.95
Using Smart	22.95

Que Order Line: **1-800-428-5331**

All prices subject to change without notice.

LEARN MORE ABOUT LOTUS 1-2-3
WITH THESE OUTSTANDING BOOKS FROM QUE

Using 1-2-3, 2nd Edition

by Douglas Cobb and Geoffrey LeBlond
with revisions by Thomas Carlton

Using 1-2-3, 2nd Edition, is an accelerated spin-off of
1-2-3, one of the overall, best-selling 1-2-3 books on the
market. The second edition includes over 125 pages of
new information and applications plus a tear-out
command-menu chart in the back of the book to provide
a working aid for the user. A book for all 1-2-3 user
levels, *Using 1-2-3*, 2nd Edition, teaches the program's
major features for the Release 1, 1A, or 2 beginner.
Experienced users who have mastered an earlier release
will be taught quickly the new features of Release 2.
Hundreds of examples help develop personal business
applications by showing how others use 1-2-3 every day.

1-2-3 for Business

by Leith Anderson and Douglas Cobb

Step-by-step instructions show you how to build
fourteen practical business applications, using all
the features of 1-2-3. The book includes models for
Fixed Asset Management, Ratio Analysis,
and Project Management.

1-2-3 Macro Library

by David Ewing

This easy-to-use reference contains more
than 100 examples of 1-2-3 macros.
Explanations help you apply many of these
macros to your 1-2-3 worksheets. Included
are examples of macros for 1-2-3's
spreadsheet, data management, and
graphics applications, as well as macros for
file and print operations. Whether you're
just getting started or looking for help
with advanced macro applications, this
comprehensive library provides the
information you need. (A companion
disk is available.)

1-2-3 Tips, Tricks, and Traps

by Dick Andersen and Douglas Cobb

A must for 1-2-3 users. This book explains
1-2-3's little-known features and offers
advice in problem areas. Tips include
shortcuts for creating macros, producing
graphs, and using Data Tables. Traps help
with special problems that may arise
when using 1-2-3.

Mail to: Que Corporation • P. O. Box 50507 • Indianapolis, IN 46250

Item	Title	Price	Quantity	Extension
130	Using 1-2-3, 2nd Edition	$19.95		
34	1-2-3 for Business	$18.95		
174	1-2-3 Macro Library	$19.95		
127	1-2-3 Tips, Tricks, and Traps	$19.95		

Book Subtotal

Shipping & Handling ($1.75 per item)

Indiana Residents Add 5% Sales Tax

GRAND TOTAL

Method of Payment:

☐ Check   ☐ VISA   ☐ MasterCard   ☐ American Express

Card Number _____ Exp. Date _____

Cardholder's Name _____

Ship to _____

Address _____

City _____ State _____ ZIP _____

If you can't wait, call **1-800-428-5331** and order TODAY.
All prices subject to change without notice.

Que Corporation
P. O. Box 50507
Indianapolis, IN 46250

Work Smarter With *IBM PC UPDATE* And Get Your First Issue FREE!

Working longer hours and getting less accomplished? Take two aspirin and subscribe to *IBM PC UPDATE*, the monthly journal for PC and PC-compatible users. *UPDATE* is the only PC publication featuring *only* articles that can help you improve your productivity.

With *UPDATE* as your tool, you can:

- select hardware enhancements for the "plain vanilla" PC
- establish a PC policy
- use tax software effectively
- make your hard disk hum
- learn to "foolproof" 1-2-3®
- use Symphony® as an office automation standard

You'll also learn from authoritative reviews which hardware and software are right for you. Columns on word processing, spreadsheets, database management, and integrated software go above and beyond the manual in helping you get the most out of your software.

If you've got a software or hardware problem, *UPDATE's* got the solution. You'll benefit from case studies of manufacturers, a health care organization, a transportation firm, a nonprofit organization, and others. *UPDATE's* tips, techniques, and applications will force you to work smarter.

Your PC productivity tool is just a phone call or envelope away. Subscribe and get your FIRST ISSUE FREE by returning the coupon below or calling

1-800-227-7999, Ext. **605**. If this FREE FIRST ISSUE offer doesn't convince you that *IBM PC UPDATE* is the best way to work smarter with your PC, simply write *cancel* on the invoice and return it to us. You may keep your FREE FIRST ISSUE, compliments of *IBM PC UPDATE* and Que Corporation.

Call 1-800-227-7999, Ext. 605

FOLD HERE

_____

_____

_____

_____

Que Publishing, Inc.
P. O. Box 50507
Indianapolis, IN 46250

Control Your Work Load With *Absolute Reference* And Get Your First Issue FREE!

If you're spending too much time poring over 1-2-3® or Symphony® because you don't have time to develop applications, *Absolute Reference* has the answers.

For example, the monthly *Absolute Reference* can help you

- create a cash flow ledger
- compute a goal from a worksheet
- create a check writer system
- do regression analysis
- simplify investment analysis

You'll also learn from authoritative reviews which hardware works best with 1-2-3 and Symphony. And tips on the uses of various functions and commands will show you how to get the most out of your software. "Elegant" macros are a regular feature that will take the drudgery out of your work.

Find out why *Absolute Reference* is a leading 1-2-3 and Symphony productivity tool. Subscribe and get your FREE ISSUE by returning the coupon below or calling 1-800-227-7999, Ext. **500**. If this FREE FIRST ISSUE offer doesn't convince you that *Absolute Reference* is the best way

to control your work load, simply write "cancel" on the invoice and return it to us. You may keep your FREE FIRST ISSUE, compliments of *Absolute Reference* and Que Corporation.

Call 1-800-227-7999, Ext. 500!

FOLD HERE

Que Publishing, Inc.
P. O. Box 50507
Indianapolis, IN 46250

Place
Stamp
Here